Digital Design Concepts and Technical Guide

FOUNDATIONS OF WEB DESIGN

Using Fireworks® MX 2004, Dreamweaver® MX 2004, and Macromedia Flash™ MX 2004

Official Macromedia Education Curriculum

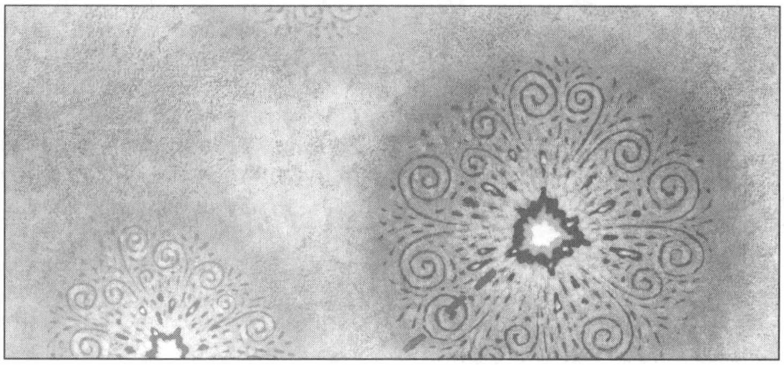

Dharkar • Underwood • Tapley

THOMSON
COURSE TECHNOLOGY™

Australia • Canada • Mexico • Singapore • Spain • United Kingdom • United States

THOMSON
COURSE TECHNOLOGY

Digital Design Concepts and Technical Guide: Foundations of Web Design Using Fireworks MX 2004, Dreamweaver MX 2004, and Macromedia Flash MX 2004

Executive Editor
Cheryl Constantini

Managing Editor
Chris Katsaropoulos

Product Manager
Robert Gaggin

Associate Product Manager
Meagan Putney

Sr. Marketing Manager
Kim Ryttel

Authors
Anuja Dharkar, Dale Underwood, Scott Tapley

Editor
Kirsti Aho

Macromedia Project Manager
Denise Costello

Development
Custom Editorial Productions Inc.

Photography
Michael Epstein, Matthew Aho

Director of Production
Patty Stephan

Production Management
Custom Editorial Productions Inc.

Print Buyer
Trevor Kallop

Cover Design
Abby Scholz

Illustrator
Paul Vismara

Compositor
GEX Publishing Services

Printed in the United States of America

3 4 5 6 7 8 9 GP 07 06 05

For more information, contact Course Technology, 25 Thomson Place, Boston, Massachusetts, 02210.

Or find us on the World Wide Web at: www.course.com

ISBN 0-619-18397-7

Introduce a Dynamic Web Multimedia Curriculum

With these *Macromedia-Approved New Products!*

Our exciting new series of Macromedia books will provide everything needed to learn about multimedia and Web site design.

NEW! Macromedia Studio MX 2004 Step-by-Step
For Macromedia Flash MX 2004, Dreamweaver MX 2004, Fireworks MX 2004, and FreeHand MX for Windows and Macintosh, Kirsti Aho, Editor
40+ hours of instruction

0-619-18390-X	Student Textbook, Soft-Perfect Cover
0-619-18391-8	Instructor Resources (CD-ROM), includes testing software (Windows platform)
0-619-18392-6	Instructor Resources (CD-ROM), includes testing software (Macintosh platform)
0-619-18393-4	Review Pack (Data CD)

NEW! Multimedia Projects for Macromedia Flash MX 2004 and Dreamweaver MX 2004, Kirsti Aho, Editor
20+ hours of instruction

0-619-18394-2	3-ring binder (extra projects)
0-619-18391-8	Instructor Resources (CD-ROM), includes testing software (Windows platform)
0-619-18392-6	Instructor Resources (CD-ROM), includes testing software (Macintosh platform)
0-619-18393-4	Review Pack (Data CD)

NEW! Digital Design Curriculum Guide, Kirsti Aho, Anuja Dharkar, and Gloria Miller
150+ hours of instruction

0-619-18396-9	3-ring binder (for instructors)
0-619-18397-7	Digital Design Concepts and Technical Guide
0-619-18399-3	Instructor Resources (CD-ROM)
0-619-18400-0	Review Pack (Data CD)

HOW TO ORDER

To Order by Phone
Call toll free:
1-800-824-5179
8:00 AM – 8:00 PM EST (Mon.-Fri.)

To Order by Fax
Fax toll free 24 hours
1-800-487-8488

To Order by Mail
Write to:
Thomson Learning
Distribution Center
ATTN: Order Fulfillment
P.O. Box 6904
Florence, KY 41042-6904

To Order by Web
Go to:
www.course.com

Customer Support
Call toll free:
1-800-824-5179

Each Order Must Include

- Your complete name, shipping and billing address, ZIP Code, and daytime phone number with area code
- Your account number
- Complete title ISBN and quantity for each title ordered
- Purchase order number (for orders not accompanied by payment)
- Any special instructions or information clearly noted
- Credit card orders must be accompanied by the cardholder's complete name, address, phone number, card number, card expiration date, and shipping instructions (e.g., UPS, Federal Express, RPS). The school name, college name, or company name is essential. All written orders must contain the signature of the cardholder.

Join Us On the Internet **www.course.com**

ACKNOWLEDGMENTS

Contributors:

Cindy Agnew
Michael Epstein
Joanne Fevergeon
Ann Gallenson
Joseph Halpin
Brian Martin
Jane McKillip
Mark Morgan
Skipper Pickle
Shannon Thissen

Pilot Teachers:

Lou August – Wilderness Technology Alliance
Mary Ann Campo – Havermale Alternative School
Dave Farnell – North River High School
Joanne Fevergeon – Ellensburg High School
Leanne Fike – Lake Washington High School
Will Fry – Chief Leschi High School
Lance Groesbeck – Edmonds-Woodway High School
Nancy Jensen – Mt. Rainier High School
Shane Loucks – White Pass High School
Sara McReynolds – Kennewick High School
Doug Reppe – Quincy High School
Ralph Rise – Lake Roosevelt High School
Chris Sande – Rogers High School
Peggy J. Soong-Yaplee – Cleveland High School
Loretta Speed – Ingraham High School
Anne Taylor – Wishkah Valley High School
Shannon Thissen – Sumner High School
Bre Urness-Straight – Anacortes High School

About This Guide

This student text is a companion publication designed to be used with *Digital Design Curriculum Guide: Foundations of Web Design.*

This text provides the guides designed for project activities in *Digital Design.* (Teachers may need to reproduce any worksheets they want to use from *Digital Design.*) This guide is not designed as a standalone, independent-study text.

Two types of student guides are included—concept guides and technical guides.

Concept guides provide information about topics relating to Web design and development such as rules of copyright, Internet citations, and professional design processes.

Technical guides contain step-by-step explanations to help students complete software-related tasks such as creating graphics, building Web pages, and creating interactive movies. These guides illustrate interface features and techniques in Fireworks MX 2004, Dreamweaver MX 2004, and Macromedia Flash MX 2004.

Table of Contents

UNIT 5 INTERACTIVITY DESIGN WITH MACROMEDIA FIREWORKS MX 2004 95

UNIT 6 REVIEW WORKSHOP 107

UNIT 7 BUILDING A BASIC CLIENT WEB SITE 111

UNIT 8 REDESIGNING A CLIENT WEB SITE 133

UNIT 9 ENHANCING USER EXPERIENCE ON THE WEB 199

Unit 1: Introduction to the Internet

Activity Guides

Activity 1.1: Acceptable Use Policies

Bellingham Public Schools Acceptable Use Policy

Washington State K-20 Network Conditions of Use

Yakima School District Acceptable Use Policy

Activity 1.2: Introduction to the Internet

Web Browser

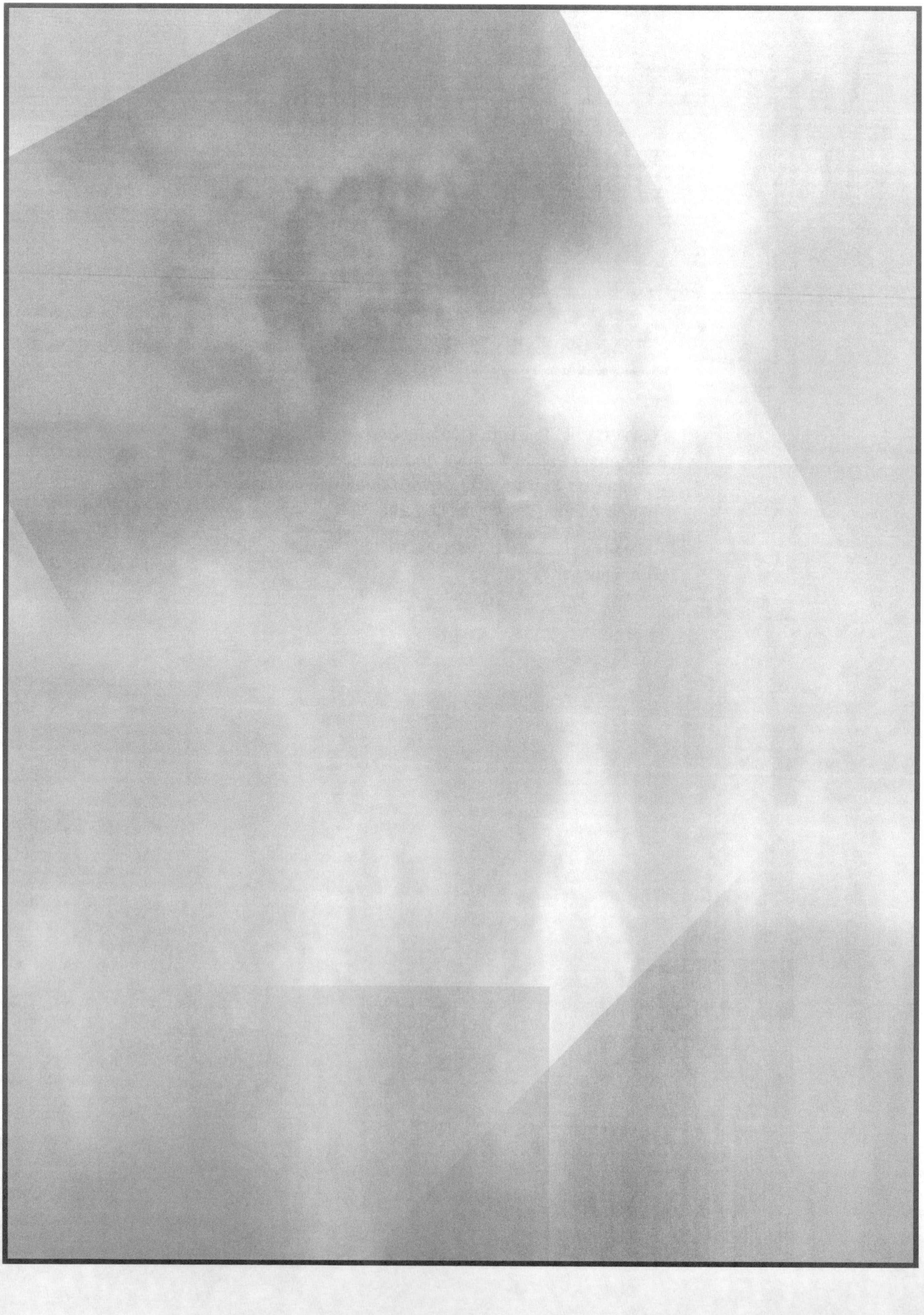

Bellingham Public Schools Acceptable Use Policy

Bellingham Public Schools

You may copy this form. Go to *http://www.bham.wednet.edu/perform.htm*

Parent Permission Letter
Internet and Electronic Mail Permission Form

The Bellingham Public Schools

We are pleased to offer students of the Bellingham Public Schools access to the district computer network for electronic mail and the Internet. To gain access to e-mail and the Internet, all students under the age of 18 must obtain parental permission and must sign and return this form to the LIBRARY MEDIA SPECIALIST. Students 18 and over may sign their own forms.

Access to e-mail and the Internet will enable students to explore thousands of libraries, databases, and bulletin boards while exchanging messages with Internet users throughout the world. Families should be warned that some material accessible via the Internet may contain items that are illegal, defamatory, inaccurate or potentially offensive to some people. While our intent is to make Internet access available to further educational goals and objectives, students may find ways to access other materials as well. We believe that the benefits to students from access to the Internet, in the form of information resources and opportunities for collaboration, exceed any disadvantages. But ultimately, parents and guardians of minors are responsible for setting and conveying the standards that their children should follow when using media and information sources. To that end, the Bellingham Public Schools support and respect each family's right to decide whether or not to apply for access.

District Internet and E-Mail Rules

Students are responsible for good behavior on school computer networks just as they are in a classroom or a school hallway. Communications on the network are often public in nature. General school rules for behavior and communications apply.

The network is provided for students to conduct research and communicate with others. Access to network services is given to students who agree to act in a considerate and responsible manner. Parent permission is required. Access is a privilege—not a right. Access entails responsibility.

Individual users of the district computer networks are responsible for their behavior and communications over those networks. It is presumed that users will comply with district standards and will honor the agreements they have signed. Beyond the clarification of such standards, the district is not responsible for restricting, monitoring or controlling the communications of individuals utilizing the network.

Network storage areas may be treated like school lockers. Network administrators may review files and communications to maintain system integrity and ensure that users are using the system responsibly. Users should not expect that files stored on district servers will always be private.

Within reason, freedom of speech and access to information will be honored. During school, teachers of younger students will guide them toward appropriate materials. Outside of school, families bear the same responsibility for such guidance as they exercise with information sources such as television, telephones, movies, radio and other potentially offensive media.

As outlined in Board policy and procedures on student rights and responsibilities (3200), copies of which are available in school offices, the following are not permitted:

Sending or displaying offensive messages or pictures

Using obscene language

Harassing, insulting or attacking others

Damaging computers, computer systems or computer networks

Violating copyright laws

Using another's password

Trespassing in another's folders, work or files

Intentionally wasting limited resources

Employing the network for commercial purposes

Violations may result in a loss of access as well as other disciplinary or legal action.

User Agreement and Parent Permission Form - 1995

As a user of the Bellingham Public Schools computer network, I hereby agree to comply with the above stated rules—communicating over the network in a reliable fashion while honoring all relevant laws and restrictions.

Student Signature ____________________

As the parent or legal guardian of the minor student signing above, I grant permission for my son or daughter to access networked computer services such as electronic mail and the Internet. I understand that individuals and families may be held liable for violations. I understand that some materials on the Internet may be objectionable, but I accept responsibility for guidance of Internet use—setting and conveying standards for my daughter or son to follow when selecting, sharing or exploring information and media.

Parent Signature ____________________ Date ________

Name of Student ____________________

School ______________ Grade _____

Soc. Sec. # ______________ Birth Date ______________

Street Address ______________________________

Home Telephone ______________

WASHINGTON STATE K-20 NETWORK CONDITIONS OF USE AND ACCEPTABLE USE POLICIES

http://www.k12.wa.us/k20/aup/default.asp

(Including all connections, circuits, switching and uplink-downlink resources and applications).

This document contains two sections. Section 1, "Conditions of Use," establishes the conditions of use of the K-20 Network for purposes of technical connections, operation and management. Section 2, "Acceptable Use Policies," provides guidance to institutions on non-technical policies relating to user eligibility for participation in the K-20 network, acceptable uses of network resources, and procedures for enforcement.

Section 1: Conditions of Use

1. Only institutions authorized by statute and approved by the K-20 Educational Network Board (K-20 Board) may maintain connections to the state-funded K-20 network, with the exception that certain external interface connections which are engineered by the K-20 Network Technical Steering Committee (NTSC) to provide interconnections with other networks are permitted. Such connections are permitted with the proviso that no network transit is allowed for such external connections other than traffic to or from authorized K-20 members. Two examples of such exceptions are local peerings and commodity and research internet transit arrangements that are engineered by the K-20 NTSC.
2. Only traffic to or from legitimate K-20 members may be transmitted over the K-20 network.
3. Uses of the network that may jeopardize the proper technical operation of the network, or uses of the network that may cause the network to be disconnected from external networks, are strictly prohibited. Where such uses occur, the K-20 Operations Cooperative (KOCO) is authorized by the K-20 Board to suspend such connections until the problem is resolved to its satisfaction. A party that believes a connection has been improperly suspended may request that the NTSC review the KOCO's action; such review shall be undertaken and completed in a timely manner (not to exceed five working days). The NTSC may, upon review, direct the KOCO to reconnect the party. A party may appeal a decision of the NTSC to the Information Services Board, the decision of which shall be final.

Section 2: Acceptable Use Policies

1. Use of the network is restricted to educational purposes, i.e., activities consistent with the educational missions of the institutions and sectors. The determination of what is an "educational purpose" rests with each institution or sector. The term is intended to be defined broadly, and may include activities that directly or indirectly support the delivery of educational services. However, the following are presumed not to be educational uses:
   - Organized political or religious advocacy.

- Resale or lease of K-20 shared bandwidth, electronics, or other equipment to private entities for commercial purposes. However, non-educational entities may utilize K-20 services under certain conditions set forth in paragraphs (2) and (3) below. For purposes of this document, resale or lease does not include educational institutions' arrangements with private entities for the transmission of (1) digital content developed by the educational entities as part of university-sponsored research; or (2) course materials, library resources, or ancillary materials, the dissemination of which is consistent with the institution's educational purpose.
- The transmission of obscene material.
- For the use of K-20 resources for videoconferencing services, priority shall be given to educational activities at K-20 Board-approved sites on a first-come, first-served basis. An institution may permit public sector non-educational entities to use its own (non-shared) videoconferencing facilities provided the following conditions are met:
  - The use involves facilities that would otherwise go unused.
  - The use involves only the on-site facilities and related equipment, and does not utilize K-20 transport or MCU capacity.

2. Where a shared component of a K-20 satellite uplink/downlink facility is underutilized, the trustee institution may find that the lease of the facility for non-educational commercial purposes is appropriate for limited periods to help offset the operational costs of the facility. Such lease arrangements are authorized provided the following conditions are met:
   - The lease involves air time or equipment that would otherwise go unused.
   - The lease involves only the uplink/downlink facility and related equipment, and does not utilize K-20 transport or other shared equipment.
   - The institution agrees to account to the K-20 Board for all monies obtained as a result of the lease.
3. The participants authorized by statute to use the K-20 network may only do so for activities which they are legally allowed to conduct and which do not conflict with state or federal law or policy which governs their endeavors. The network may not be used for illegal purposes. Entities have primary responsibility for enforcing the provisions of this document. While it is understood that enforcement here cannot be done through technology, it will instead be achieved at the end-sites and via the normal legal or policy channels relevant to appropriate investigation and adjudication.
4. Where an entity is alleged to have violated one or more provisions of this document other than Section 1(3), the K-20 Board shall take appropriate remedial action, which may include suspension of an entity's network connection, only after providing the entity with notice of the specific allegations against it and an opportunity to respond to those allegations in writing or, at the entity's option, in public hearing. The K-20 Board shall set forth in writing the basis for any remedial action. Any entity whose connection to the network has been suspended by the K-20 Board may request reconnection to the network upon a showing that it has taken appropriate steps to correct the matter or matters that are the basis for the action.
5. Nothing in this document is intended to preclude an entity from developing or enforcing its own acceptable use policies to supplement Section 2 of this document, provided its policies are not inconsistent with those set forth above. Where an entity proposes a policy that is inconsistent, it may at any time petition the K-20 Board for a waiver of one or more specific

provisions. A petition for waiver shall set forth the provision or provisions for which waiver is sought; the grounds for such a waiver; the impact of a waiver, if any, on the technical operation of the network; and the fiscal impact, if any, on the network. The decision to grant or deny a waiver shall rest solely with the K-20 Board.

Note: At its March 23, 2000 meeting, the K-20 Educational Network Board approved and adopted these conditions of use and acceptable use policies on a permanent basis.

Yakima School District Acceptable Use Policy

http://www.esd105.wednet.edu/

ESD 105/K-20 policy

1. Use of the K-20 Network shall be solely for the purpose of facilitating the exchange of information in furtherance of education and research, and otherwise be consistent with the purposes and objectives of OSPI, Educational Service District 105 and other members of K-20.
2. Any use of the network for commercial or for-profit purposes is prohibited.
3. Use of the network for private business is prohibited.
4. Extensive use of the network for personal use is prohibited.
5. Any use of the network for product advertisement or political lobbying is prohibited.
6. K-20 e-mail accounts are to be used only by the authorized owner of the account for the authorized purpose. Student usage of any kind, including under a teacher's username, is only permitted after student and parent/guardian sign-off of the Acceptable Use Policies attached or an equivalent school district policy approved by ESD 105/K-20.
7. Users shall not intentionally seek information on, obtain copies of or modify files or passwords belonging to other users, or represent other users on the network.
8. All communications and information accessible via the network should not be assumed to be private property.
9. No use of the network shall serve to disrupt the use of the network by others; hardware or software shall not be destroyed, modified or abused in any way.
10. Malicious use of the network to develop programs that harass other users or infiltrate a computer or computer system and/or alter the software components of a computer or computer system is prohibited.
11. Hate mail, harassment, discriminatory remarks and other similar behaviors are prohibited.
12. The illegal installation of copyrighted software for use on personal computers is prohibited.
13. Use of the network to access obscene or pornographic material is prohibited.
14. Diligent effort should be made to delete mail regularly from your personal mail directory to avoid excessive use of ESD 105 servers' hard disk space.
15. Any use of K-20 that accesses sources beyond K-20 itself shall conform to the Acceptable Use Policies of those other sources.
16. Interpretation, application, and modification of this Acceptable Use Policy shall be within the discretion of ESD 105 and WSIPC. Questions about any issue arising under this Policy should be directed to ESD 105 or WSIPC.

At random intervals, the local School District, Educational Service District 105 and K-20 will make determinations on whether specific uses of the network are consistent with the acceptable use practice. Local School Districts and Educational Service District 105 reserve the right to log Internet use and to monitor fileserver space utilization by users while respecting the privacy of user accounts. Local School Districts and Educational Service District 105 reserve the right to remove a user account on the network to prevent further unauthorized activity. K-20 and Educational Service District 105 reserve the right to disconnect a School District to prevent further unauthorized activity.

ESD 105 Publishing Policies

All ESD 105 School Districts and K-12 private schools are invited to use ESD 105 servers to house and serve World Wide Web pages and related files. As this is a shared resource for the entire region, districts and schools choosing to use this service are subject to the following policies, procedures and expectations:

1. One staff member from each district, private school or large school building will be responsible for the content, uploading and maintenance of all presented information and materials. This staff member must be an active ESD 105 Internet account holder and have completed the Web Publishing Application Form with all required signatures.
2. The authorized staff member must be indicated in the "webmaster" or "mailto:" references on all pages.
3. All pages and materials presented must be school district, building, classroom or educationally orientated. The presentation of classroom-based student projects is acceptable and encouraged; however, no personal information may be included. "Personal" home pages are not permitted.
4. Due to privacy and student safety concerns, personal information about students is to be limited to "first-name only." Pictures which individually identify students (even just by first name), family members or parents are not permitted. Group pictures which do not identify individual members are acceptable.
5. Materials must be utilized and presented in the most efficient manner available at the time. For example, large graphics should be stored in the lowest resolution of practical quality, allowing the graphic to be loaded more quickly while demanding fewer server resources. Large graphics should also be presented in "interlaced" or gif89 format. Any sounds, movies or other large file downloads should also be in the lowest resolution of practical quality and therefore able to be presented as efficiently as possible.
6. All download references should be to resources at ftp.esd105.K-20.edu as appropriate.
7. All presented information and materials must be free of copyright and/or trademark restrictions.
8. No derogatory, inflammatory, libelous or illegal information may be presented.
9. All backgrounds, dots, buttons, lines and similar gif or jpeg images must be accessed from a common directory.

10. The main page in all school district directories and subdirectories will be named "index.html."
11. No software programs or scripts in any form may be uploaded.
12. Each school district is limited to 15 MB of disk space for WWW materials.
13. ESD 105 reserves the right to remove any page, file or material from any district or building directories or to remove the WWW publishing service altogether in response to policy violations or to protect the efficient operation of ESD 105 servers and networks.
14. A program to convert RGB (Red, Green, Blue) color numbers into hexadecimal is provided to assist you to add color backgrounds and text on your pages.
15. There is a fee of $25 per district or school site.

Web Browser

Command Menus: Provide access to the complete set of commands and features.

Title Bar: Contains the title of the Web page.

Back and Forward: Retrace your steps as you move from page to page.

Refresh: Reload the current page.

Favorites: Quick access to sites you've added to your Favorites menu.

Print: Print the current page.

Stop: Interrupts the current download.

Search: Find Web content using a key word or phrase.

History: List the sites you've visited recently.

Edit: Launch the current page in an external program for HTML editing.

Status Bar: Identifies the path of links, displays the status of pages as they download, and displays security information.

Go: Sends you to the site in the Address box.

Mail: Read e-mail or send e-mail containing a link to (or a copy of) the current Web page.

Links Bar: Add or remove links to your favorite sites.

Address Box: Enter the Internet address (URL) or location of the Web site or file you wish to view.

Home: Takes you directly to a Web page you designate as your starting page.

Discuss: Attach comments to a Web page or any document that can be opened with a browser.

Unit 2: Graphic Design Using Macromedia Fireworks MX 2004

Activity Guides

Activity 2.1: Introduction to Graphics and Copyright

Principles and Rules of Copyright

Internet Citations

Sample Student Document

Activity 2.2: Introduction to Scanning

Scanning

How to Scan Images without Image-Editing Software

Activity 2.4: Optimizing Graphics for the Web

Fireworks Optimize Panel

How to Optimize GIF Images

How to Optimize JPEG Images

Activity 2.5: Making a Nameplate

Fireworks Panels

How to Build a Nameplate

How to Create Effects

Activity 2.12: Naming Conventions

Naming Conventions

Principles and Rules of Copyright

Copyright is protection for intellectual property.

Intellectual property consists of anything an individual has written or created. It might be music, text, pictures, photographs, sounds, and so on.

Fair use doctrine is part of the copyright laws. It states that "limited portions" of material may be used without written permission for certain purposes, such as reporting the news or schoolwork. It doesn't define "limited," though, so be sure you don't overuse material. The fair use doctrine requires you to give credit to the author or creator of any material you use.

Derivative works are copyrighted materials that have been altered or changed. Such material is protected by copyright laws. If you alter a copyrighted photograph by using computer software, that photograph is still protected, and you may not use it without written permission.

Academic standards for copyrighted material are higher than others. Because scholars and researchers study so many different ideas and are responsible for sharing those ideas with the world, they are required to satisfy higher standards of honesty. They must give credit not only when quoting the exact words of someone else but also for the ideas those words represent. As a researcher, you cannot paraphrase what someone else says and not give credit for it.

Bibliographies are lists of sources that have been used in research. When using the Internet for research or for design work, you need to give credit where it is due. Often, people who use graphics and images from the Internet for publication on their own Web page create a list of image credits, rather than a bibliography.

Rules of Copyright

1. You cannot use copyrighted material without written permission from the creator of the material (or from its copyright holder).
2. Material can be protected even if it does not display the © symbol. Even if no mention is made regarding copyright, you must assume that all material from another source is protected.
3. Penalties for violating copyright laws can range from mild to severe. If you break the copyright law, you might simply receive an e-mail message from the author asking you to stop using the material. If you publish the material on a Web site, the Webmaster might shut down your site. In addition, you could be sued by the author or prosecuted by federal authorities.
4. To make sure you are not violating any copyright law, it is important that you do the following:
   - Write or send e-mail to the author or creator and ask permission to use the material. Do not use it until you are given permission.
   - Follow the directions on the site regarding use of material. You might be asked to create a link on your page or to notify the author or creator.
   - Most important: *Do not* use any material if you don't have written permission.

INTERNET CITATIONS

Any information you use from a book or magazine for a report should be noted or cited in your bibliography. Citing information means you are giving credit for the work to its author. There are specific forms to follow for each kind of source.

Citation format

Be sure you fill in the citation exactly as it is written, with information from your source. Your school's preferred citation method must be followed exactly. Following are examples of citation formats for specific Internet resources.

World Wide Web

Author. Title of item. [Online] Available http://address/filename, date of document or, if not available, date of download.

Example:

Cintas, Benjamin. The Cold War Revisited: A splintered Germany. [Online] Available http://usa.coldwar.server.gov/index/cold.war/countries/former.soviet.block/Germany/germany.htm, November 5, 1996.

Online image

Description or title of image. (Online Image) Available http://address/filename, date of document or, if not available, date of download.

Online sound

Description or title of sound. (Online Sound) Available http://address/filename, date of document or, if not available, date of download.

Online video clip

Description or title of video clip. (Online Video Clip) Available http://address/filename, date of document or, if not available, date of download.

Other Resources to Cite

- e-mail
- newsgroups

Sample Student Document

Filename: planetary_nebula_mz3.jpg
File size: 35.5 KB
Found at http://heritage.stsci.edu/2001/05/index.html

Planetary Nebula Mz3 by the Hubble Heritage Team. Copyright 2001 by NASA and Space Telescope Science Institute.

SCANNING

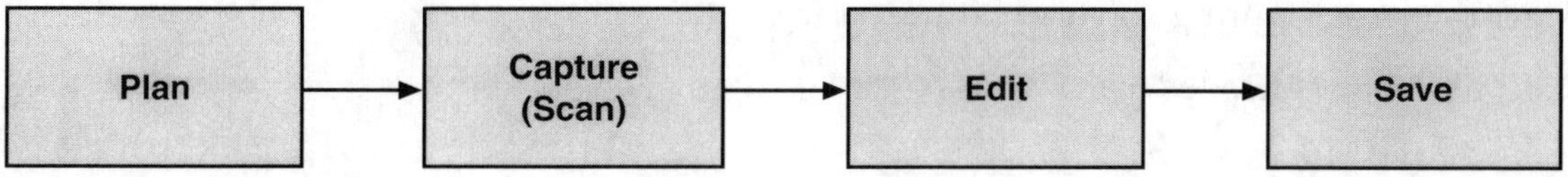

PLAN

Ask yourself:

- What message do I want to get across?
- Does this image tell the story? Focus on the message.
- Does it tell the same story as another image?
- How am I going to use this image? Displayed on a monitor? Printed?
- Will I need to modify this image again for another purpose?
- Is there any extraneous information in the image?
- Are there any distracting details?

CAPTURE

Preview Scan:

- Turn on the scanner.
- Position the image or object on the surface.
- Start the scanner software (if it did not already start when the scanner was turned on).
- Set the scan mode.
- Scan.
  - Set the final size.
  - Set the resolution.
- Final scan: Scan again to do a "final" scan.

EDIT

Edit Image:

- Start the image-editing software, if necessary.
- Correct color, if needed.
- Add special effects.
- Resize, if needed.

SAVE

Save Files:

- Save as a file I can make changes to in the future.
- Save as a Web-ready file.
- Save as a print-ready file.

How to Scan Images without Image-Editing Software

1. Lift the scanner cover. Check the orientation for the placement of the image. Notice the orientation hash marks etched into the plastic frame around the glass portion.
2. Place the image on the glass. Check to be sure it is lined up on the glass.
3. Press the Scan button (typically on the far left side of the row of buttons). If there are no buttons, you should see a dialog box where you can select the next step.
4. The scanner lamp turns on and warms up. Wait for the image to be completely scanned.
5. The scanner takes a preview scan.

   Note: Now you can make your first adjustments. Cut away the parts of the image you do not want to include in the final scan. Reset the resolution or scan type.
6. Take a final scan.
7. Save the image as a TIF (TIFF), GIF, or JPEG. These are the most common file types.
8. If you have image-editing software, you can open the scanned file and use the image editor to make edits.

Fireworks Optimize Panel

You can select your optimization settings by using the Optimize panel. The first step is to determine which type of file you plan to export, such as GIF or JPEG. You can then select the detailed settings. GIF images are generally used for line art and images with solid colors. GIF images can contain transparent areas and can be used for animation files. The disadvantage of GIF images is that they are restricted to 256 colors. JPEG is generally used for photographic images or images with gradients and more colors. JPEG files cannot be transparent or animated.

Options for GIF Optimization

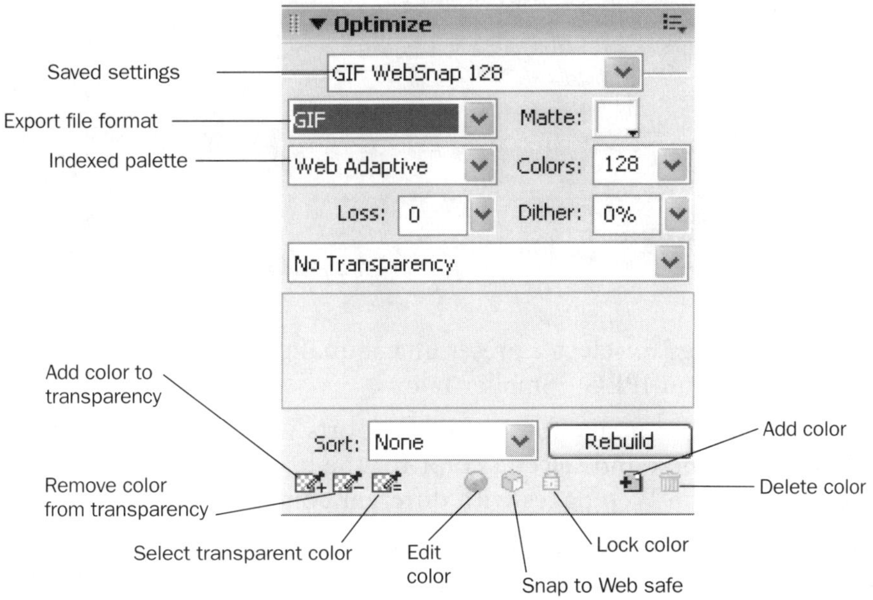

Saved settings: Use Saved settings to select a preset image quality for export. For GIF these include GIF Web 216, GIF WebSnap 256, GIF WebSnap 128, GIF Adaptive 256, and Animated GIF Websnap 128.

Matte: If you want to anti-alias an image for multiple exports with different-colored backgrounds, click the Matte color box and select a color for the background of the image. This is useful if the image will appear on Web pages with different colored backgrounds.

Colors: Control the number of colors in the image. This number is automatically configured from the Settings selection. Decreasing the number of colors lowers file size and can lower image quality.

Dither: The Dither option is useful for images with many color gradations. Dithering approximates colors not in the current color palette by alternating two similar colors. Increasing the Dither setting can greatly increase file size.

Loss: Lower the image quality on export. Higher loss settings can yield smaller files but lower image quality. A loss setting between 5 and 15 typically yields the best results.

Transparency: Remove the background color or halos around the image so that in a Web browser the background of the Web page is visible through those areas. (This capability is a key advantage of exporting images as GIFs.) The Index Transparency option removes the background color. The Alpha Transparency option removes the background of an image if its canvas color is transparent. The Add color to transparency button enables you to remove specific colors from the image. The No Transparency option exports an image without any transparency.

Options for JPEG Optimization

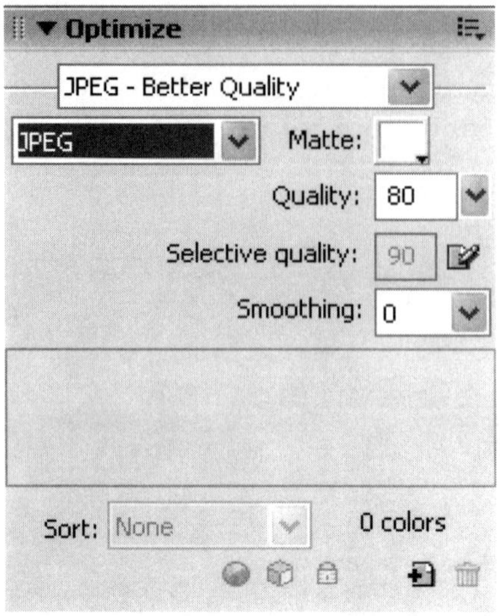

Saved settings: Use Saved settings to select a preset image quality for export. For JPEG these include JPEG - Better Quality and JPEG - Smaller File.

Matte: If you want to anti-alias an image for multiple exports with different colored backgrounds, click the Matte color box and select a color for the background of the image. This is useful if the image will appear on Web pages with different colored backgrounds.

Quality: Adjust the quality of the image. Lower quality decreases file size; higher quality increases file size.

Selective Quality: Adjust the quality of only the selected part of the image while leaving the rest of the image intact. Used with a JPEG mask.

Smoothing: Blur hard edges in the image and reduce file size.

How to Optimize GIF Images

GIF (Graphic Interchange Format) is a graphic file format best used for images with large areas of solid flat color, such as simple illustrations, logos, and text. With Macromedia Fireworks MX 2004, you can compare different versions of the same graphic to create the best quality with the smallest file size. Before optimizing, complete the graphic (size, effects, color, and design).

Optimize a GIF Image

1. Open a completed graphic in Fireworks.
2. On the Optimize panel, choose **GIF** from the Export file format drop-down menu. Then choose the type of GIF you want from the Indexed palette drop-down menu.
3. Select the **4-Up** button to compare different versions of the image. Make sure the image is visible. (If necessary, use the **Hand** tool to drag the image into the middle of the display area.)

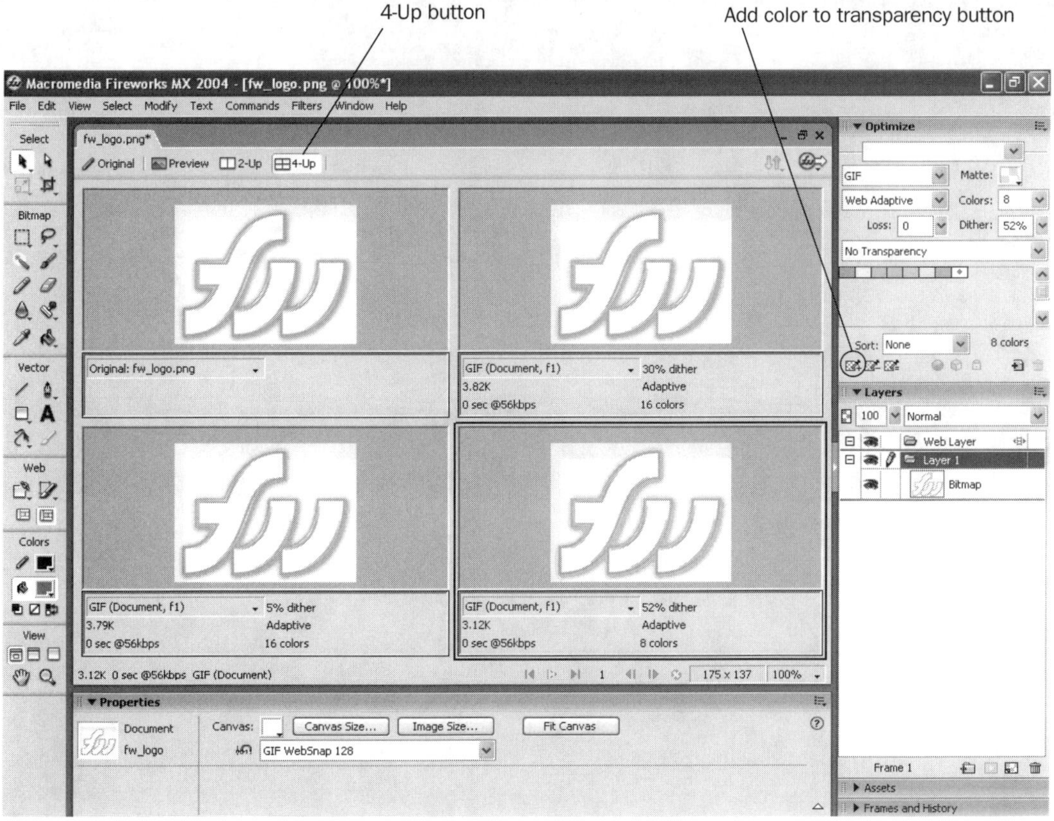

4. Use the **Pointer** tool to select each of the three alternate versions of the original image in turn, and try different settings on the Optimize panel to find the smallest file size with the most acceptable quality:
   - To adjust the image for many color gradations, increase the Dither setting.
   - To make the file smaller, increase Loss (usually between 5 and 15).
   - To remove the background color or halos around the image, select **Index Transparency**.
   - To remove specific colors from the image, use the **Add color to transparency** button. This capability is a key advantage of exporting images as GIFs.

   As you try different settings, note the file size and download time for each quality level.
5. To export the image version you prefer, click it and choose **File > Export**. Name the file with a .gif extension.
6. To also save the richest version of the file, choose **File > Save** to save the image as a Macromedia Fireworks PNG file (with a .png extension).

How to Optimize JPEG Images

JPEG (Joint Photograph Experts Group) is a graphic file format best used for photographs or for images with subtle changes in color, gradations, or lighting. With Fireworks, you can compare different versions of the same graphic to create the best quality with the smallest file size. Before optimizing, complete the graphic (size, effects, color, and design).

Optimize a JPEG Image

1. Open the completed graphic in Fireworks.
2. On the Optimize panel, choose **JPEG** from the **Export file format** drop-down menu.
3. Select the **4-Up** button to compare different versions of the image. Make sure the image is visible in the display area. (If necessary, use the **Hand** tool to drag the image into the middle of the display area.)

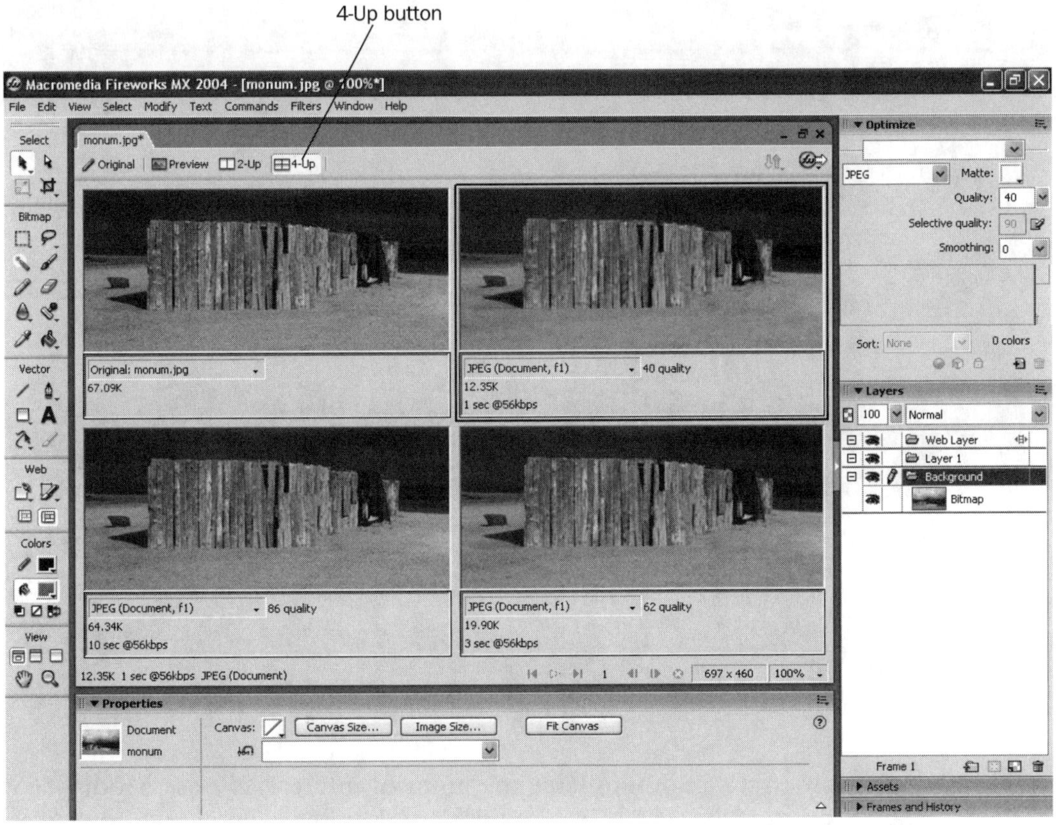

4. Use the **Pointer** tool to select each of the three alternate versions of the original image in turn, and try different settings on the Optimize panel to find the smallest file size with the most acceptable quality. On the Optimize panel, increase Smoothing to decrease the file size.
   - On the **Saved settings** drop-down menu, choose **JPEG - Better Quality** or **JPEG - Smaller File** for preset Quality values.
   - Try other values for the Quality setting.
   - To make the file smaller, increase the Smoothing.

As you try different settings, note the file size and download time for each quality level.

5. To export the image version you prefer, click it and choose **File > Export**. Name the file with a .jpg extension.
6. To also save the richest version of the file, choose **File > Save** to save the file as a Macromedia Fireworks PNG file (with a .png extension).

Use a JPEG Mask for Further Optimization (optional)

You can further optimize the size of a graphic by selecting a specific area of the image and changing its quality setting.

1. Click the **Original** button to return to the (single) original image.
2. Using the **Marquee** tool, outline the point of interest in your image.
3. With the point of interest selected, choose **Select > Select Inverse**. This selects everything *except* the point of interest of the image.

4. To make changes only to the region outside the point of interest, choose **Modify > Selective JPEG > Save Selection as JPEG Mask**. A highlight color appears on everything except the point of interest of the image.
5. On the Optimize panel, you can now make changes to the Selective Quality. Reducing this number retains the image quality of the point of interest, but reduces the quality of the background and thereby reduces the file size. Click the **Preview** tab to see the effect of your changes.

Fireworks Panels

Floating and Docked Panels

Panels provide easy access to controls that help you edit selected objects or elements of the document. Panels let you work on frames, layers, symbols, color swatches, and more. Each panel is "draggable," so you can group panels together in custom arrangements. By default, the panels are docked to the right side of the workspace. You can undock panel groups, add panels to a group, undock individual panels, rearrange the order of docked panel groups, and collapse and close panel groups. To undock a panel, drag the panel gripper in the upper left corner of the panel's title bar. Many of the panels are tabbed, with two or more panels combined.

Tools Panel

The Fireworks Tools panel is divided into clearly labeled sections for easy tool selection. If the Tools panel is not visible, you can display it by choosing Window > Tools. To select a tool, just click it or use the shortcut key shown in parentheses. If a tool has a small black triangle in the bottom right corner, it is part of a group of tools; click and hold the pointer over the tool to access the pop-up tool group.

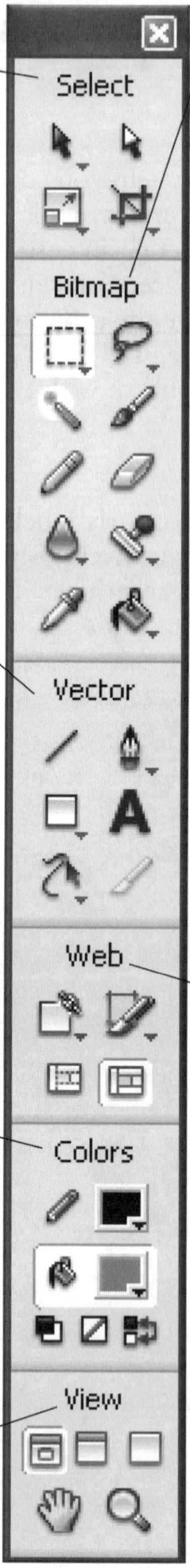

Selection, movement, and transformation tools:

Pointer tool (black arrow): Click an object to select it. Drag a selected object to move it.

Scale tool: Enlarge or reduce an object; rotate, flip, distort, or skew objects or groups. Press and hold the small arrow at the bottom right to choose the Skew or Distort tools.

Subselection tool (white arrow): Select and move points of an object or edit paths between adjacent points.

Crop tool: Remove the part of an image outside a selected rectangular region. Press and hold the small arrow at the bottom right to choose the Export Area tool.

Drawing and writing tools:

Line tool: Draw straight lines.

Rectangle tool: Draw rectangles. Press and hold the small arrow at the bottom right to choose a different shape to draw.

Freeform tool: Draw freeform shapes. Press and hold the small arrow at the bottom right to choose the Reshape Area or Path Scrubber tools.

Pen tool: Click to place points; the Pen tool connects successive points with straight lines. Drag a point to form a curve. Press and hold the small arrow at the bottom right to choose the Vector Path or Redraw Path tools.

Text tool: Type text.

Knife tool: Cut a path into two or more paths.

Color tools:

Stroke color: Set the color of the outline of an object.

Fill color: Set the color of the region inside an object.

Three bottom icons:

Set Default Stroke/Fill Colors: Automatically set colors for stroke and fill; defaults are black for stroke and white for fill.

No Stroke or Fill: A white box with a red line means there is no color (completely transparent). You cannot modify a stroke or fill with no color.

Swap Stroke and Fill Colors: Swap the stroke and fill colors.

View tools:

Hand tool: Move the visible portion of an image without using the document scroll bars.

Zoom tool (magnifying glass): Zoom in or out for a closer or farther view of an image.

Three top icons: Standard Screen mode, Full Screen with Menus mode, or Full Screen mode.

Image modification tools:

Marquee tool: Select a rectangular region of pixels. Press and hold the small arrow at the bottom right to choose a different shape for your selection tool.

Magic Wand tool: Select pixels of a similar color.

Pencil tool: Draw a vector path with a 1-pixel stroke.

Blur tool: Blur the focus of parts of an image. Press and hold the small arrow at the bottom right to choose the Sharpen, Dodge, Burn, or Smudge tools.

Eyedropper tool: Sample a color from swatches or anywhere on the screen.

Lasso tool: Similar to Marquee tool, but lets you freeform-select an area of pixels. Press and hold the small arrow at the bottom right to choose the Polygon Marquee tool.

Brush tool: Select from a variety of brush strokes, such as spray paint, calligraphy, crayon, and air brush.

Eraser tool: Erase parts of an image.

Rubber Stamp tool: Duplicate an area of an image. Press and hold the small arrow at the bottom right to choose the Replace Color or Red Eye Removal tools.

Paint Bucket tool: Change the color of selected pixels. Press and hold the small arrow at the bottom right to choose the Gradient tool.

Interactive objects tools:

Rectangle Hotspot tool: Draw a special area on top of an image; click to link to a new Web page. Press and hold the small arrow at the bottom right to choose a different shape for your hotspot.

Hide slices and hotspots tool: Hide all slices and hotspots drawn on an image.

Slice tool: Draw slice areas on an image to enable user interaction with the image on a Web page. Press and hold the small arrow at the bottom right to choose a different shape for your slice.

Show slices and hotspots tool: Show all slices and hotspots drawn on an image.

Property Inspector

The Property inspector displays options that change according to the current object or tool selection. Open a document, and the Property inspector displays document properties. Choose a tool, and it displays tool options. Select a vector object, and it displays options such as stroke and fill. You can change these and other options right from the Property inspector. By default, the Property inspector is visible, but you can hide or show it by choosing Window > Properties. The examples below show the properties for a text object and a rectangle shape. The options will vary depending on the type of object or tool you have selected.

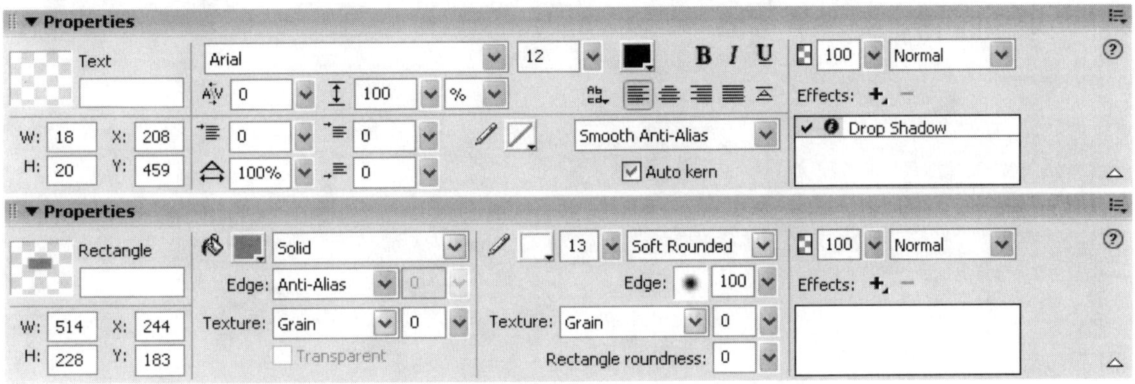

Note: On the Macintosh, the Property inspector does not include a title bar.

The left side of the Property inspector provides information about the selected object. You can also use this area to size or position the object on the canvas.

Fill: Change the Fill color by clicking the color box. For example, you can choose the fill type for a shape, such as solid, patterned, or dithered, from the menu beside the color box. This menu also provides various gradient effects. Other options include changing the type and amount of texture.

Stroke: Change the Stroke category or color. Change the Tip size (thickness of the stroke) by typing a number in the text box beside the color box or by clicking the down arrow and then setting the slider. Choose the Stroke category, such as pencil, felt tip, or crayon, from the menu in the upper right. Other options include changing the Edge softness, the type and amount of Texture, and the degree of Corner roundness.

Effects: Add effects by clicking the Add effects button (the plus sign). You can add effects to either the inside or border of objects. Effects include glows, shadows, bevels, and color adjustments. Delete existing effects by selecting the effect and clicking the Delete effects button (the minus sign). After you choose an effect from the menu, various options are available for adjusting that effect, such as lighting changes, angles, and depths of effects and colors of the effects.

How to Build a Nameplate

To build a nameplate, you create a shape, add text, and then add effects to the shape and text. You create the design by adding various effects and colors to the fill, stroke, and text.

Build a Nameplate

1. Start Fireworks, open a new document, and specify canvas dimensions (at least 400 pixels wide and 200 pixels high).
2. Save the file.
3. Create a background for your nameplate by using the **Rectangle** tool from the Tools panel. Leave some white space on the canvas around the rectangle to add effects later.

   The rectangle shows a light blue outline with small blue squares in the corner when it is selected.
4. Change the color of the stroke (outline) or the fill (inside) of the rectangle by using the **Stroke Color** and **Fill Color** tools on the Property inspector or the Tools panel.
5. To add your name to the rectangle, select the **Text** tool on the Tools panel, then click and drag to draw a text box over the rectangle you just created. Using the Property inspector, select the font, size, color, and style you want. Key your name.

   (The example below was created with Comic Sans MS, 32pt, white, bold, and all caps.)

6. To move your name around inside the rectangle, click the **Pointer** tool on the Tools panel, select the text object, and drag it to the desired position.
7. To customize the look of the nameplate, select the rectangle or text. Then click the **Add effects** button on the Property inspector, select an effect, and choose your settings. You can also change the type of fill and stroke.

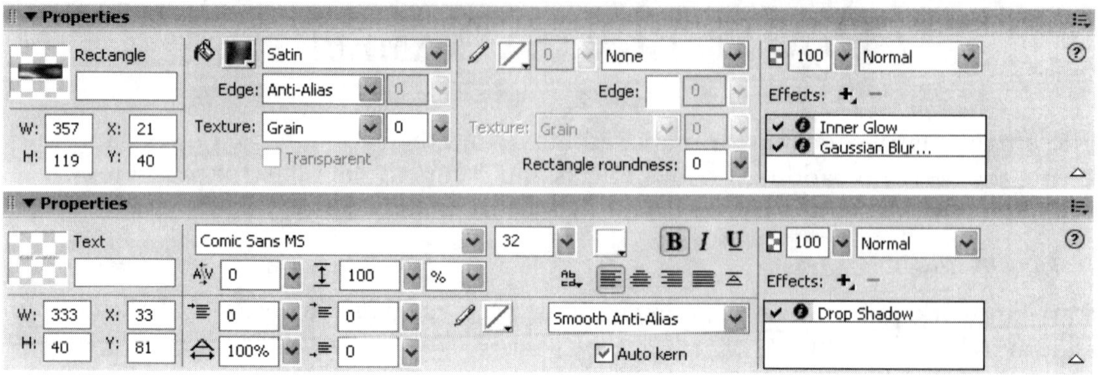

The illustrated nameplate uses a Satin fill pattern, no stroke, with Inner Glow and Gaussian Blur effects for the rectangle. The text on the nameplate uses the Drop Shadow effect.

8. After you complete all the desired effects, choose **Modify > Canvas > Trim Canvas** from the main menu bar. This action removes any excess white space around the image.

9. Save the nameplate.

How to Create Effects

Effects are applied to graphic and text objects, either to the interior of an object, to the border, or to both. Effects add dimension and contrast between the object and its background. These effects can be found on the Property inspector, in the Fill pane, the Stroke pane, and the Effects pane. Each effect has variables you can change to customize the effect. The following are the effects you can use.

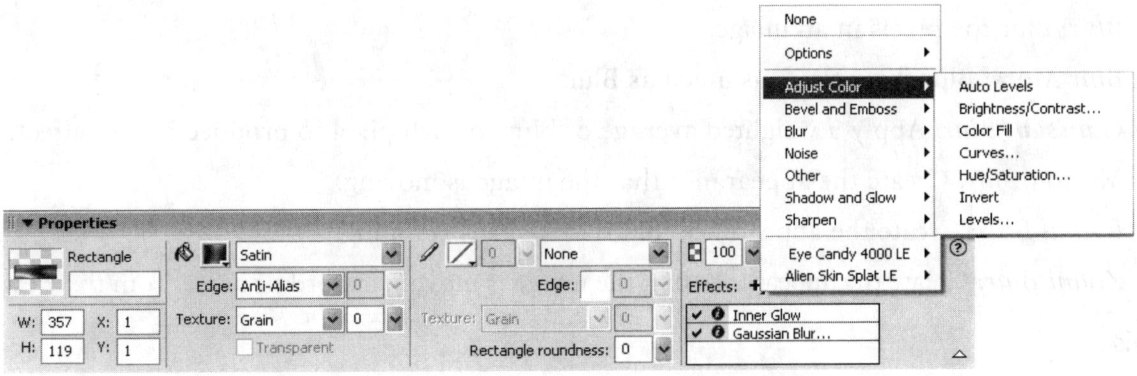

Effects Pane

Adjust Color

- *Auto Levels:* Same as the Levels filter, but Fireworks automatically changes the lightest to darkest pixel range.
- *Brightness/Contrast:* The *Brightness* makes the object brighter or darker. The *Contrast* makes the distinction between light and dark greater or smaller.
- *Color Fill:* Place another color on top of the object and change how transparent it is and/or how it blends with the original color.
- *Curves:* Adjust any color along the tonal range (the light-to-dark spectrum) without affecting other colors.
- *Hue/Saturation:* Adjust the color by changing the purity and lightness of the color in the image.
- *Invert:* Change a color to the inverse color on the color wheel. For example, apply Invert to a red object to change its color to light blue.
- *Levels:* Change the tonal range (the light-to-dark spectrum) by changing the number of pixels that are highlights, midtones, or shadows.

Bevel

You can alter a bevel's color, its type (raised, highlighted, inverted, or inset), the shape of the bevel edge (flat, smooth, sloped, and so on), its contrast, its softness, and the angle of light that falls on it.

- *Inner Bevel:* Give an object a 3D look by making the inside of the object look lower than the outside of the object.
- *Outer Bevel:* Give an object a 3D look by making the inside of the object look higher than the outside of the object.

Emboss

You can alter the way the embossing looks by altering its width, contrast, and softness, and the angle of light that falls on it.

- *Inset Emboss:* Make an image appear inset from its background.
- *Raised Emboss:* Make an image appear raised from its background.

Blur

- *Blur:* Blur the pixels in an image.
- *Blur More:* Blur three times as much as Blur.
- *Gaussian Blur:* Apply a weighted average of blur to each pixel to produce a hazy effect.
- *Motion Blur:* Create the appearance that the image is moving.
- *Radial Blur:* Create the appearance that the image is spinning.
- *Zoom Blur:* Create the appearance that the image is moving toward or away from the viewer.

Noise

You can add to an image to control random variation in color for the image. Somtimes, such as when you are pasting part of one image into another, the difference in the amount of random color variation in the two images can stand out, preventing the images from blending together smoothly. In such a case, you can add noise to one or both images to create the illusion that both images come from the same source.

Other

- *Convert to Alpha:* Convert an object into a gradient transparency based on the transparency of the image.
- *Find Edges:* Identify the color transitions and change those transitions to lines to give a sketched look.

Shadow and Glow

The Shadow and Glow effects simulate angles of light falling on the object. You can alter the color of the shadow or glow. You can alter the distance of the shadow from the object or width of the glow, the opacity of the shadow or glow, its softness, and the angle of light that falls on a shadow or the offset of the glow from the object.

- *Drop Shadow:* Make the object appear to be casting a shadow.
- *Glow:* Make the object appear to glow.
- *Inner Glow:* Highlight the object.
- *Inner Shadow:* Darken the object so it looks as though something is casting a shadow on it.

Sharpen

- *Sharpen:* Adjust the focus of a blurred image.
- *Sharpen More:* Adjust the focus three times more than Sharpen.
- *Unsharp Mask:* Adjust the contrast of the image edges to sharpen an image.

Eye Candy 4000 LE

Like the other effects, Eye Candy 4000 LE effects have attributes for altering them. Because Eye Candy combines many of the previously mentioned effects, you can alter combinations of subattributes for customizing the effect of Eye Candy.

- *Bevel Boss:* Create a beveled, embossed, and highlighted look all at once.
- *Marble:* Create a marbled look.
- *Motion Trail:* Draw a trail from the object to simulate rapid movement.

Alien Skin Splat LE

- *Edges:* Apply a halftone dot pattern to the edges.

Fill Effects

Fill effects alter only the inside of an object. These effects add texture to a graphic or text object. The Fill category menu allows you to select from a list of Fill types. These include:

- *None* (white box with red diagonal line): Use no color to fill the object.
- *Solid:* Fill the object with a solid color.
- *Web Dither:* Approximate colors not in the current palette.
- *Gradient:* Fill the object with a color that gradually changes shape or color following a pattern that you select. Gradient options include Linear, Radial, Ripples and so on.
- *Pattern:* Create a textured pattern as the fill.

Stroke Effects

Stroke effects alter only the stroke or outline of a graphic or text object. In this pane you can change the type of medium used to create the outline. Each medium has options such as tip size, texture of the ink, and sharpness of the pen tip. The following mediums are available:

- *Basic:* Several types of pens.
- *Air Brush:* Several types of airbrushes.
- *Calligraphy:* Several types of calligraphy pen tips.
- *Charcoal:* Several colors and types of charcoal pens.
- *Crayon:* Several types and colors of crayons.
- *Felt Tip:* Several types of felt pens.
- *Oil:* Several types of oil paintbrushes.
- *Pencil:* Several types of pencils.
- *Watercolor:* Several types of watercolor brushes.
- *Random:* Several types of elements surrounding the object (Confetti, Dots, Fur, Squares, Yarn).
- *Unnatural:* Several looks created with multiple pens to the stroke of the object (3D, 3D Glow, Chameleon, Fluid Splatter, Outline, Paint Splatter, Toothpaste, Toxic Waste, and Viscous Alien Paint).

NAMING CONVENTIONS

- Give files unique names that indicate the contents of the file. The name might also identify the type of object.

  Example: "feedback_button.gif" instead of "button3.gif"
- Use lowercase letters instead of uppercase (capital) letters.

  Example: "class_picture.gif" instead of "Class_Picture.gif"
- Use a hyphen (-) or an underscore (_) instead of spaces.

  Example: my-dog.gif" or "my_dog.gif" instead of "my dog.gif"
- Use letters and numbers. Many special symbols aren't recognized by Web browsers.

  Example: "my2friends.gif" instead of "me&friends.gif"
- Use filenames that help others recognize the contents of the file.

  Example: "class-pet.gif" instead of "roo-roo.gif"

Unit 3: Electronic Portfolios and Macromedia Dreamweaver MX 2004

Activity Guides

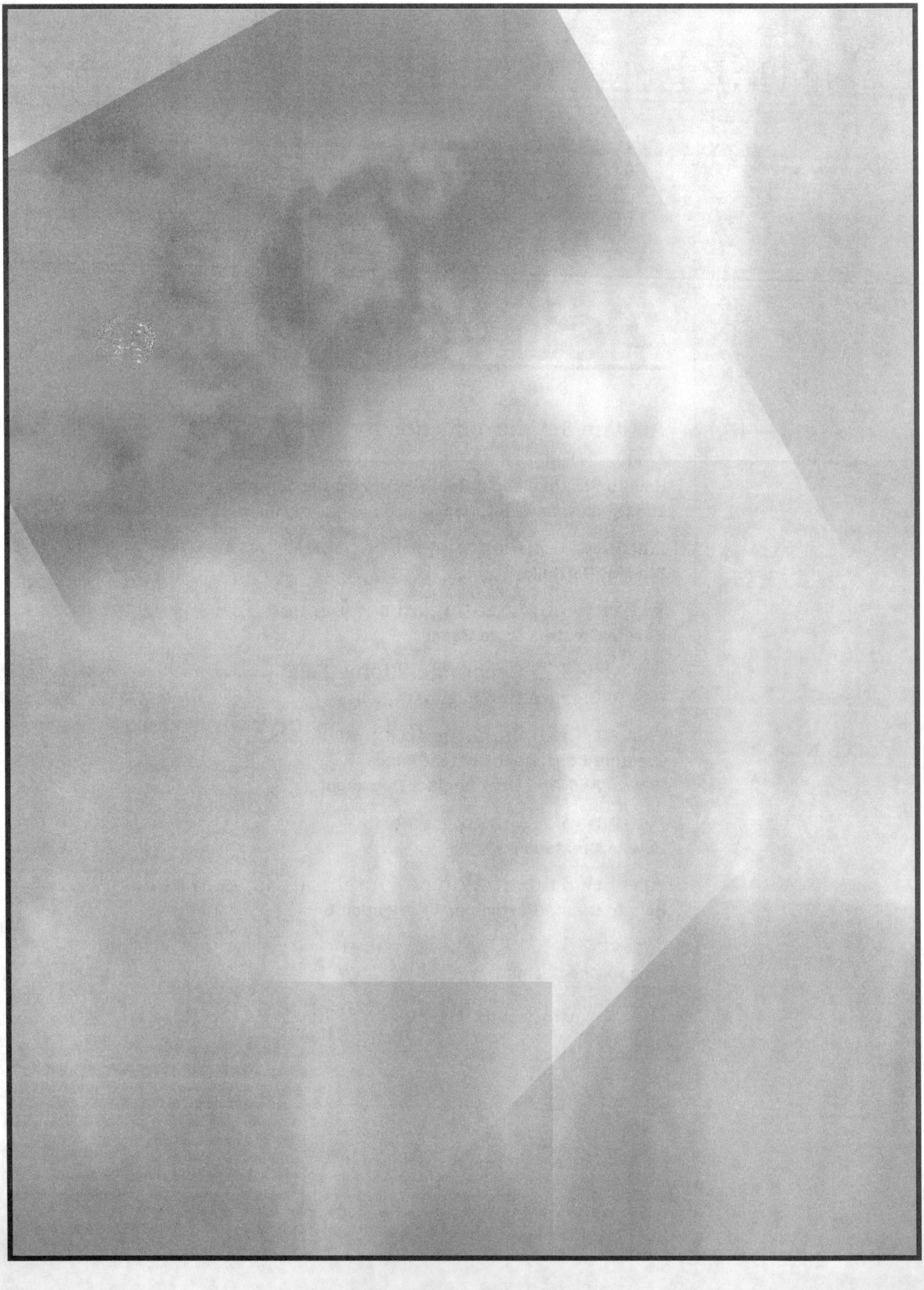

How to Set Up a Local Root Folder and Site Structure

The first thing to do when creating a new Web site using Macromedia Dreamweaver MX 2004 is to define a site and identify a root folder where you will save all files, images, and other elements for the Web pages.

Setting Up a Local Root Folder

1. Create a folder on your computer to serve as the main folder for your Web site. Give the folder a name that identifies the Web site. This folder is called the *local root folder*.

   Note: When creating a root folder for a site on your computer, it is highly recommended that you place it at the top level of your hard drive. For example C:\my-site (Windows) or Macintosh HD: my-site (Macintosh).

2. Start Dreamweaver.
3. From the menu bar, choose **Site** > **Manage Sites**.

   The Manage Sites dialog box opens.

4. Click **New** and select **Site**

   The Site Definition dialog box opens.

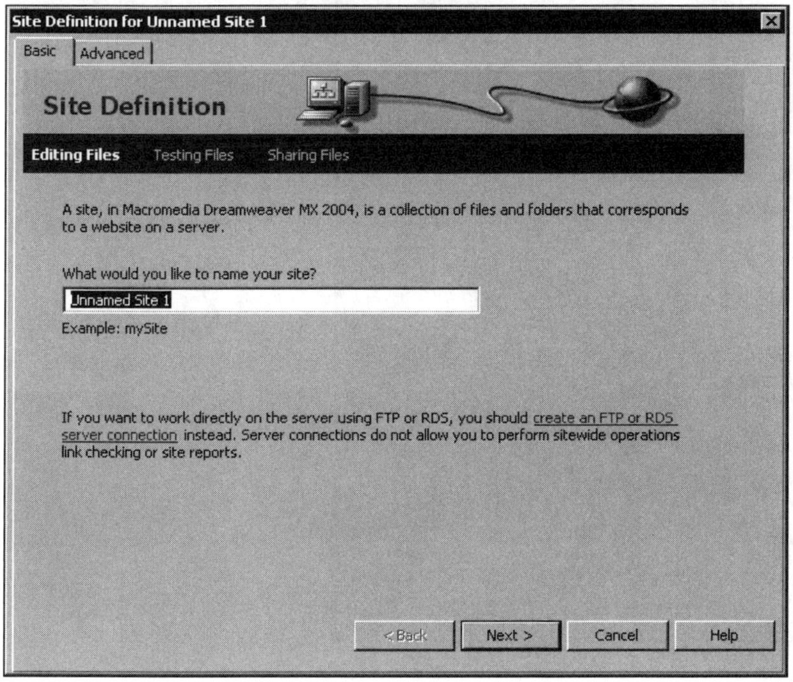

5. Delete the temporary name, *Unnamed Site 1*. Enter a new name for the site and click **Next**.

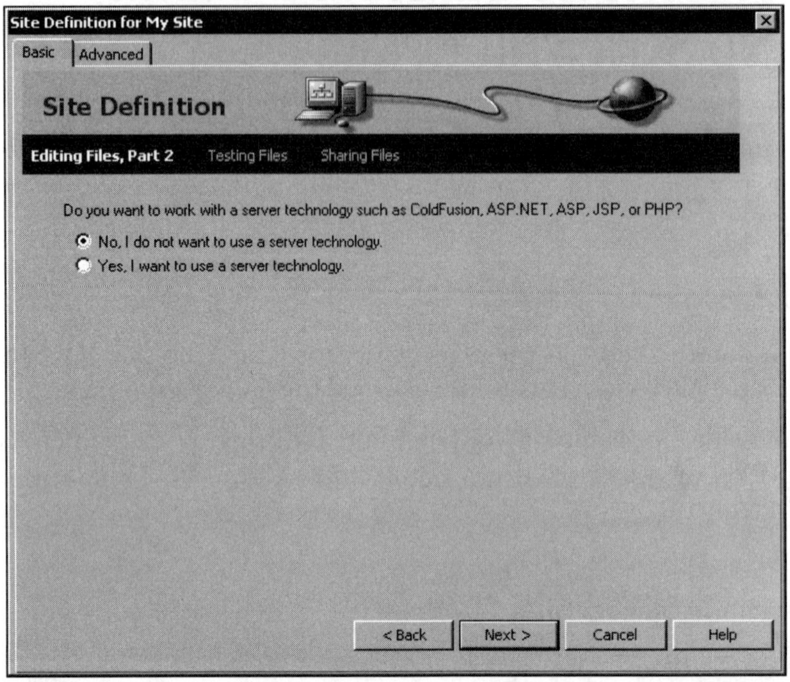

6. If necessary, select **No, I do not want to use a server technology**, and click **Next**.

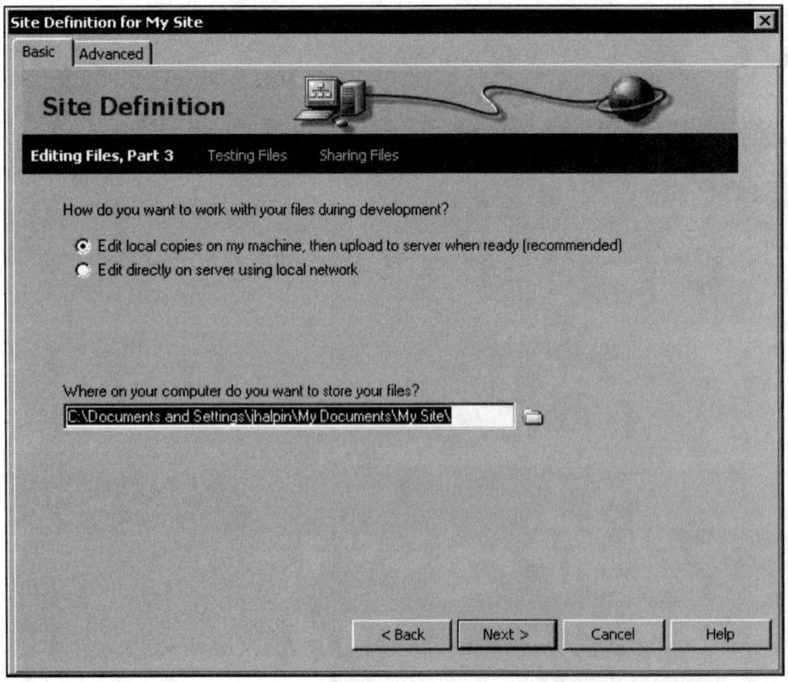

7. If necessary, select **Edit local copies on my machine, then upload to server when ready (recommended)**.

8. Click the **Folder** icon to the right of *Where on your computer do you want to store your files?*

   The Choose local root folder for site dialog box opens.

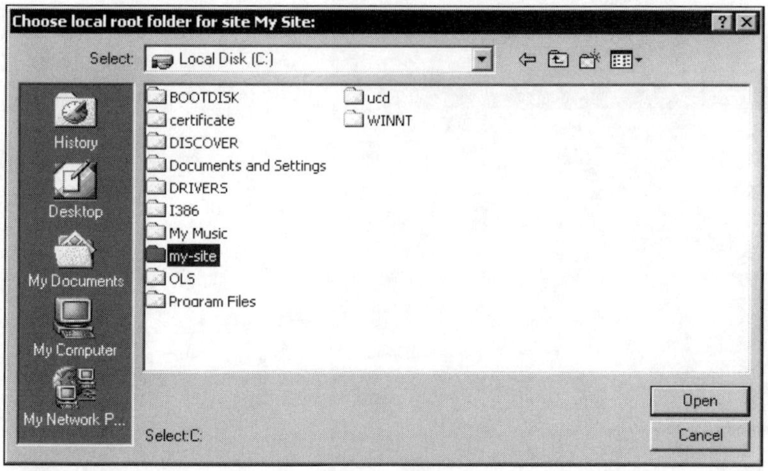

9. Locate and select the root folder you created for your site. Click **Open** and then **Select** (Windows), or click **Choose** (Macintosh).
10. Click **Next**.

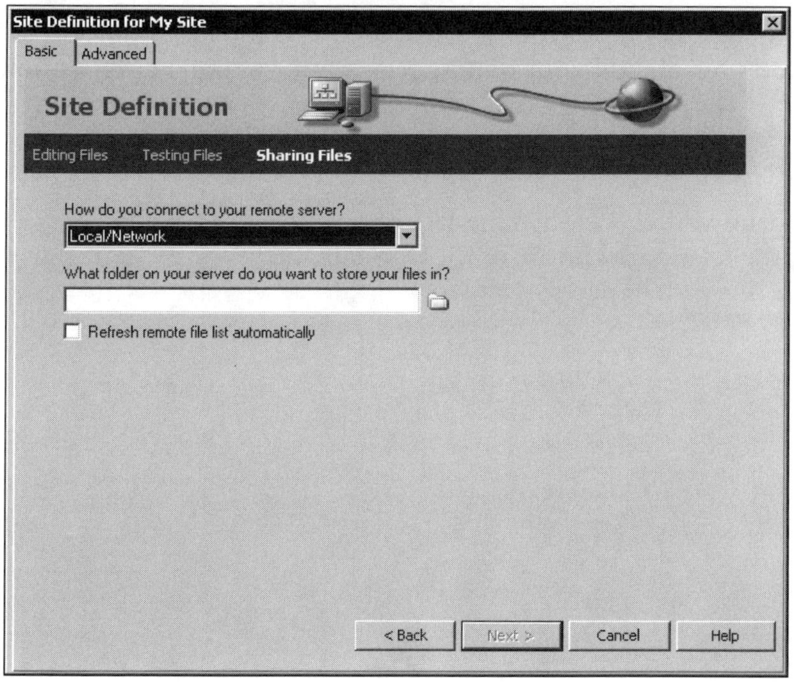

11. Select **None** in the box for *How do you connect to your remote server?* Click **Next.**

You are presented with a summary of your settings.

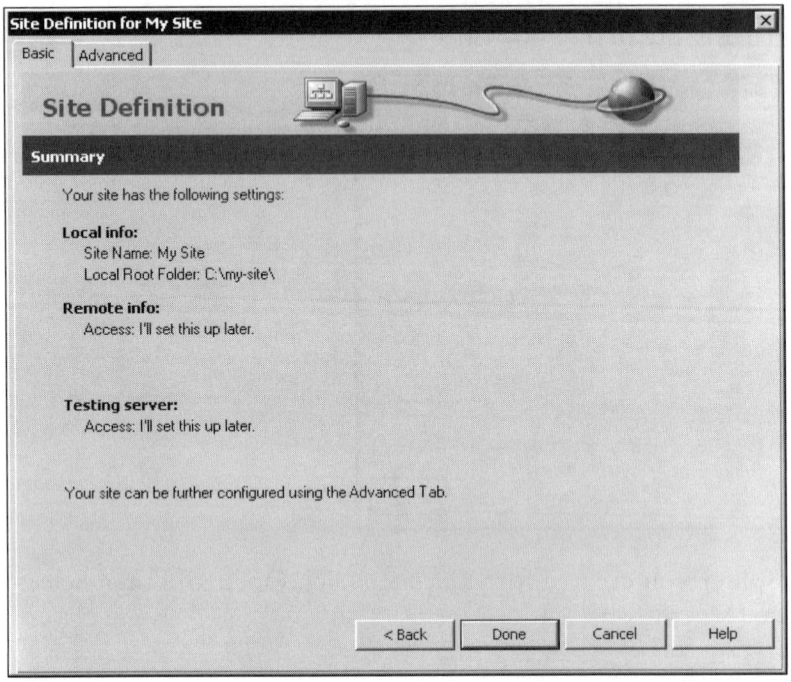

Note: For now you are defining the site on your local system. If you plan to publish to a remote site, you can edit the site and add your remote server information at a later time.

12. Click **Done**. Your local root folder is defined.
13. You return to the Manage Sites dialog box. Click **Done**.

On the right side of the Dreamweaver window, the Files panel displays the folders and files of your site. In Windows, the Files panel is one of the docked panels on the right side of the window. You can leave this panel open as you work.

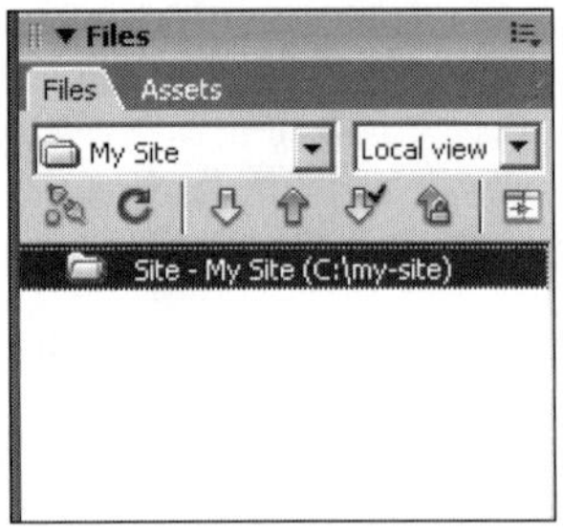

Modifying Site Information

1. If you want to change the settings for your site at any time, choose **Site** > **Manage Sites** from the menu bar.

   The Manage Sites dialog box opens.

   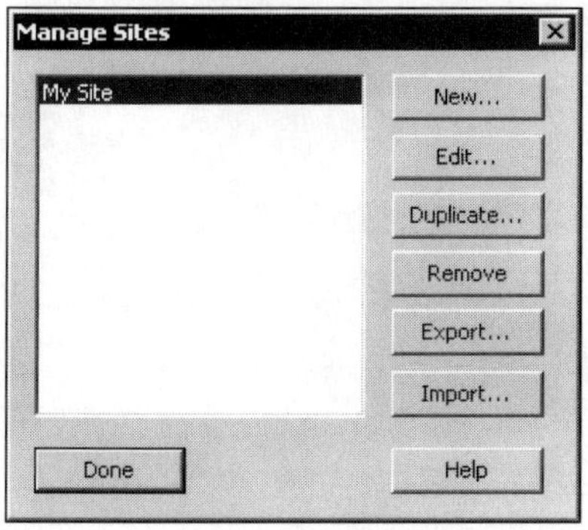

2. Select the site name and click **Edit**.

   The Site Definition dialog box opens.

3. Change any of your original settings as desired.

The Dreamweaver Interface

You can access Dreamweaver tools, commands, and features by using menus or by selecting options from one of the Insert bars or from Dreamweaver panels. The most commonly used areas of the Dreamweaver interface are the Document window, the Insert bar, panels, and the Property inspector.

The *Document window* displays the current document as you create and edit it. The *Insert bar* contains buttons for creating and inserting objects such as images, tables, layers, and frames you might want to add to your Web pages. The *Property inspector* displays properties for the selected object or text and lets you modify those properties. The right side of the window, by default, displays *panels* that you can expand or collapse as you need them.

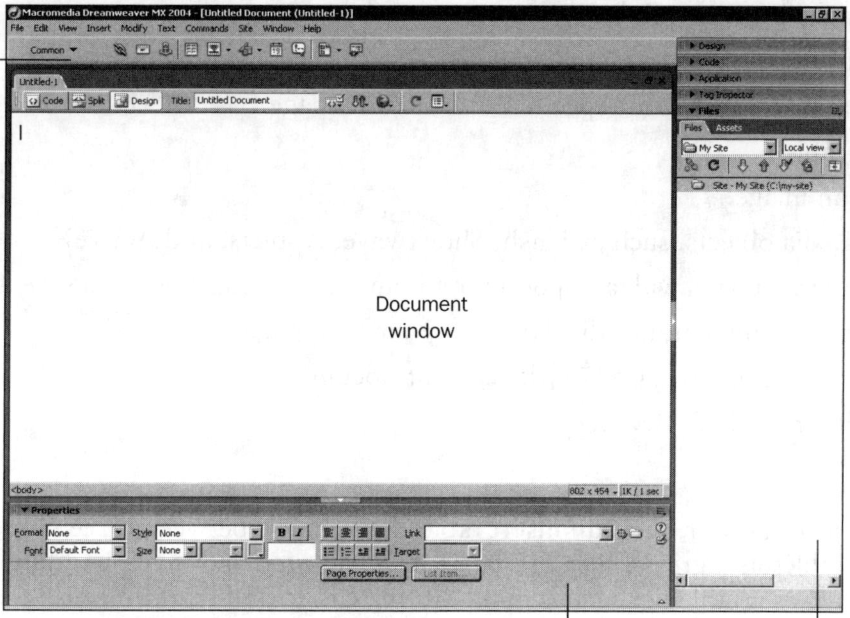

The Document Window and Panels

You can add and manipulate text, images, menus, tables, and other elements in the Document window, and it will display an approximate representation of your Web page.

The Insert Bar

The *Insert bar* contains buttons for inserting various types of objects, such as images and tables, into a document. The Insert bar contains several categories, such as Common and Layout. The *Common Insert bar* contains buttons for inserting the most commonly used objects.

Common Insert Bar

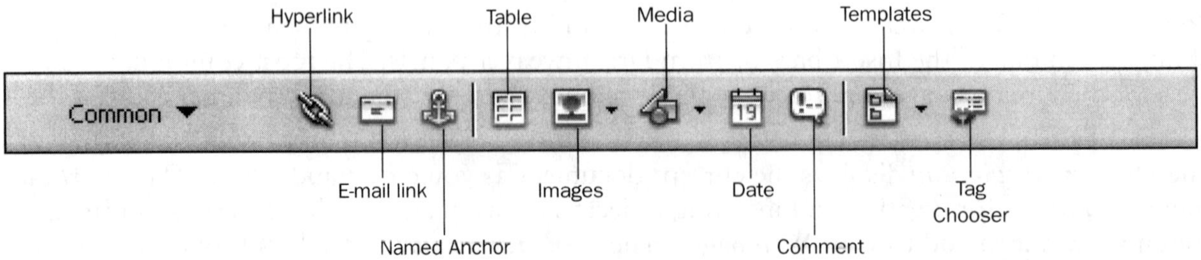

Hyperlink: Insert a hypertext link.

E-mail Link: Insert a link to an e-mail address.

Named Anchor: Insert a link to a specific location on a page.

Table: Insert a table.

Images: Insert an image.

Media: Insert media objects, such as Flash, Shockwave, Applets, and ActiveX.

Date: Insert the current date, with an option for automatic updating when you save the document.

Comment: Insert a comment, not displayed on your Web page.

Templates: Make a template based on the current document.

Tag Chooser: Insert an HTML tag.

Layout Insert Bar

From the *Layout Insert bar*, you can insert tables and choose between three modes. *Standard mode* displays tables as a grid of lines. *Expanded Tables mode* adds cell padding and spacing to tables and increases table borders to make editing easier, and *Layout mode* displays tables as boxes that can be drawn, dragged, and resized.

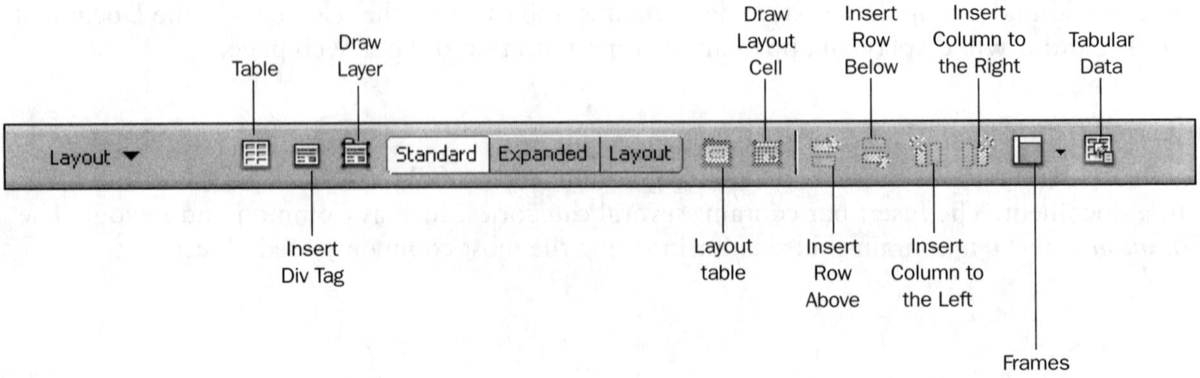

Table: Insert a table.

Insert Div Tag: Insert a div tag to create a content block.

Draw Layer: Insert a layer to hold content at any location on a page.

Standard mode: Switch to the Standard mode of editing documents.

Expanded Tables mode: Add extra spacing and cell padding to tables to make editing easier.

Layout mode: Layout and adjust cells and tables on the page before adding content.

Layout Table: Draw a whole table with cells to hold information or objects.

Draw Layout Cell: Draw individual cells in a table.

Insert Row Above: Insert a row above the current row in a table.

Insert Row Below: Insert a row below the current row.

Insert Column to the Left: Insert a column to the left of the current column.

Insert Column to the Right: Insert a column to the right of the current column.

Frames: Insert a frame.

Tabular Data: Insert tabular data, such as from a spreadsheet.

The Property Inspector

The *Property inspector* enables you to view and change a variety of properties for the currently selected object or text. Each kind of object has different properties. The illustration shows the Property inspector for a selected table. It displays column and row attributes, cell colors, and border colors. You can change cell padding and cell spacing as well. When you select text, you can alter font, size, color, and alignment in the Property inspector.

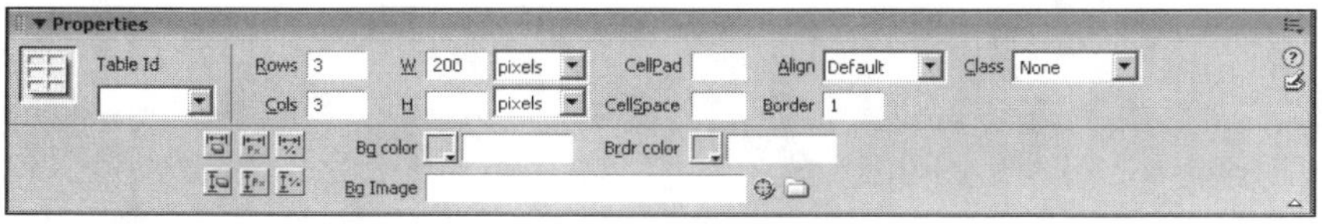

Student Portfolios

The content and purpose of a portfolio can vary widely. Student portfolios typically contain examples of work as well as text descriptions and reflections on each piece. Three types of electronic portfolios are those that showcase work, document progress through a project, or highlight skill growth. Examples of these three types follow.

Showcase Portfolio

A showcase portfolio highlights its owner's expertise by showing examples of best work. A student showcase would include a selection of finished images, designs, and Web sites. It might also provide a reflection on the piece or document the process students followed to create it. Following is a sample category outline with associated files:

Image work

- Digital camera photographs
- Optimized images
- Web photo album (to be completed in Unit 4)

Design work

- Logo
- Business card
- Macromedia Fireworks interactive image (to be completed in Unit 5)

Client Web site

(To be completed later)

This is a sample site map for a showcase portfolio:

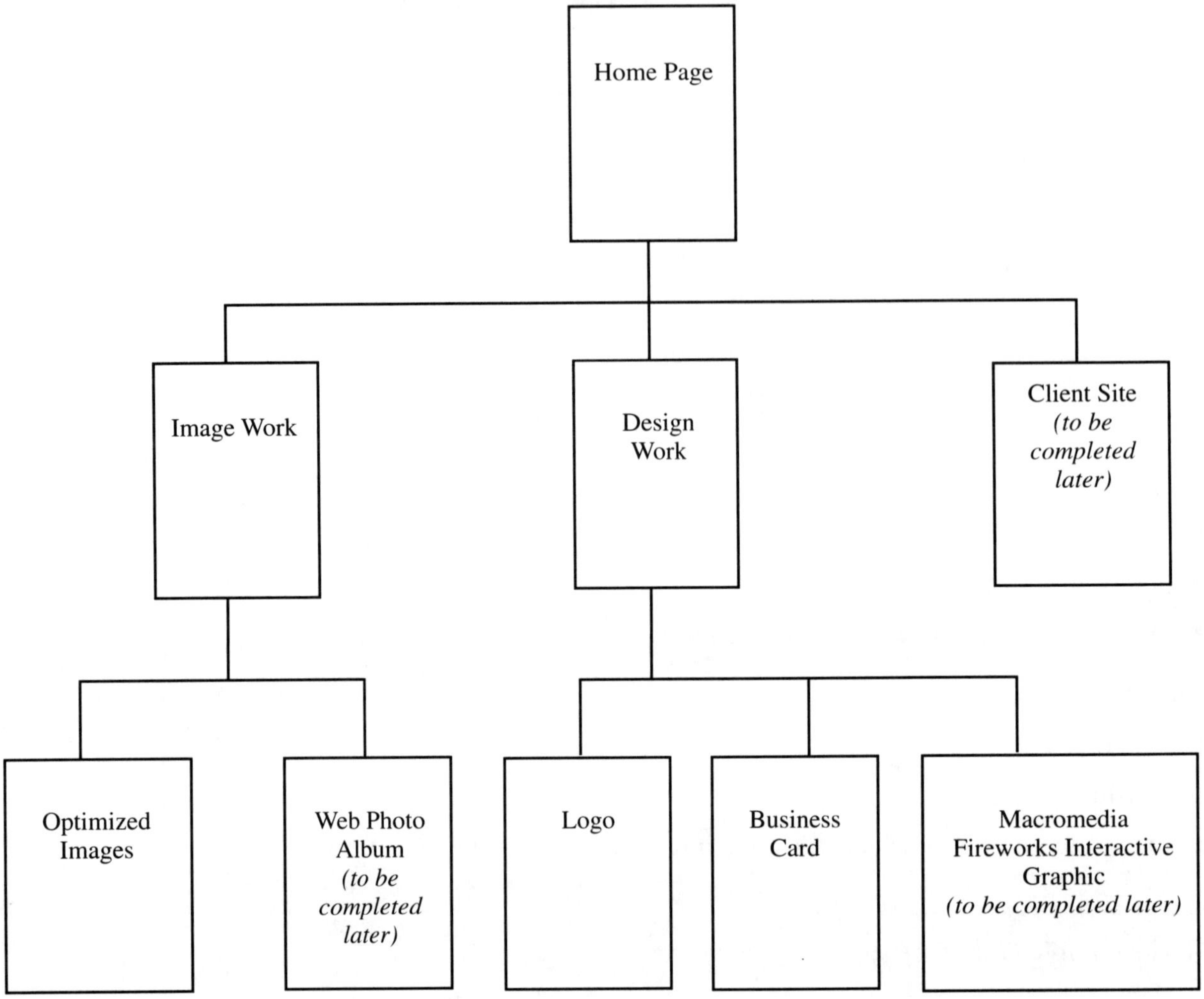

Skill Growth Portfolio

A skill growth portfolio shows multiple samples of work on the same project to demonstrate increasing skill. For example, students include several versions of their business card to show how the design evolved. This portfolio can also include reflection and discussion of redesigns. Following is a sample category outline with associated files:

Design work

- **Logo**
  - Logo (early version)
  - Logo (final version)
  - Logo self-review
- **Business card**
  - Business card (early version)
  - Business card (final version)
  - Business card peer review
- **Interactive graphic (to be completed later)**
- **Client site (to be completed later)**
  - Client site (early version)
  - Client site (final version)
  - Client site reflections

This is a sample site map for a skill growth portfolio:

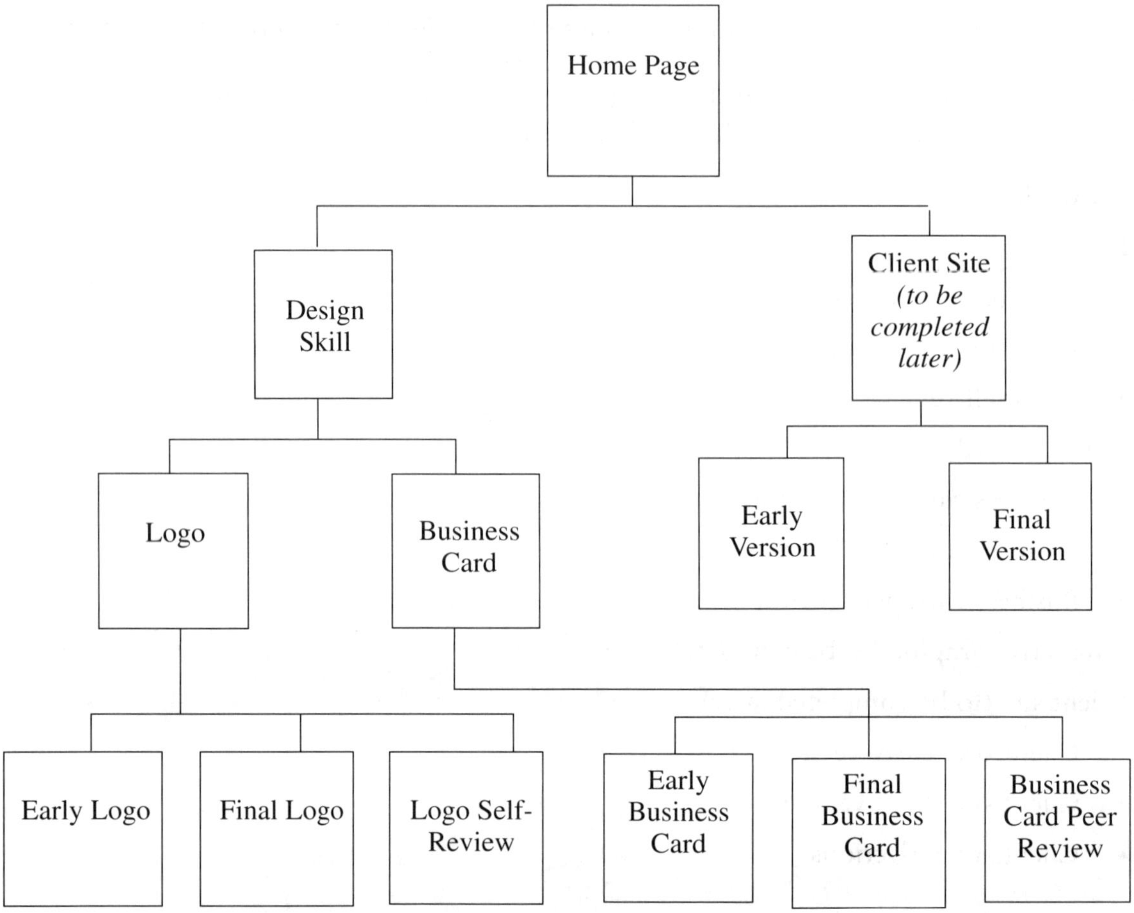

Project Progress Portfolio

A project progress portfolio contains a more complete selection of work around a particular project. The portfolio reflects the span of work done on a project—showing different stages from early ideas to completion. An example would be to show all the work students did while learning Macromedia Fireworks. The portfolio would include sketches and storyboards, early versions, final versions, peer-review, and self-review. For this portfolio type, students will need to scan worksheets and other handwritten documents to create electronic versions.

How to Create a Page Banner

The purpose of a page banner is to establish a consistent identity on all pages so viewers know they are on a page of your Web site and recognize what the Web site is about.

Create a Page Banner

1. Start Macromedia Fireworks MX 2004.
2. Create a new file with dimensions at least 400 pixels wide and 100 pixels high. (Match your banner width to the pixel width of the Web page you're designing.)
3. Turn on **Guides** and **Rulers** from the **View** menu so you can align banner elements easily.
4. Use the **Rectangle** or **Ellipse** tool to create a background shape (such as a rectangle or oval) for the page banner.
5. Add effects to the background shape.
6. Add text to the banner.
7. Add effects to the text, as you desire.
8. Add images to your banner, as you desire.

The following images of the Property inspector show the effects used for the text and the background ellipse in the sample banner.

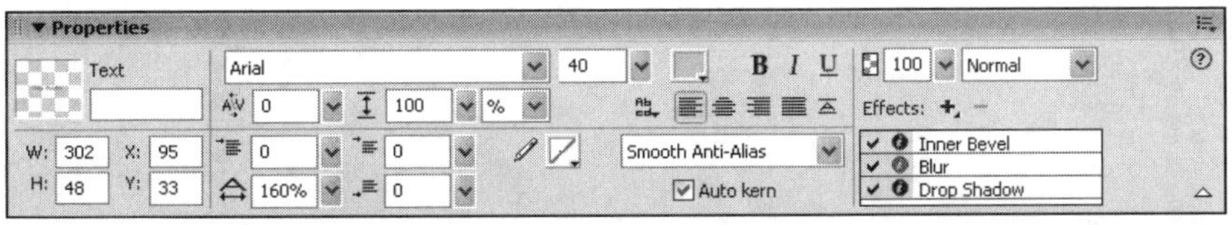

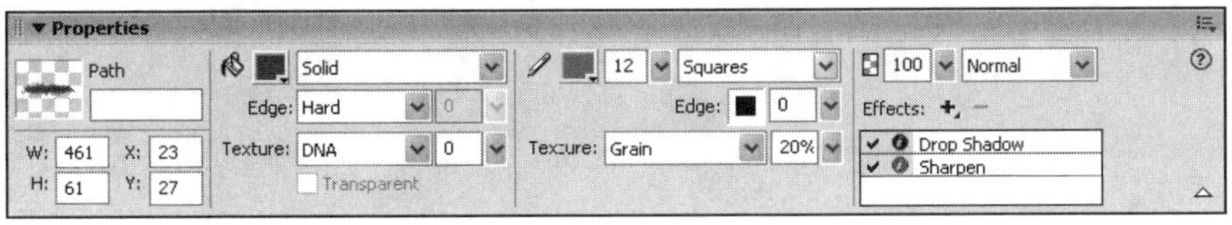

9. Save the file.
10. Export the file as a GIF or JPG image, depending on the level of color gradation or the presence of photographic elements in the banner.

How to Create a Web Page with Tables

Most HTML pages use tables to control the position of text and images on the page. One way to create a table in Macromedia Dreamweaver MX 2004 is to use the Layout mode, which lets you insert images and text on a page and automatically generate table cells around them.

Create a New Page

1. Start Macromedia Dreamweaver MX.
2. Make sure the Files panel is visible. In Windows it will be docked on the right side of the screen. If the Files panel is not open, choose **Window > Files**.

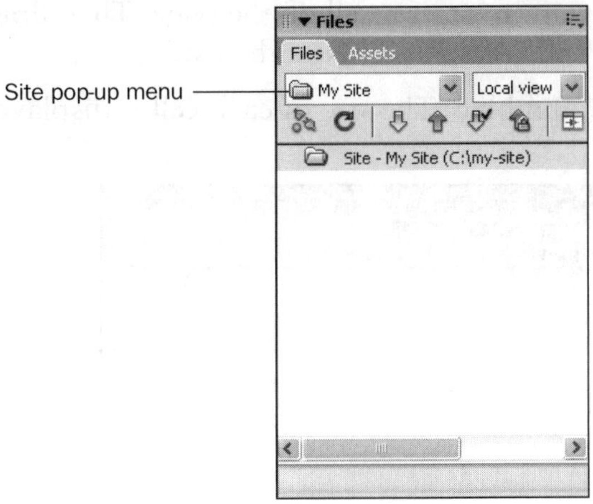

3. Make sure your portfolio site is selected. If it is not, click the site pop-up menu and select your portfolio site.
4. On the **Start** page, select **HTML** in the **Create New** list to open a new Untitled document.
5. To save the Untitled document as your home page, choose **File > Save As** to open the Save As dialog box.

   The Save As dialog box opens to the root folder of your portfolio site automatically.
6. Name the new page **index.html** and click **Save**.

   The new file, index.html, is added to the root folder on the Files panel.

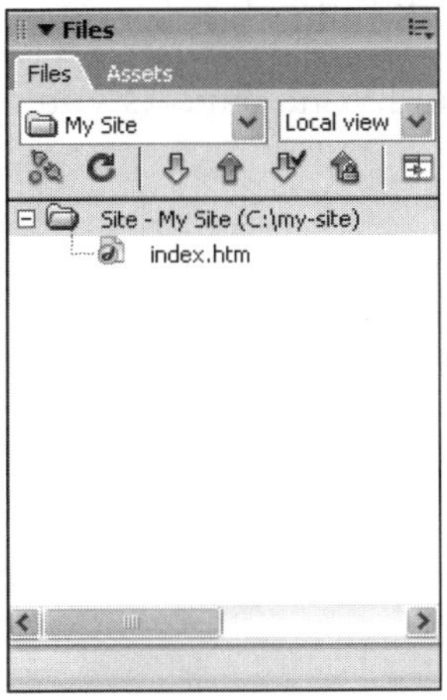

Create a Table in Layout Mode

1. Select the **Layout** category on the Insert bar, and click **Layout Mode** to switch to Layout mode.

   Note: If this is the first time you are switching to Layout mode, you may be presented with a Getting Started in Layout Mode message. Read the message and click OK.

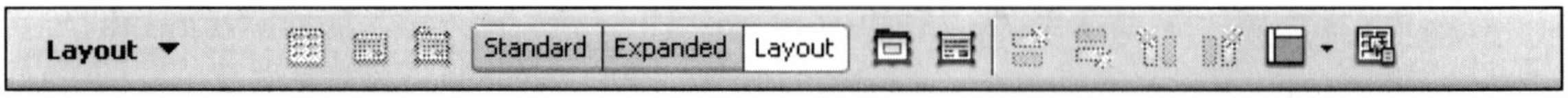

   In Layout mode you can draw a table that accommodates the layout planned in your storyboard. The rectangles (graphics, text, and navigation elements) on your storyboard correspond to cells in the table.

2. Click the **Draw Layout Cell** button in the **Layout** category on the Insert bar.
3. Position the pointer where you want to start a cell on the page. Then drag to create a layout cell that matches the size of the area on your storyboard.

   The current cell appears, outlined in blue. The size of each cell is displayed in the column header at the top of the cell.

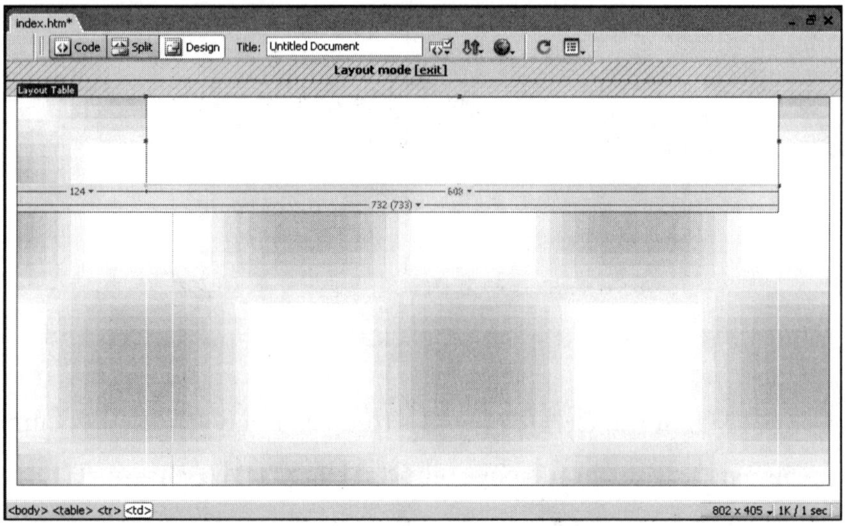

   Note: Typical screen dimensions are 800 × 600 pixels. Allowing space for the browser window, you might want to create a table that is approximately 750 × 400 pixels.

4. Draw a cell for each rectangle on your storyboard.
5. To move a cell, click an edge of the cell and drag the cell by its solid blue border.

   Note: In Layout mode, you can create cells and move them around your page as you're making a table.

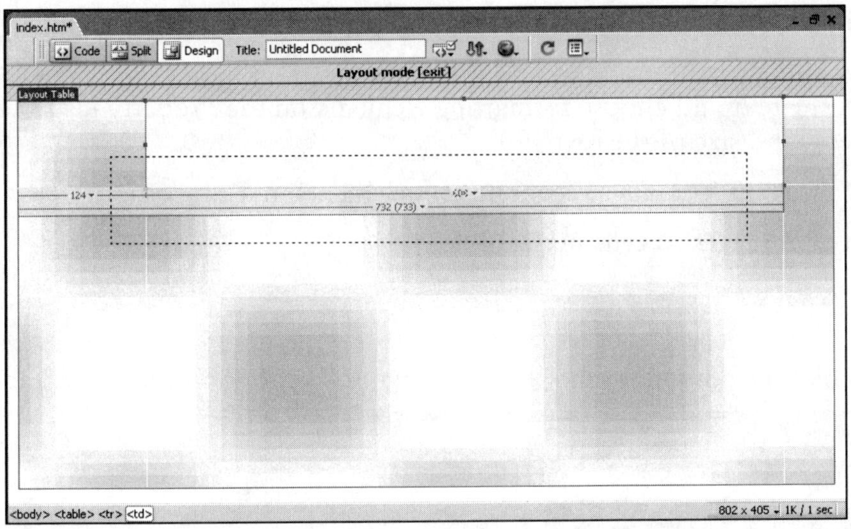

6. To resize a cell, click an edge of the cell and drag one of the handles (blue dots) along its border.

   Note: Cells cannot overlap each other.

7. Choose **File > Save** to save your work.

Add Text and Images

1. To insert an image in a cell, click in the cell to position the insertion point and choose **Insert > Image** on the menu bar.
2. In the Select Image Source dialog box, locate and select an image to insert (such as your Page Banner). Then click **OK** (Windows) or **Choose** (Macintosh).
3. To format the image in the cell, select the image and choose formatting elements on the Property inspector.

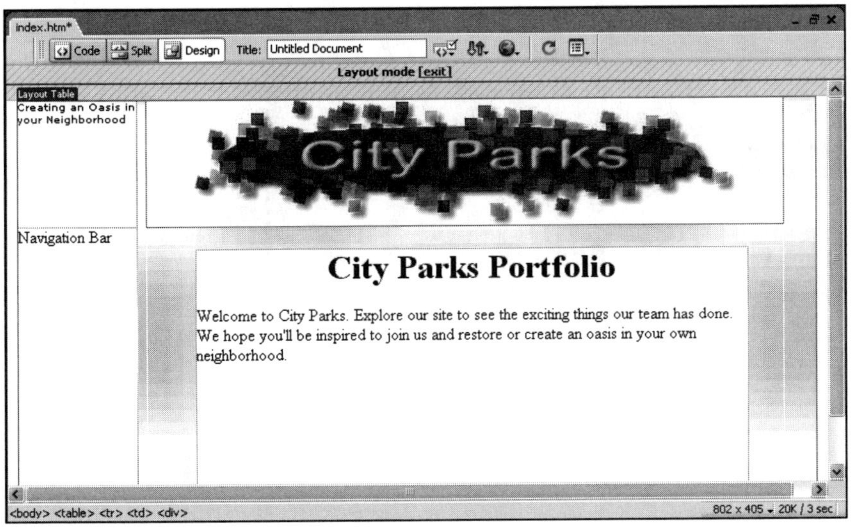

4. To add text to a table cell, click in the cell and type text or paste text copied from another document.
5. To format text, select the text and choose formatting elements on the Property inspector, such as font, alignment, and size of the text.

   Note: You can apply different formats to separate text elements in a single cell.
6. Continue to add text and images to cells in the table.

Preview a Page

1. To see the finished table, click **Standard mode** in the **Layout** category on the Insert bar.

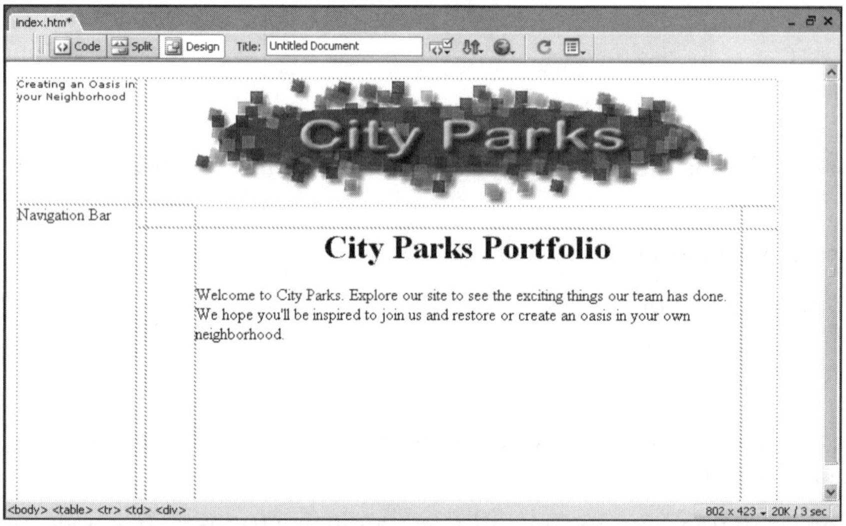

2. To preview the page in a browser, choose **File > Preview in Browser** and then choose a browser from the submenu (or press **F12**).

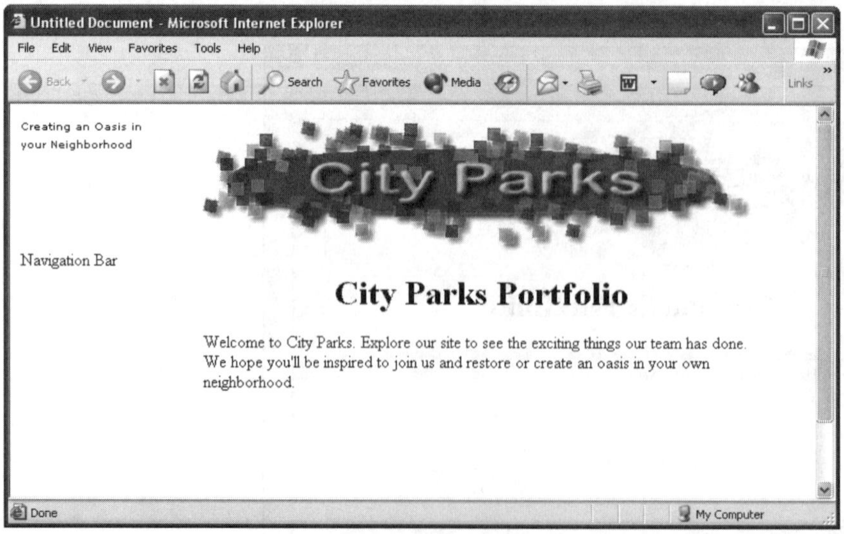

   Note: It is important to preview in a browser to make sure your design fits in a standard browser window.

Creating Consistent Content Pages

Content pages link from the electronic portfolio's home page. Using the ideas from the class discussion, determine the consistent elements of your content pages and plan your navigation bar. Create a checklist of items that will appear on each page by answering the following questions. Then draw a general layout of a content page, drawing and labeling the elements that will appear on all content pages.

Organizing Content

How you organize content on a page highlights important features and elements of your site. Important elements might be higher on the page, larger in size, or in stronger colors. Include rough descriptions of navigation, copy layout, graphic allocation, key headers, and other elements that appear on a screen. Identifying common structures between pages helps users understand they are on the same site as they navigate from page to page.

- Will your name banner be on each page? If yes, is it in the same place? Is it the same size?
- What font will you use for titles or headings in your content pages?
- What color will you use for titles or headings in your content pages?
- What font will you use for descriptions in your content pages?
- What color will you use for descriptions?

Navigation

For users of your Web site to understand the content, you must provide clear navigation. Users need to know where they are in a site, where they need to go, and how to get back to where they came from. Having a consistent layout grid helps orient users and keeps them from feeling lost. Using consistent buttons, links, and graphics on each page maintains a sense of place. As users move from page to page, provide familiar visual cues and navigational aids. For more on interface design, see *www.macromedia.com/resources/techniques/resources/*.

Here are some questions to answer:

- Where will you place the navigation bar on the page?
- What content will be in the navigation bar?
- Will the navigation bar be on every page?
- How will your navigation bar help users know which page they are on?

How to Add Text from Another Document

Copy Text from Another Document

1. Open the document from which you want to copy text.
2. Select the text and choose **Edit > Copy**.
3. Open the Dreamweaver document in which you want to paste the text.
4. Position the insertion point on the page where you want to paste the copied text.
5. Choose **Edit > Paste**.
6. The new text appears in the Dreamweaver document.

   Note: Copied text may lose some of its original formatting, including line breaks and paragraph breaks. To insert a blank line after a section of text, position the insertion point at the end of the last text line and press **Enter** (Windows) or **Return** (Macintosh). To create a line break at the insertion point, press **Shift-Enter** (Windows) or **Shift-Return** (Macintosh).
7. To change the format of any new text in the document, select the text and set options on the Property inspector.

Import Microsoft Word HTML

1. Open the Dreamweaver document in which you want to add the text.
2. Choose **File > Open**.

   The Open dialog box opens.
3. Navigate to and select the HTML file you want to open, and click **Open**.

   The Word HTML file is opened in Dreamweaver.

4. Choose **Commands > Clean Up Word HTML**

   The Clean Up Word HTML dialog box opens.

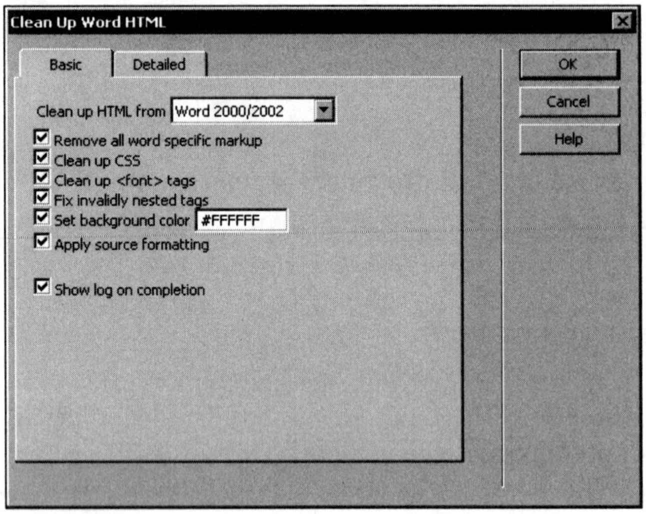

5. Click **OK**.

   You are presented with a summary of the cleanup process.

6. Click **OK**.

   Use the Property inspector to edit the text as necessary.

How to Create Links

There are several different types of links:

- Internal link (document-relative pathname link or site-root-relative pathname link) goes to another page in your site.
- External link (absolute pathname link) goes to another site.
- Named Anchor link goes to a specific position on a page in your site.
- E-mail link opens a blank e-mail message window instead of linking to a page.

Create an Internal Link

1. Open the Web page in Macromedia Dreamweaver MX 2004 and select an image, a word, or phrase of text that you want to format as a link.
2. In the Link text box on the Property inspector, type the name of the document to which you want to link. Alternatively, you can click the **Browse for File** (file folder) icon next to the Link text box and select the document to link from the Select File dialog box. If you have the Files panel open, you can also click the **Point to File** icon beside the Link box, then click and drag to draw a link line to the target file in the Files panel. The name of the file you point to will be added to the Link box automatically.

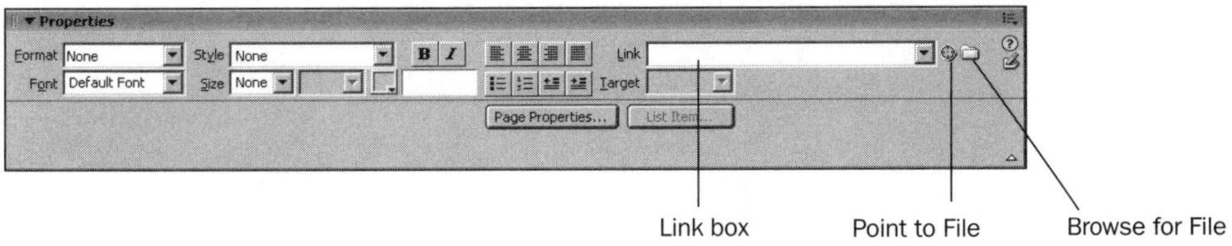

Create an External Link

1. To link to another Web site, select an image, a word, or phrase of text that you want to format as a link.
2. In the Link text box on the Property inspector, type or paste the address (URL) of the site to which you want to link. (Remember to include "http://" in the address.)

Link to a Named Anchor

To link to a specific location on a Web page, first create a named anchor at that location, then link to the named anchor.

1. Position the insertion point at the desired location on the page.
2. Choose **Insert > Named Anchor**.

   The Named Anchor dialog box opens.

3. Enter a short anchor name without any spaces.
4. Click **OK**.
5. Select an image or text that you want to link to the named anchor.
6. In the Link text box on the Property inspector, type # and type or paste the anchor name.

How to Create Buttons and Navigation Bars

Macromedia Fireworks MX 2004 enables you to design the look and functionality of buttons, including links and rollover features. You can then import these buttons into Macromedia Dreamweaver MX 2004.

Build a Button

1. Start Fireworks. Create a new document.
2. Save the document in the **images** folder of your Dreamweaver Web site.
3. Choose **Edit > Insert > New Button.**

   The Button Editor opens. Buttons contain four states:

   - Up (button untouched)
   - Over (pointer over button)
   - Down (button being clicked)
   - Over While Down (pointer over after button clicked)

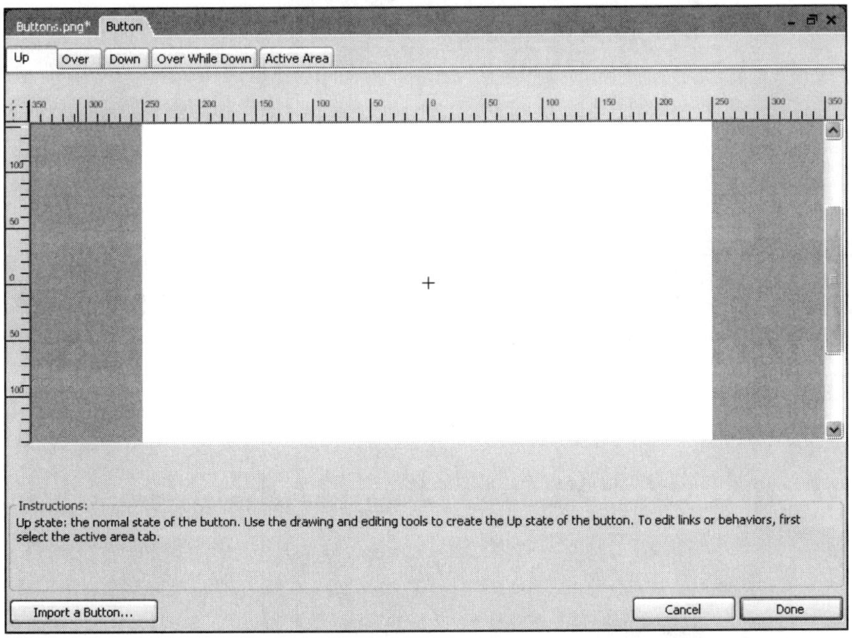

4. Use the **Rectangle** tool or the **Ellipse** tool from the Tools panel to draw a shape for the Up state. Make the dimensions of the shape fit the size of your navigation bar.
5. Add dimension to the button by adding an effect such as Inner Bevel from the Effects pop-up menu on the Property inspector. (To learn more about effects, see the *How to Create Effects* guide from Activity 2.5 in Unit 2.)

6. Add color and text to the button to match the color and font design of your home page. Since you will duplicate this first button to create the other buttons on your navigation bar, be sure to center-align the text.

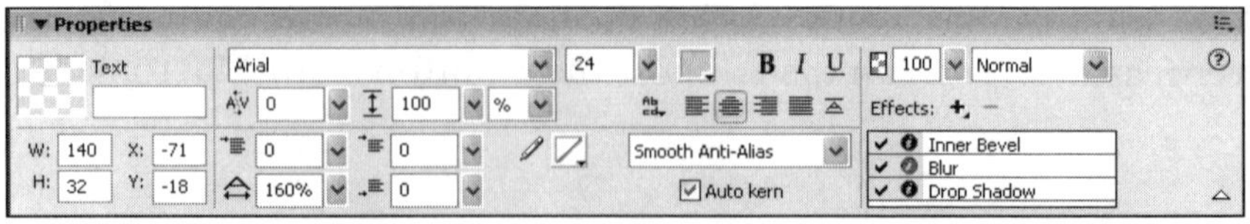

7. Click the **Over** tab at the top of the Button Editor.

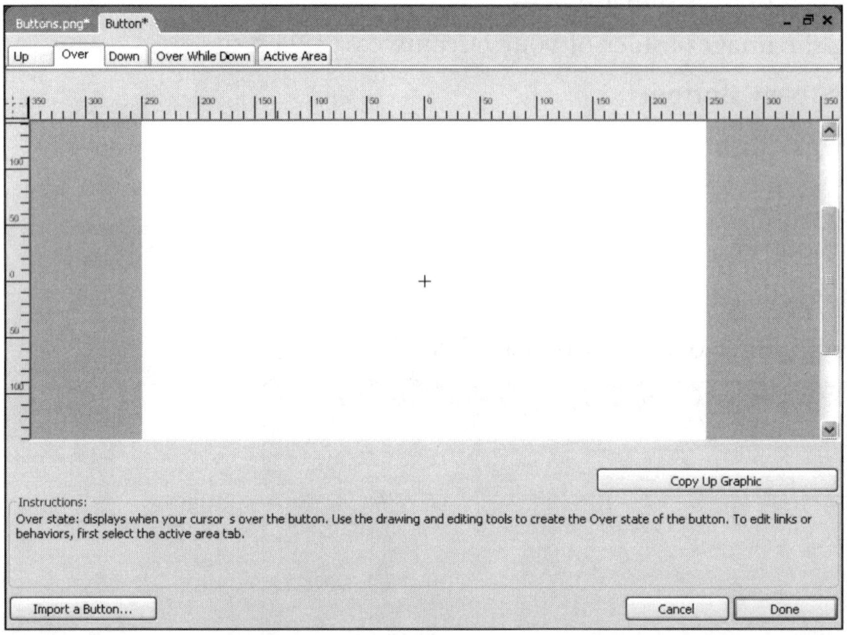

8. Click **Copy Up Graphic** to copy the Up graphic to the Over button state. This saves you time and helps keep the look of the button consistent.

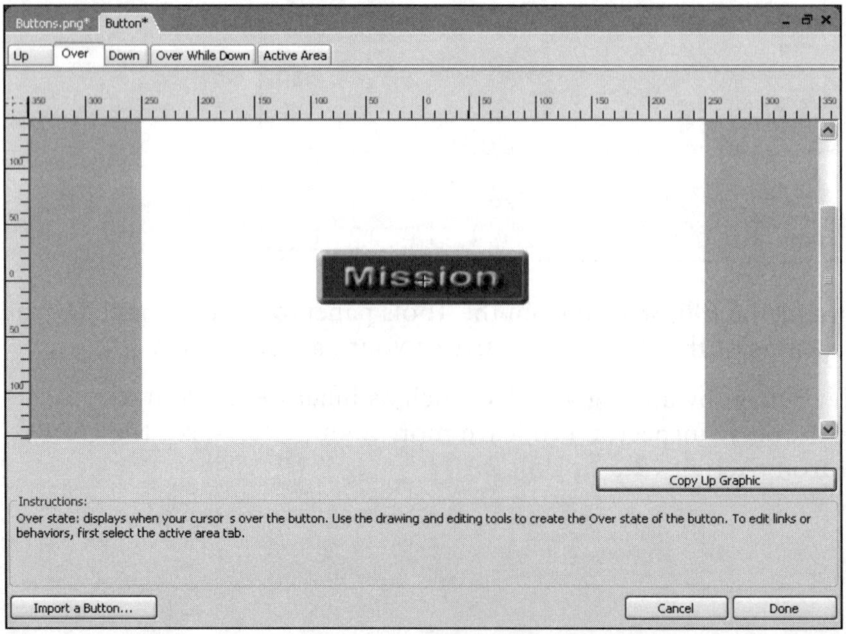

9. Decide how you want the button to look when the pointer rolls over the button. Then change the copied graphic by modifying the color or effects of the text or the shape of the button.
10. Click the **Down** tab.
11. Click **Copy Over Graphic** to copy the Over graphic to this button state.
12. Decide how you want the button to look when users click the button. Add effects such as changing to an Inner Bevel, darkening the color, or adding a drop shadow to the shape.
13. For this project, skip the Over While Down state.
14. Click the **Active Area** tab. The active area of the button is shown by green shading and red lines. This shading indicates the area users can click to activate the button.
15. To change the size of the active area, drag the red guides (Windows) or green shading (Macintosh) to extend or decrease the green shaded active area.
16. When you are satisfied with the states of your button in the Button Editor, click **Done**.

    Your button is displayed on the Fireworks canvas.
17. Click the button to select it. In the Link text box on the Property inspector, enter the name of the Web page in your portfolio to which you want to link this button.

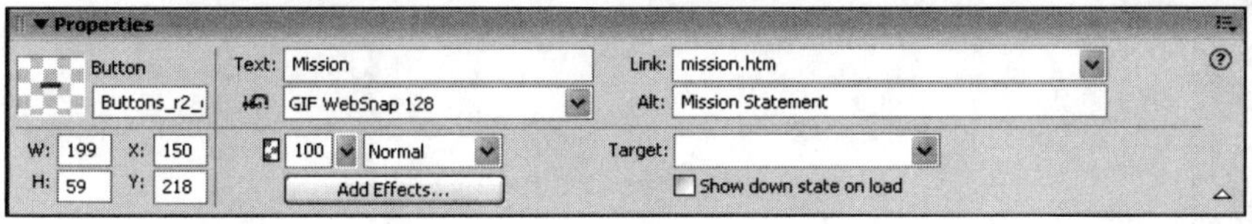

18. In the Alt text box, enter an alternative text label (Alt tag) for the button.

    Alternative text is displayed in place of the image when users elect not to display images in their browser. Such text can also be voiced for visually impaired users.
19. Choose **Modify > Canvas > Fit Canvas** to fit the canvas to the size of your button.

Copy Buttons and Make the Navigation Bar

1. Change the size of the canvas to accommodate all the buttons on your navigation bar. Choose **Modify > Canvas > Canvas Size** and edit the value for height or width in the Canvas Size dialog box.

   If you have four buttons, for example, multiply the height or width of the first button by four (depending on whether your navigation bar is vertical or horizontal).
2. Select the first button. Move it to the top of the canvas. Choose **Edit > Clone**.

   A new instance of the button appears on top of the original button.
3. Drag the new button instance below the original button. You can also use the arrow keys to move the button.

4. Repeat steps 2 and 3 as many times as necessary to create the rest of your navigation bar.

5. Click the second button and use the Property inspector to edit it. In the text box labeled "Text," change the text to the name of the second button. Edit the information in the Link text box and the Alt text box as appropriate for this button.
6. Repeat step 5 for the remaining buttons.

7. Fit the canvas to your navigation bar: Choose **Modify > Canvas > Fit Canvas.**
8. Save the file.

Export a Navigation Bar for Use in Dreamweaver

Fireworks enables you to save interactive graphics (a button, for instance) as HTML, so you can import working buttons into a Dreamweaver document.

1. To export your navigation bar, choose **File > Export.**

The Export dialog box opens.

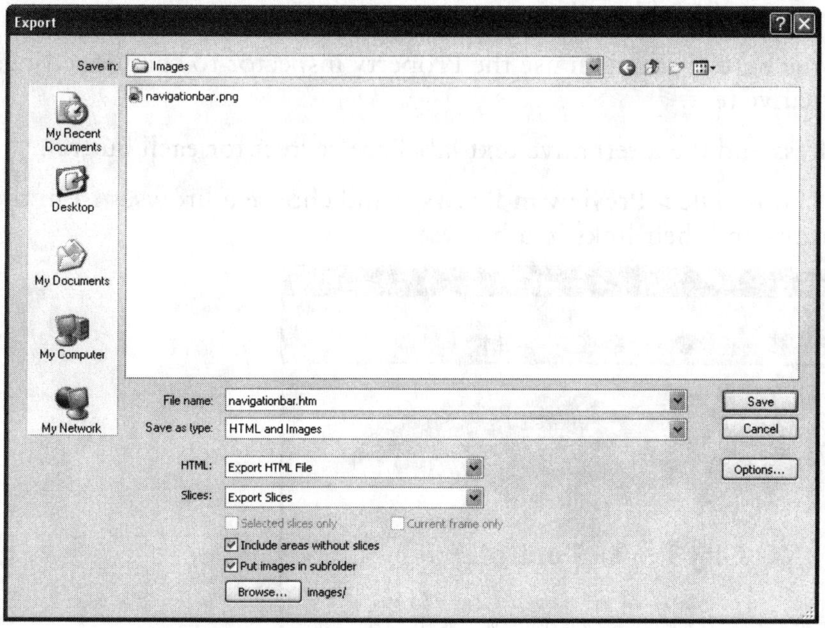

2. Navigate to the folder in your local root folder where you want to save the navigation bar.
3. Give the navigation bar file a short descriptive name.
4. Make sure the **HTML and Images** option is selected in the Save as type (Windows) or Save As (Macintosh) box.
5. Make sure the **Include areas without slices** option is selected.
6. Select the **Put images in subfolder** option.
7. Click **Save**.

Insert the Navigation Bar into a Dreamweaver Document

1. Start Dreamweaver.
2. Open the page on which you want to insert the navigation bar.
3. Position the insertion point in the cell where you want the navigation bar to appear.

   In the **Common** category on the Insert bar, click the **Images** pop-up menu and select **Fireworks HTML.**

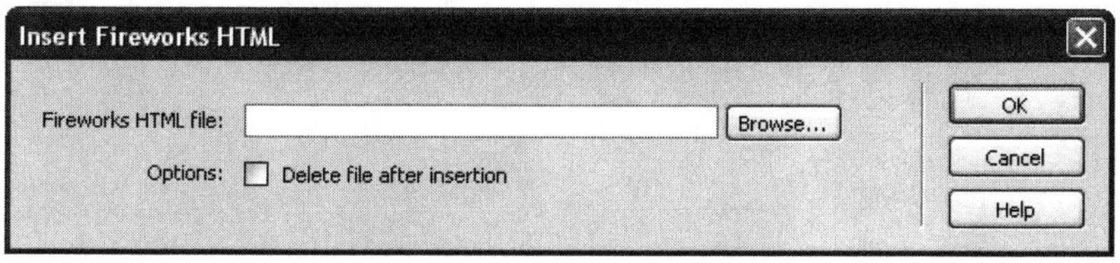

4. In the Insert Fireworks HTML dialog box, click the **Browse** button, then locate and select the navigation bar HTML file. Click **Open**.

5. In the Insert Fireworks HTML dialog box, click **OK**.

   The navigation bar appears in the table cell.

6. To edit a button, select the button and then use the Property inspector to change settings such as the link or alternative text.

7. Check that the link address and the alternative text label are correct for each button.

8. Save your file and then choose **File > Preview in Browser** and choose a browser from the submenu to test the buttons and their links in a browser.

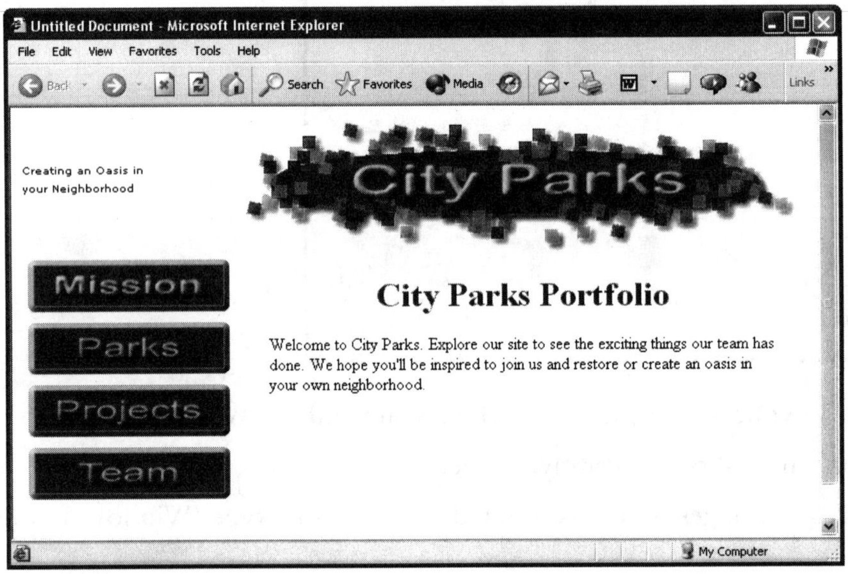

How to Check Links

A key technical testing task is to check all the links. Macromedia Dreamweaver MX 2004 enables you to do this automatically in the Site window.

1. Start Dreamweaver.
2. Make sure your site is open.
3. On the menu bar, choose **Site > Check Links Sitewide.**

   The Link Checker tab displays all the broken links on the site.

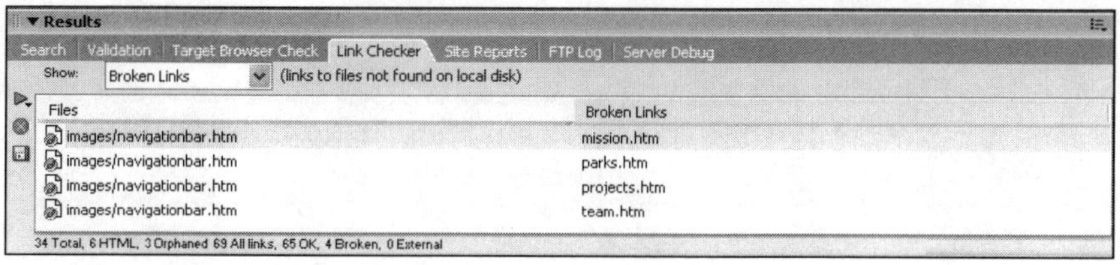

   Note: Even though links are listed as broken, check them in the browser to confirm.

4. Fix the broken links and check the links again.

HTML Tags

The following is a quick reference guide for common tags used in HTML pages.

Main setup tags for an HTML document

```
<HTML>
  <HEAD>
    <TITLE>
    </TITLE>
  </HEAD>
  <BODY>
  </BODY>
</HTML>
```

<HTML> </HTML> encompasses all tags in an HTML document and defines it as an HTML document.

<HEAD> </HEAD> encompasses the title tag and contains document titles and authoring information for the document.

<TITLE> </TITLE> encompasses the title for the document.

<BODY> </BODY> encompasses all the tags that make up the document.

<BODY BGCOLOR = "*name of color*"> </BODY> encompasses all the tags that make up the document and gives the document a background color.

<BODY BACKGROUND = "*title of image*"> </BODY> encompasses all the tags that make up the document and gives the document a background image.

Main formatting tags for the document

<H1> </H1> is a heading tag that creates the largest size text. The heading tag number can range from one to six. Increasing the number will make the text smaller.

<P> </P> creates paragraphs.

 </BR> creates a line break.

<B> </B> bolds text.

<I> </I> italicizes text.

<U> </U> underlines text.

<CENTER> </CENTER> centers text.

<FONT COLOR = "*name of color*"> </FONT> changes the font color.

Links

<A HREF> </A> inserts a link.

Tables

<TABLE> </TABLE> creates a table. This pair of tags encompasses all the row and cell tags in the table.

<TR> </TR> creates the rows of a table. This pair of tags encompasses all the cell tags in the table.

<TD> </TD> creates a cell in a table.

Ordered lists

<OL> </OL> creates an ordered list. This pair of tags encompasses all the list tags for each item in the numbered list.

<LI> </LI> encompasses the list items.

Unordered lists

<UL> </UL> creates an unordered list. This pair of tags encompasses all the list tags for each item in the bulleted list.

<LI> </LI> encompasses the list items.

UNIT 4: WEB PHOTO ALBUM

Activity Guides

How to Create a Web Photo Album

You can create an interactive catalog of photographs or graphics by using the Create Web Photo Album command in Macromedia Dreamweaver MX 2004. All you need is a folder of images.

1. Assemble all the images for your album in one folder (preferably outside your local root folder).
2. Start Dreamweaver. If necessary, open your portfolio site.
3. Open a new HTML page and then choose **Commands > Create Web Photo Album**.

   The Create Web Photo Album dialog box opens.

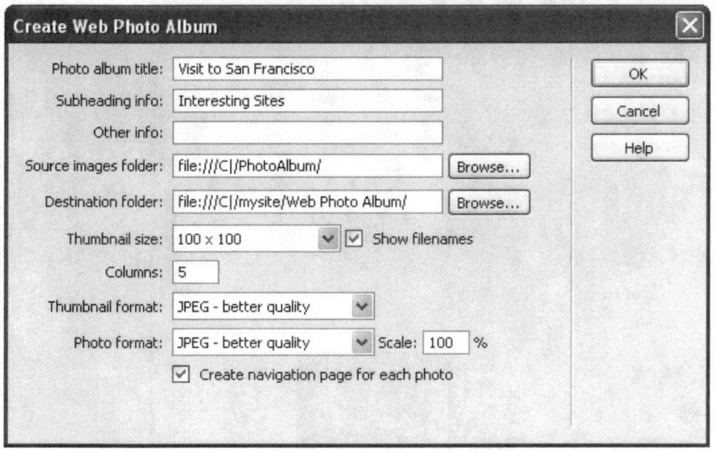

   In the dialog box, provide the following information:

   - *Photo album title:* Title to display on the main page of the photo album, which will display thumbnails for the images in your album.
   - *Subheading info:* Subtitle to display on the main page.
   - *Other info:* Text to appear below subtitle on main page.
   - *Source images folder:* Folder for source images. Click **Browse** and locate your folder of images.
   - *Destination folder:* Folder where the HTML and image files for the photo album will be saved. Click **Browse** and create a folder within the local root folder.
   - *Thumbnail size:* The size of the thumbnail images on the main page.
   - *Columns:* Number of columns in the table that displays the thumbnails. (If you have six to nine images, three columns would work.)
   - *Thumbnail format:* GIF or JPEG format for the thumbnail images.
   - *Photo format:* GIF or JPEG format for the large-size images on the individual album pages. You can use different formats for thumbnails and full-size images.
   - *Scale:* Setting Scale to 100% creates large-size images the same size as the originals. If your images are large, you may need to scale them down.

- *Create navigation page for each photo:* Creates an individual Web page for each large-size image, containing navigation links labeled *Back*, *Home*, and *Next*. If you select this option, the thumbnails link to the navigation pages. If you don't select this option, the thumbnails link directly to the large-size images.

4. Click **OK** in the Create Web Photo Album dialog box.

   Macromedia Fireworks MX starts and creates all the thumbnail and large-size images for the photo album. A message window appears when the album is complete.

5. Click **OK**.

6. To preview the album in a browser, press **F12**.

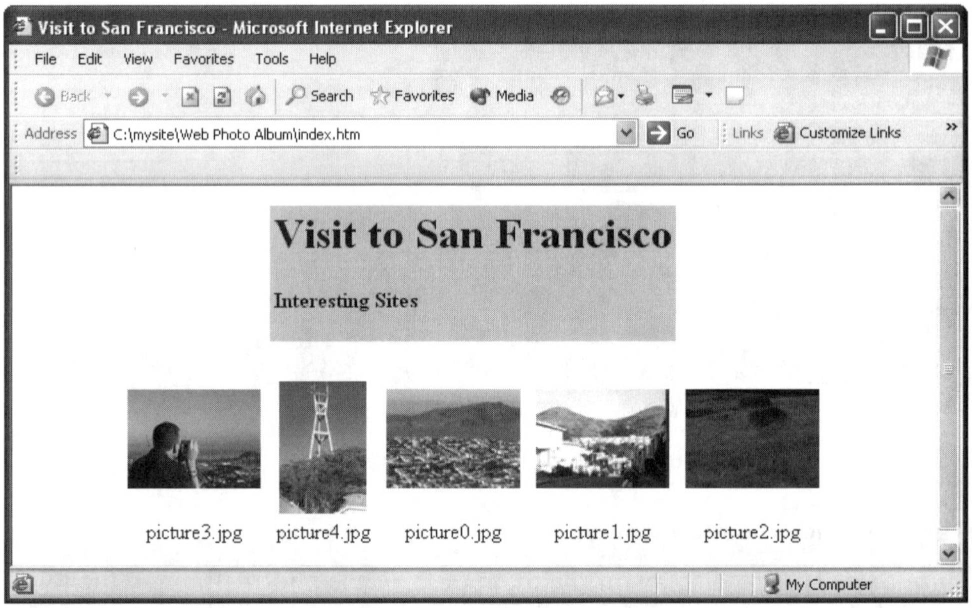

Note: If the images on the index page don't line up, return to the Document window and drag the outside edges of the table to provide more space for the images.

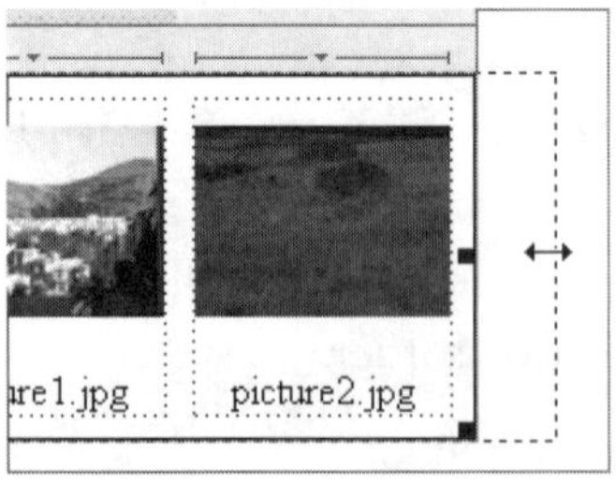

7. Replace the labels for each of the images on the home page with brief descriptive labels.

8. Select each image in turn and add alternative text (Alt tag) to make the page more accessible. Do this in the Alt box on the Property inspector.

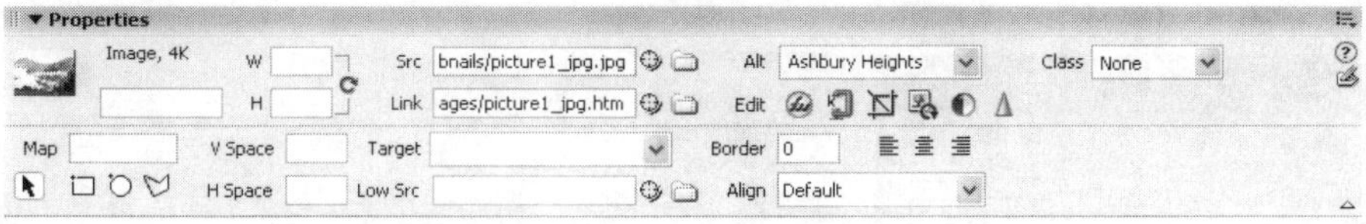

9. Using the Files panel (**Window > Files**), expand the destination folder you chose for the HTML and image files.

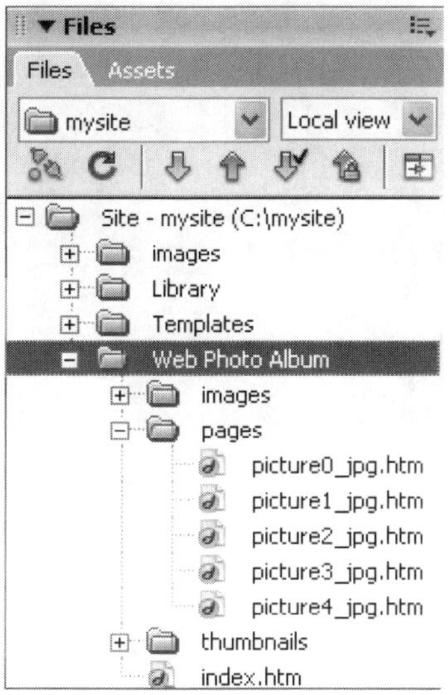

10. Open each HTML page (in the Pages folder) and replace the filenames with descriptive labels.

Note: If you have a word-processing document with description information about the images, you can copy and paste that text into your image pages.

11. On the Files panel, replace the filenames (in the Pages folder) with more descriptive names. You will be asked if you want to update the links to the file. Choose Update to maintain the links.

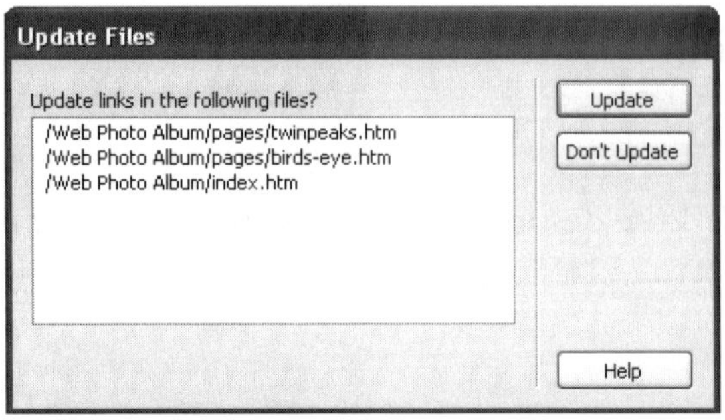

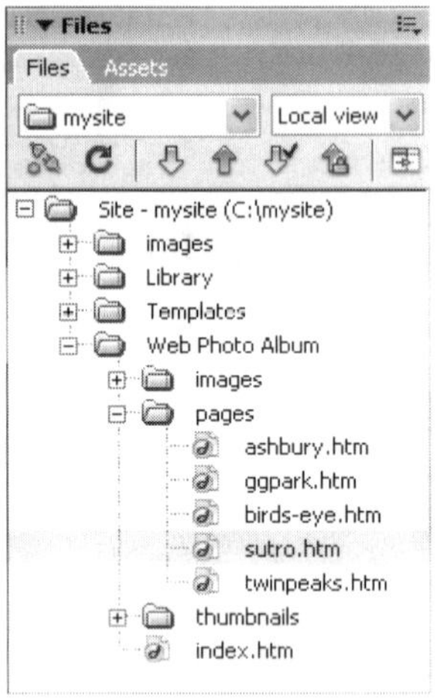

12. Save and close the index.htm page for your Web Photo Album.

How to Integrate a Web Photo Album into a Portfolio

To add a page to your portfolio, first edit the portfolio navigation bar (created in Unit 3) in Macromedia Fireworks MX 2004 and then update links and page format in Dreamweaver.

Add a Button to the Navigation Bar

You can skip this section if you have already created a button for the photo album on your navigation bar.

1. Open your navigation bar PNG file in Fireworks.
2. Choose **Modify > Canvas > Canvas Size.**

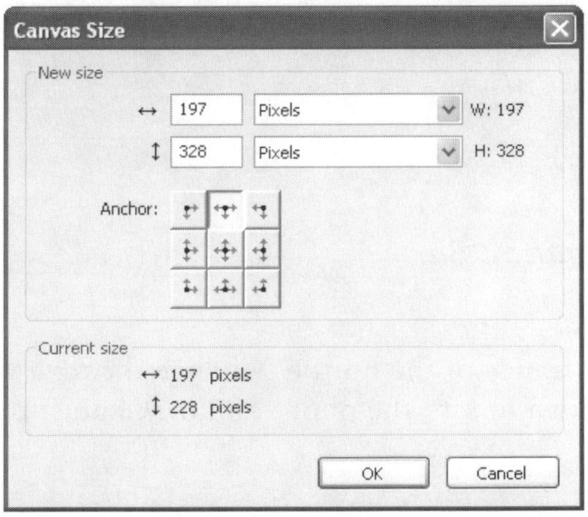

3. Change the canvas height (or width, as appropriate) to accommodate a new button. Be sure to select the top-center Anchor button. This will place the extra canvas space directly below the existing buttons.

4. Copy an existing button and paste it at the end of the navigation bar.

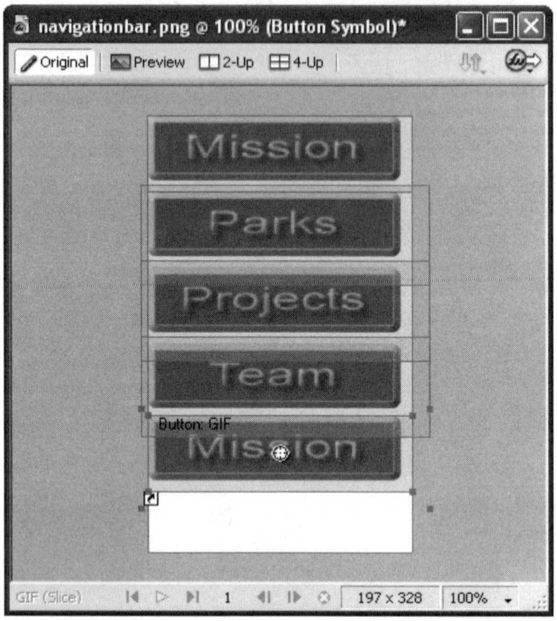

Change the Button Label and Export the Navigation Bar

5. Select the new button.
6. Use the Property inspector to edit the current instance of the button. Change the text that appears on the button in the Text box to indicate a link to the photo album. Change the Alt text to something that describes the button.

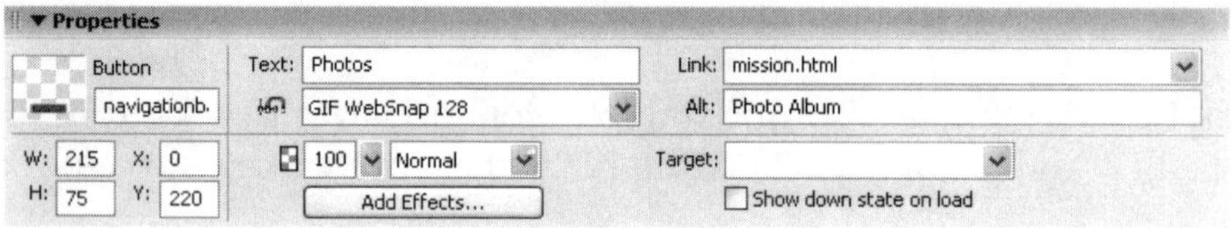

Note: You will change the link information when you return to Dreamweaver.

7. Choose **Modify > Canvas > Trim Canvas** to trim the canvas to an exact fit for the revised navigation bar.
8. Save the PNG file and export the navigation bar using the same HTML and Slice settings as you did when you originally created the navigation bar. Then click **Save**.

9. Click **OK** in each of the two dialog boxes that open prompting you to replace the existing files.

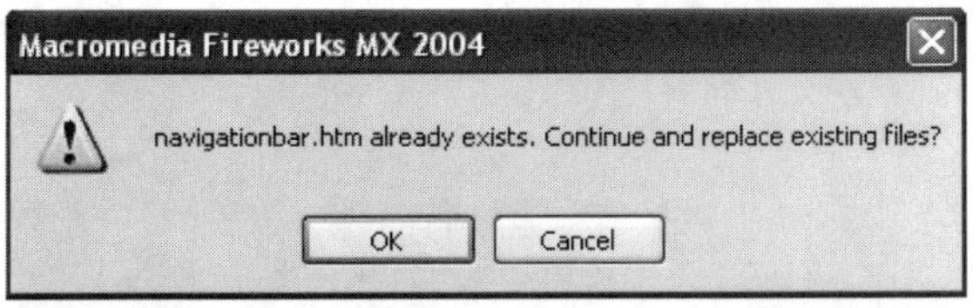

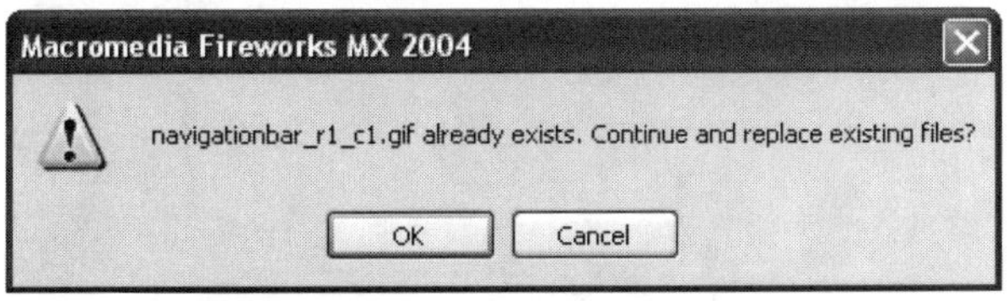

Configure the Button in Dreamweaver

10. Open the home page of your site in Dreamweaver.

    Note: The navigation bar should be updated automatically with the new photo album button.

11. Select the photo album button in the Document window.

12. In the Property inspector, click the **Browse for File** button next to the Link text box.

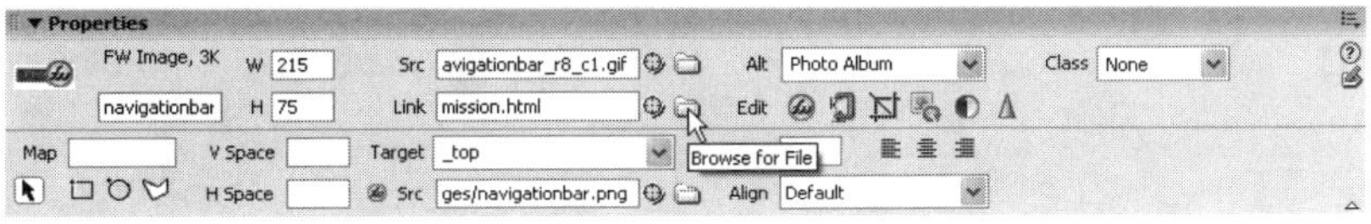

The Select File dialog box opens.

13. Locate the **index.htm** page of the photo album and click **OK**.
14. In the Property inspector, choose **_blank** for Target to open the photo album in a new window.

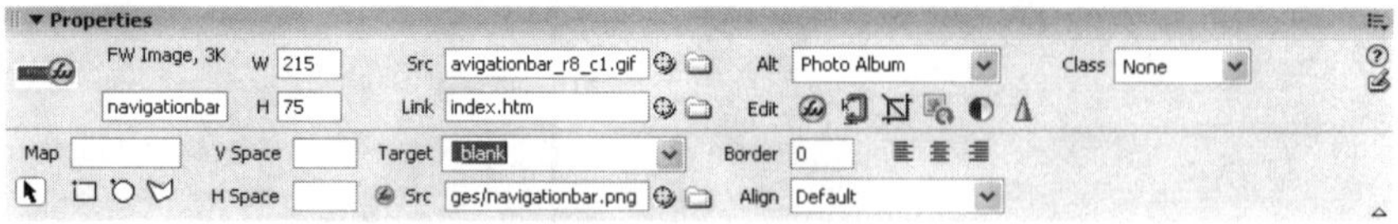

15. Press **F12** to test the button in a browser.

The Web photo album should open in a new browser window.

Unit 5: Interactivity Design with Macromedia Fireworks MX 2004

Activity Guides

Activity 5.2: Planning an Interactive Image in Macromedia Fireworks MX 2004
Layers, Frames, and Behaviors Panels

Activity 5.3: Building an Interactive Image
How to Build an Interactive Image

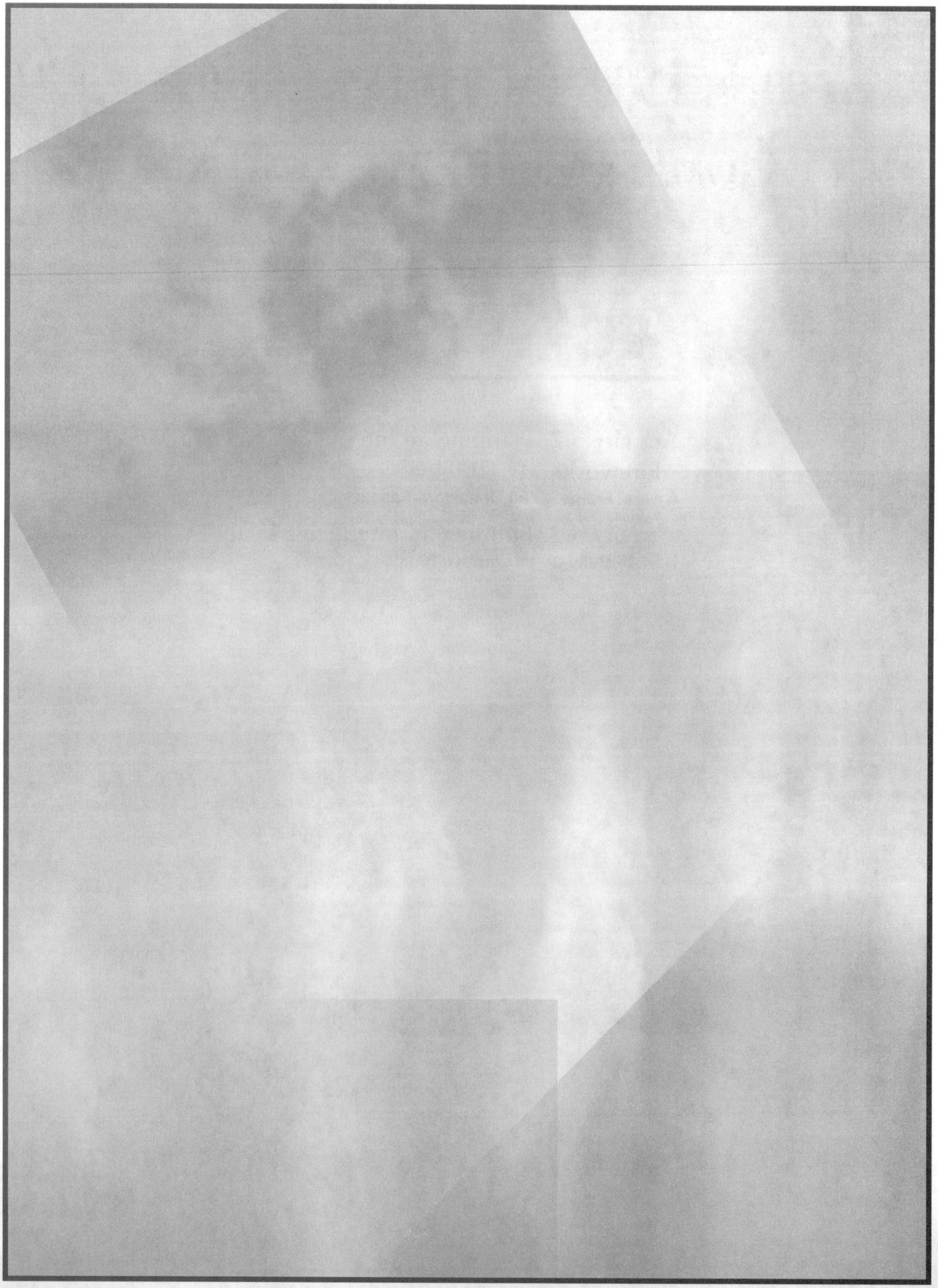

LAYERS, FRAMES, AND BEHAVIORS PANELS

The *Layers panel* displays the contents of all the layers in the current frame of a document.

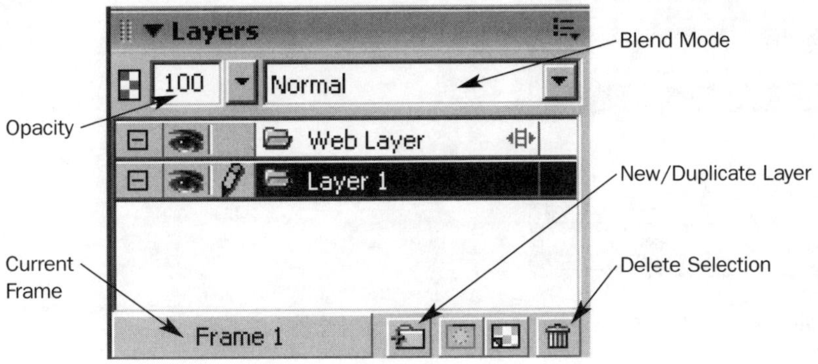

Layers Tools

On the Layers panel you can control the order of objects on the canvas. You can place each object on a different layer to create a complete image. You can also separate objects on sublayers of a single layer.

To add a new layer, click the New/Duplicate Layer button at the bottom of the panel. To delete a layer, select it and click the Delete Selection button at the bottom of the panel.

You can change the opacity of a selected object from opaque (100%) to transparent (0%).

The Blend mode enables you to vary the transparency or color interaction of two or more overlapping objects. The default (Normal) applies no blending mode.

The *Frames panel* displays all the frames used in the document.

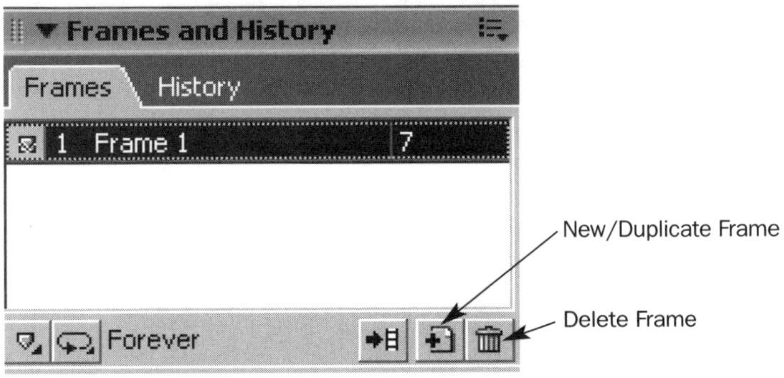

Frames Tools

The Frames panel controls which layers are active. Frames are components of animations and interactivity. By default, there is one frame in a document.

To add a frame, click the New/Duplicate Frame button at the bottom of the panel. To duplicate a frame (and its contents), select it in the Frames list and drag it to the New/Duplicate Frame button. To delete a frame, select it and click the Delete Frame button.

The *Behaviors panel* displays the behaviors attached to a selected slice or hotspot.

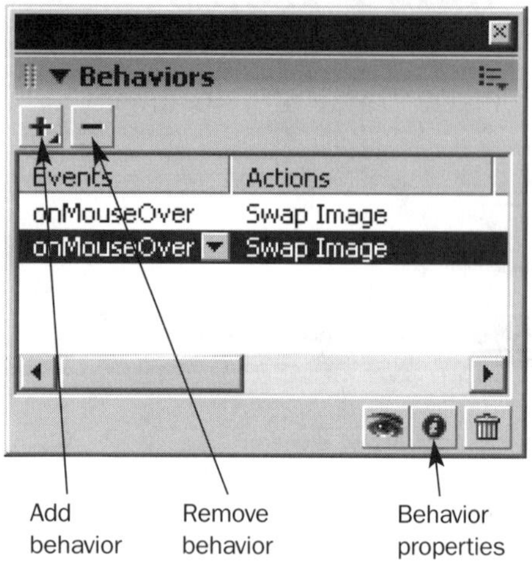

Behaviors Tools

The Behaviors panel contains behaviors for creating interactive graphics.

To add a behavior to a selected slice or hotspot, click the Add behavior button and select a behavior from the pop-up menu. To remove a behavior, select it and click the Remove behavior button.

To see information about a selected behavior or to edit the behavior, click the Behavior properties button.

How to Build an Interactive Image

Prepare the Image

Set Up the Image

1. Start Macromedia Fireworks MX 2004.
2. Open the image you want to make interactive: Choose **File > Open**, navigate to the image file, select it, and click **Open**.
3. Resize the canvas to make room for any effects or additional content you want to add to the image to appear during the rollover or interaction. (Choose **Modify > Canvas > Canvas Size.**)
4. Center the image on the canvas.

5. Open the **Layers** panel and observe that the image appears in Layer 1. The Web layer is empty.

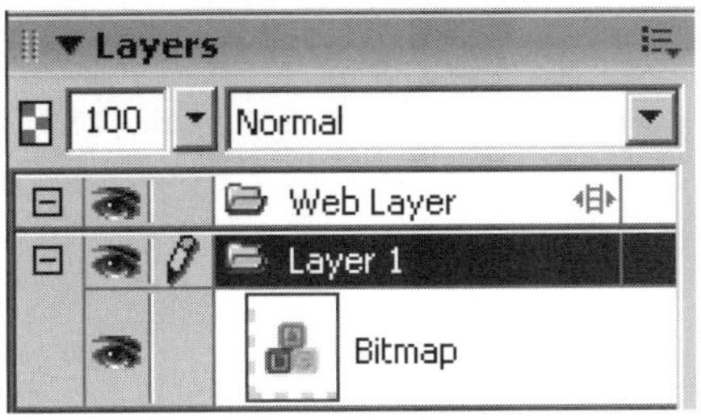

6. Save the new document.

Set Up Frames

7. Open the **Frames** panel.

   Frame 1 holds the image as it normally appears.

8. In the Frames panel, click the **New/Duplicte Frame** button at the bottom of the panel.

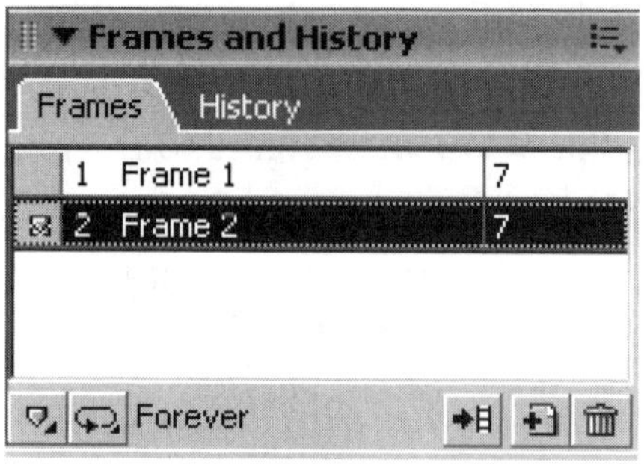

   Observe that in Frame 2 the canvas is blank. This frame will hold the image as it appears during the interaction or rollover.

Add Interactivity

Create Rollover Effects

Rollovers all work the same way. Rolling the pointer over one graphic triggers the display of another. The *trigger* is a Web object, called a *slice*. A *simple rollover* swaps an image in Frame 1 with an image directly below it in Frame 2. A *disjoint rollover* swaps an image in Frame 1 with an image or text object away from the pointer.

1. Click **Frame 1** in the Frames panel and use the **Marquee** tool to select a rectangular area of the image that you want to change on rollover (the trigger).

2. Copy the selection.
3. Click **Frame 2** on the Frames panel and paste the copied selection in Frame 2. (Choose **Edit > Paste** or use the keyboard equivalent.)

   The pasted image will be the target for the rollover. Observe on the Layers panel that the pasted image appears in Layer 1 of Frame 2.

4. If necessary, use the **Pointer** tool to select the pasted image in Frame 2. On the Property inspector, add effects such as Bevel, Glow, or Contrast (or add graphic elements) to make the target image stand out on rollover.

   Note: In a simple rollover, any added graphic elements must be within the boundary of the target image, since the trigger image and the target image are within the same slice.

5. Add text near the rollover to give pop-up information when the user rolls over the image.

   Note: In a disjointed rollover, the target, such as the text "A is for apple," is outside the boundary of the target image.

6. Save the document.

Create Slices for the Interactive Image

7. Using the **Pointer** tool, select the image in Frame 2.

8. Choose **Edit > Insert > Slice** to attach a slice to the image.

   The slice appears as a box with light green fill on the image. When you select a slice, you will see the *behavior handle* in the center, a circle with cross hairs.

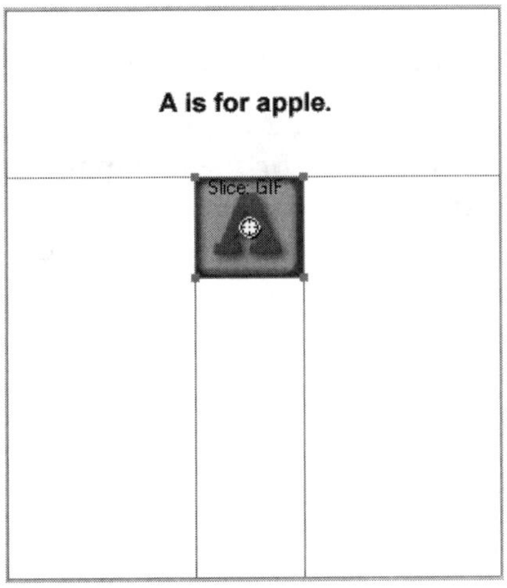

Observe on the Layers panel that the slice appears in the Web Layer. A slice is a Web object—that is, HTML code—that creates the interactivity, such as swapping out an image or displaying new text when the user rolls over the image in a browser.

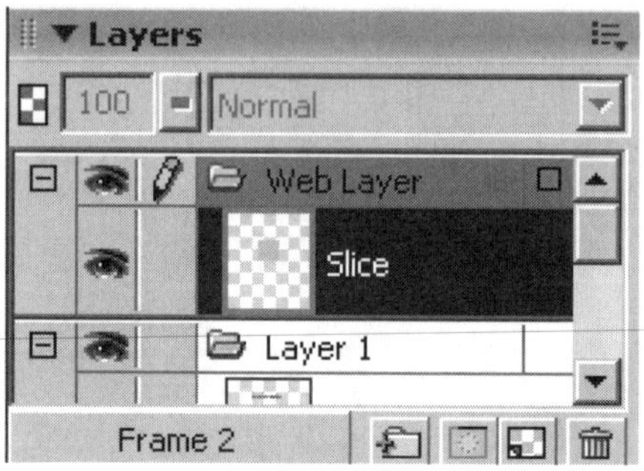

9. On the Layers panel, double-click the name **Slice** and key a short descriptive name (using lowercase letters and numbers, but no spaces, such as "*block-a*").
10. Select the text object in Frame 2.
11. Choose **Edit > Insert > Slice** to attach a slice to the text. Give the slice a short descriptive name.

    The text now has a light green slice box over it.
12. Save the document.

Add Behaviors

13. On the Frames panel, click **Frame 1**.
14. Using the **Pointer** tool, select the trigger slice that contains the area of the original image you copied in step 10.
15. To add the simple rollover (swapping the altered image on Frame 2 for the original image on Frame 1), drag the behavior handle to the upper left edge of the slice.

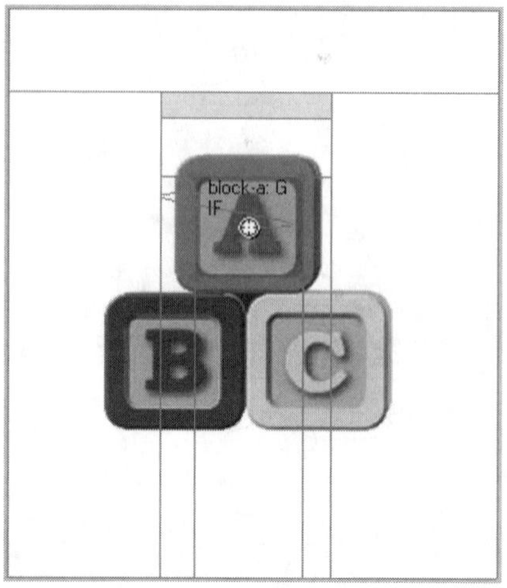

A curved blue line connects the center of the slice to the upper left edge. When you release, the Swap Image dialog box opens.

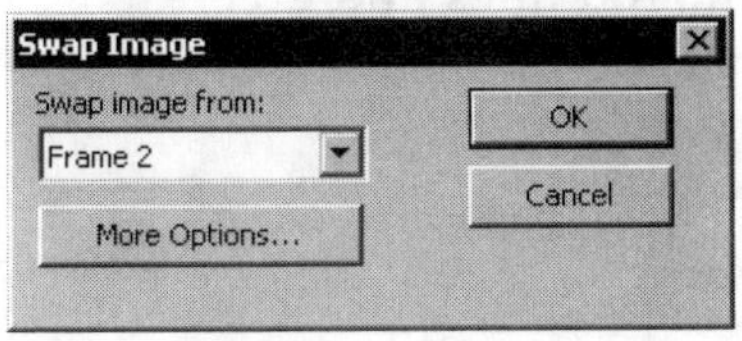

16. For Swap image from, select **Frame 2** and click **OK**.
17. To add the disjointed rollover (displaying the text away from the pointer), drag the behavior handle from the trigger slice to the upper left edge of the text slice.

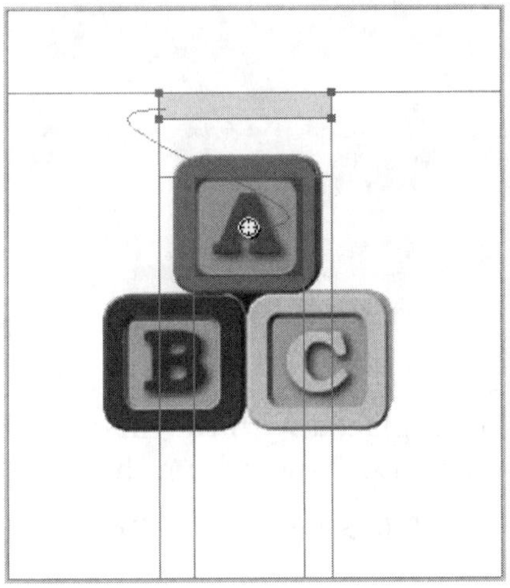

A curved blue line connects the center of the trigger slice to the upper left edge of the target (text) slice.

18. In the Swap Image dialog box, select **Frame 2** for Swap image from and click **OK**.

The trigger slice is now connected to itself (for the simple rollover) and to the text slice (for the disjointed rollover).

19. To see the behaviors you just added by dragging the behavior handle, open the **Behaviors** panel (**Window > Behaviors**) and click the trigger slice.

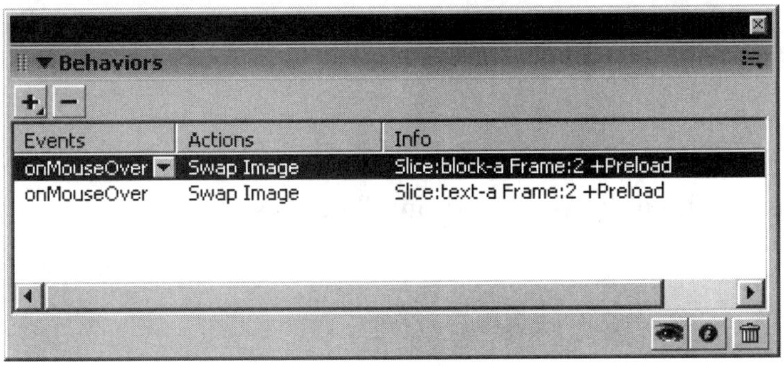

Note: You can also add or edit behaviors on the Behaviors panel.

20. Save the document.

Preview the Image

1. Click **Hide slices and hotspots** on the Tools panel to hide the red lines and green slice areas.
2. Click the **Preview** button at the top of the canvas.
3. Test your interaction by moving the pointer over the image.

As you roll the pointer over the trigger image, it should be replaced with the image from Frame 2, and the text you created in Frame 2 should be displayed away from the pointer.

You can also test your interaction in a browser by choosing **File > Preview in Browser** and choosing a browser from the submenu.

4. To add more interactivity, click the **Original** button at the top of the canvas.
5. Click **Show slices and hotspots** on the Tools panel.
6. Add interactivity to other elements of your original image.

Note: As you create more slices, be careful that they do not overlap and remember to name each one.

Export the Image

Exporting the interactive image produces an HTML file and a subfolder that contain all the sliced images used in the HTML file. You can then import all the HTML into a Macromedia Dreamweaver MX document.

1. Choose **File > Export.**
2. In the Export dialog box, make sure **Include Areas without Slices** is selected.

3. Select **Put images in subfolder.**

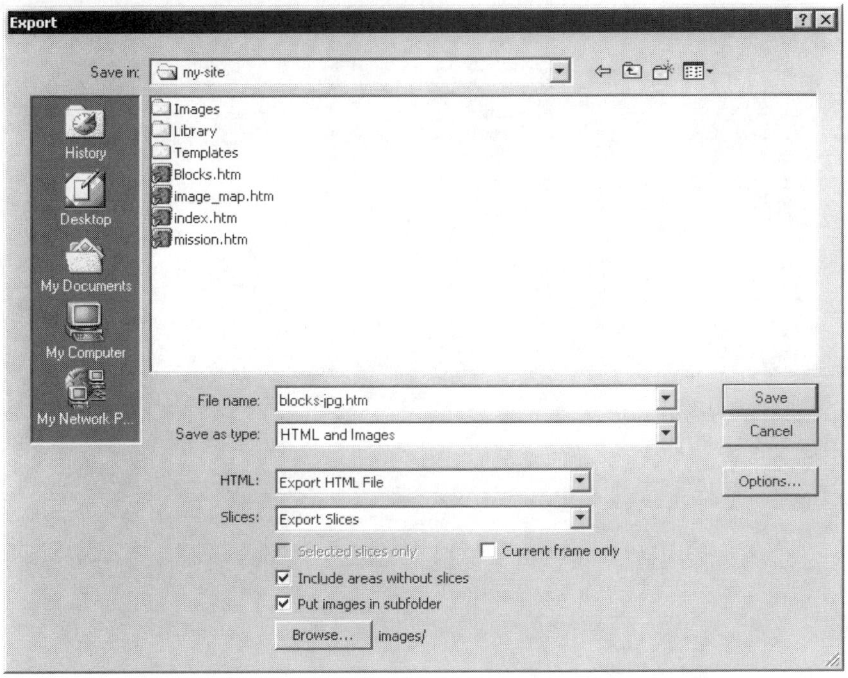

A pathname appears next to the Browse button, indicating the subfolder that Fireworks will create for the images. You can change this subfolder by clicking the Browse button.

4. Click **Save.**

Import the Image into Macromedia Dreamweaver MX 2004

1. Start Macromedia Dreamweaver MX 2004.
2. If necessary, create a new document and save it.
3. Choose **Insert > Image Objects > Fireworks HTML.**

   The Insert Fireworks HTML dialog box opens.

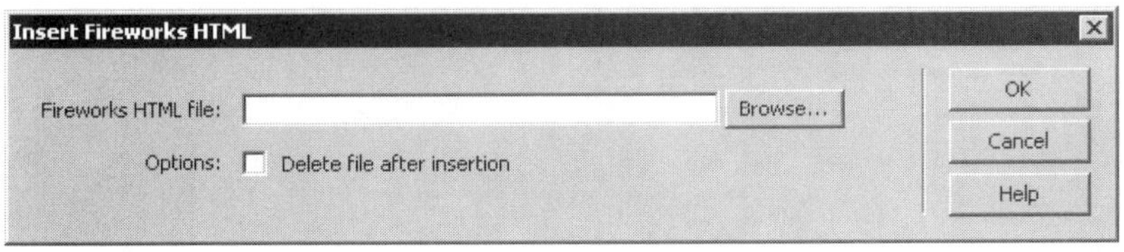

4. Click **Browse** and navigate to your interactive image HTML file you exported from Fireworks. Select the file and click **Open**.

   The pathname for the HTML file appears in the dialog box.

5. Click **OK.**
6. Save the document.

   This document is the Web page for your interactive image.

Unit 6: Review Workshop

Activity Guide

Activity 6.1: Review Workshop

Review Workshop

REVIEW WORKSHOP

A review workshop is a method for providing constructive feedback on a project's design and content. Evaluation guidelines consist of defining components or elements of both design and content to help in critiquing the work.

Each work is reviewed separately using the following process:

1. The designer briefly describes the portfolio's audience, purpose, and goals, as well as the type of information included in the portfolio, and why that information is included.
2. During the feedback session, the designer takes notes on the group's feedback. From this point on, the designer does not participate in the discussion.
3. First, one member of the group summarizes the designer's audience, purpose, and goals, as well as the type of information included in the portfolio, and why that information is included. This helps confirm that the group understood the designer's intent.
4. The group first discusses the strengths of the design in the portfolio.
5. The group discusses the strengths of the content.
6. The group discusses ways to improve the design and content.
7. Finally, one member of the group summarizes the positive aspects of the portfolio.

Unit 7: Building a Basic Client Web Site

Activity Guides

Activity 7.2: Planning a Client Project
Professional Web Design and Development Process

Activity 7.3: Structuring a Client Web Site
Sample Screen Views

Activity 7.5: Reviewing and Revising to Client Specifications
Production Storyboard

Activity 7.6: Building a Client Web Site
How to Use Templates
How to Use Libraries
How to Check Files In and Out

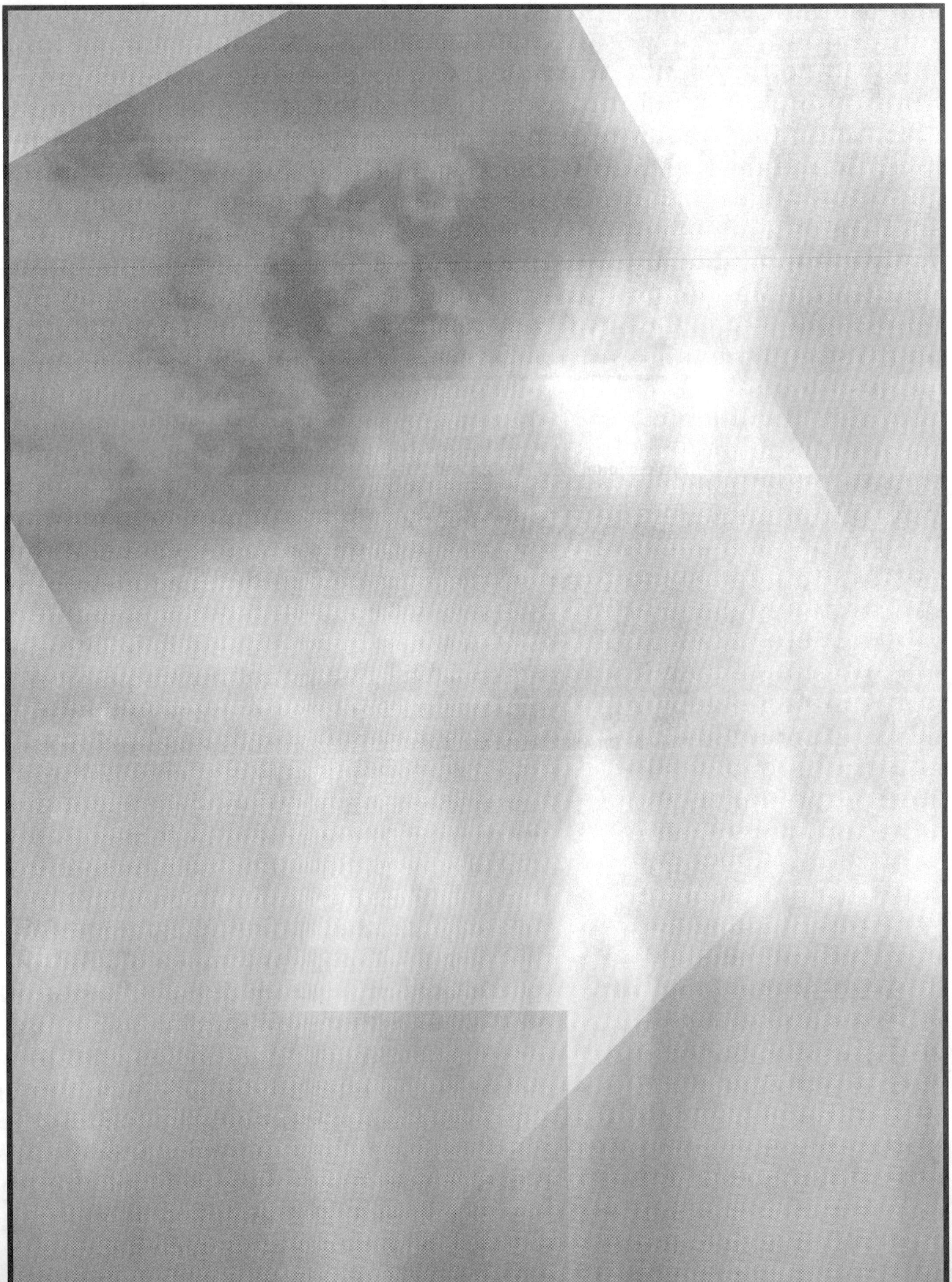

Professional Web Design and Development Process

The professional web design and development process requires a cycle of planning, design, building, and evaluating. Web professionals will circulate through these steps until the client is satisfied with the product.

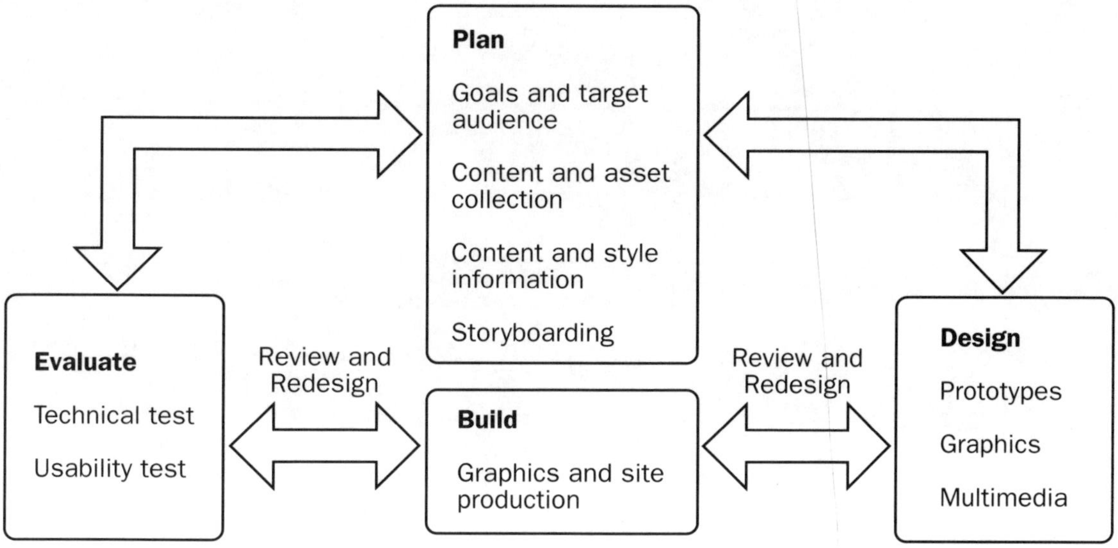

When planning a web project, professionals break the cycle down into the following phases:

Define	Structure	Design	Build and Test	Launch
Goals and target audience	Site map	Design comps	Site production	Promotion plan
Content and asset collection	Screen view sketches	Design review	Technical test and bug list	Put site online
Content and style information		Redesign	User test	
Delivery requirements		Production storyboard	Revision	
			Test revised site	
			Final presentation	
			Final revision	

SAMPLE SCREEN VIEWS

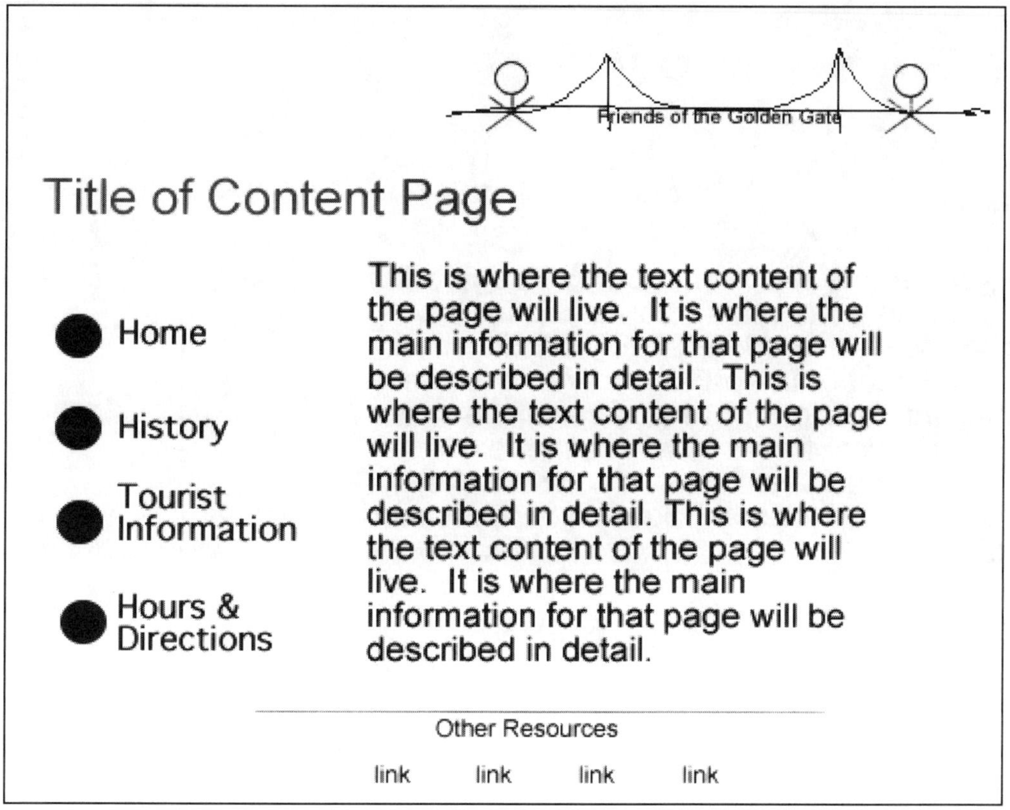

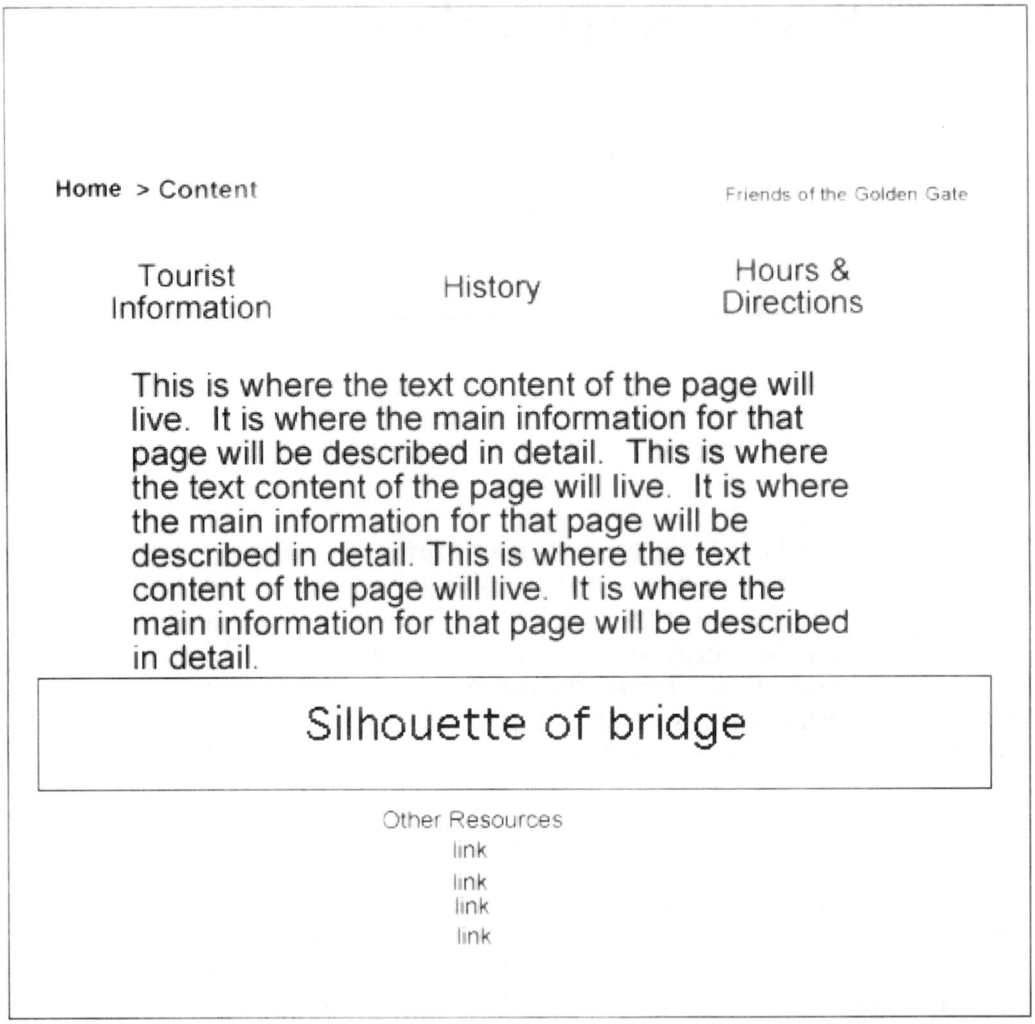
Home > Content
Friends of the Golden Gate
Tourist Information
History
Hours & Directions
This is where the text content of the page will live. It is where the main information for that page will be described in detail. This is where the text content of the page will live. It is where the main information for that page will be described in detail. This is where the text content of the page will live. It is where the main information for that page will be described in detail.
Silhouette of bridge
Other Resources
link
link
link
link

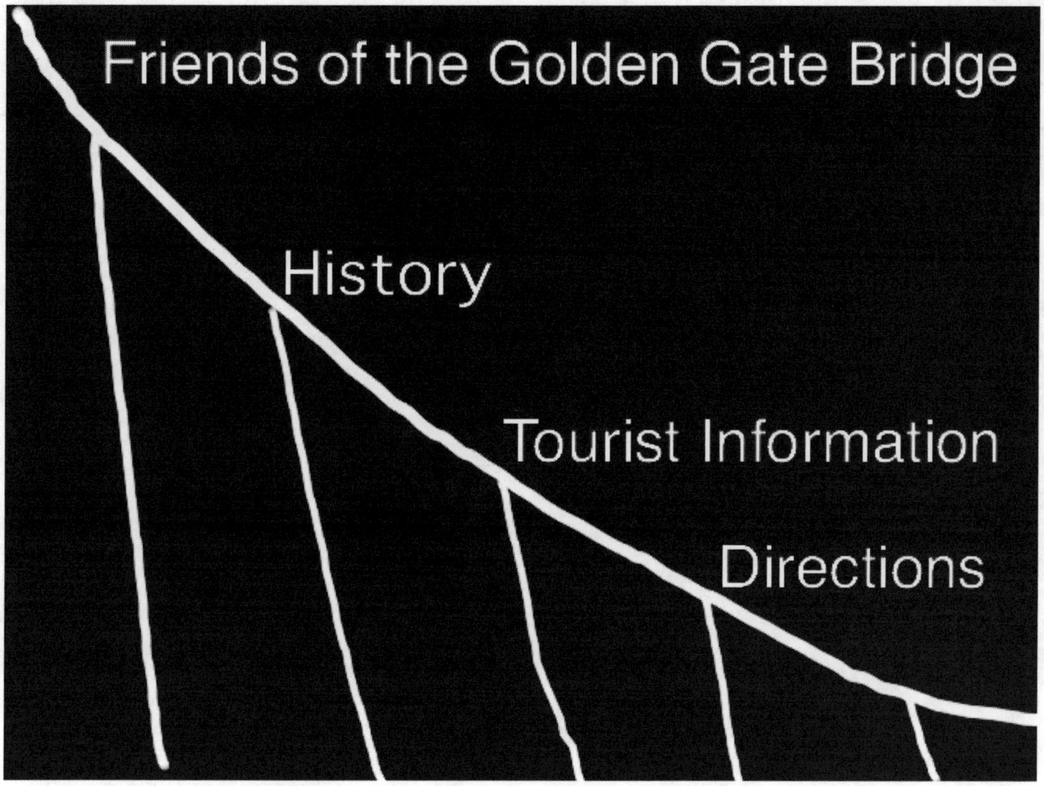
Friends of the Golden Gate Bridge
History
Tourist Information
Directions

Production Storyboard

Name: *D. Smith* Date: *08-02-04*

Site Name: *Kids Read!*

Page Title: *ABC Fruit Blocks* Filename: *abc_blocks.html*

Page sketch (everything specific to this page; common navigation elements optional)

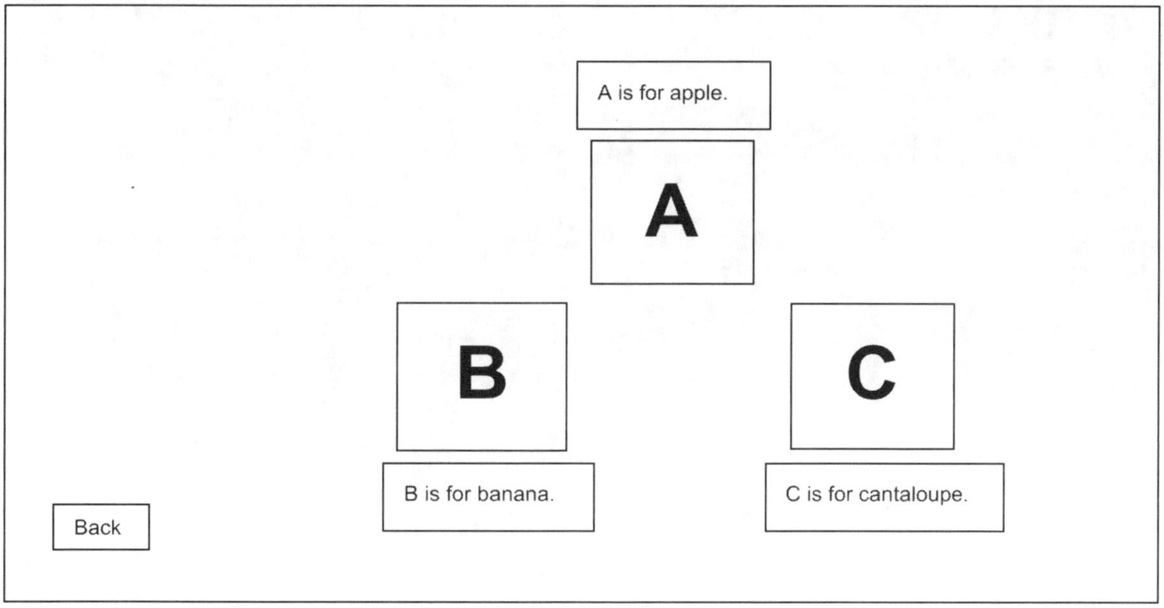

Background color (name and number): *cream (#FFFCCC)*

Description (what happens on the screen, such as order of display, text, and animation steps)

The starting image is three blocks, each with a letter as shown in the sketch. When the user rolls the pointer over a block, the face of the block changes to a darker shade and text appears next to the block, as shown in the sketch. When the pointer is not over a block, no text is displayed.

Navigation (button or link names and destinations)

Back: Goes to index.html

Graphics files (all graphics specific to this page)

blocks-example.png, plus all associated exported files that will result from the slices.

How to Use Templates

You can use a Macromedia Dreamweaver MX 2004 *template* document to create multiple pages that share the same layout. In a template, you control which elements of a page should remain constant in documents based on that template and which elements can be changed. Templates are helpful for building a Web site in which most pages have the same header, navigation system, and other elements. Using templates helps you save time as well as create and maintain a consistent look when more than one person is developing a site.

Create a Template

1. Start Dreamweaver.
2. Build a page that contains elements that will occur on all content pages such as common graphics, a navigation bar, and common layout structures such as tables.

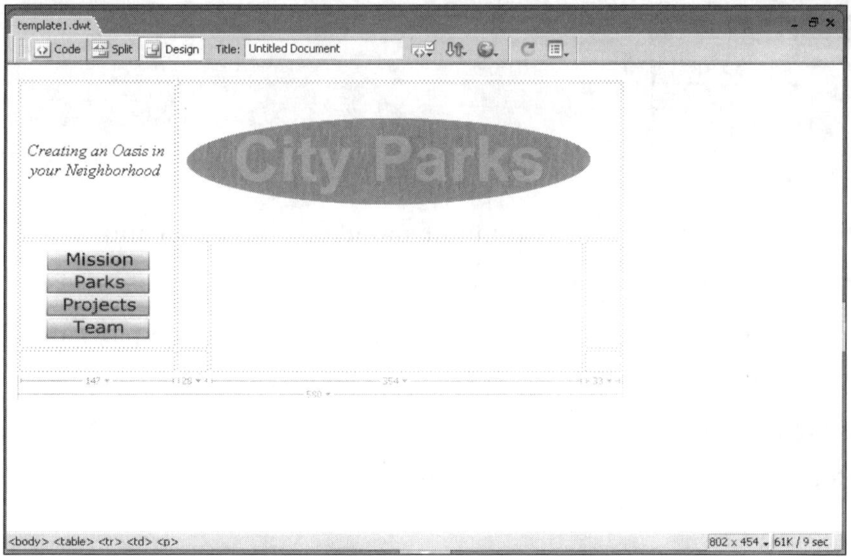

Note: You may want to create navigation elements in Macromedia Fireworks MX 2004 and export them as HTML documents.

3. Choose **File > Save as Template.**

   Dreamweaver creates a Templates folder in your site root folder and saves your template in that folder. Template files have a .dwt file extension.

Create an Editable Region

Editable regions in a template are the parts of the page that can be changed in files based on the template. Locked (non-editable) regions are the parts of the page layout that remain constant from page to page. All regions in a new template are locked, so to make the template useful, you must make some regions editable.

4. Position the insertion point where you want to insert an editable region in the template.

   For example, you might want to use a table cell for content that is specific to each page—that is, content that changes from one page to another.

5. Do one of the following to create an editable region:

   - Choose **Insert > Template Objects > Editable Region**.
   - Right-click (Windows) or Control-click (Macintosh) the region and choose **Templates > New Editable Region** from the context menu.
   - On the Common Insert bar, click the Templates button, and select **Editable Region**.

   The New Editable Region dialog box opens.

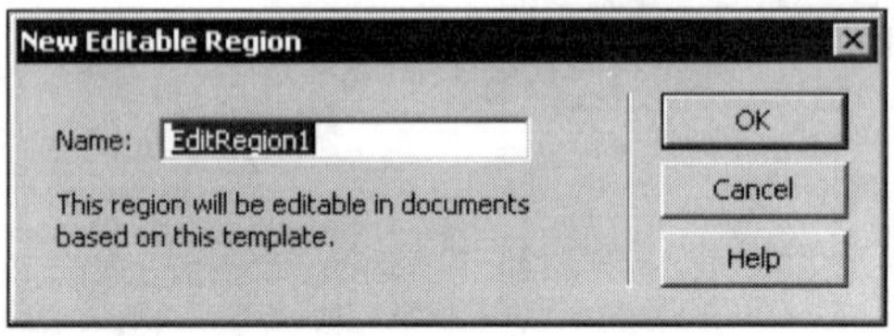

6. In the New Editable Region dialog box, enter a unique name for the region and click **OK**.
7. The editable region is enclosed in a blue rectangle on the template.

   Note: You cannot use the same name for more than one editable region in a particular template. Use only letters and numbers in the name.

Create a Document Based on a Template

Once you create a template, you can apply it to new documents.

8. Choose **File > New**.

9. In the New Document dialog box, select the **Templates** tab.

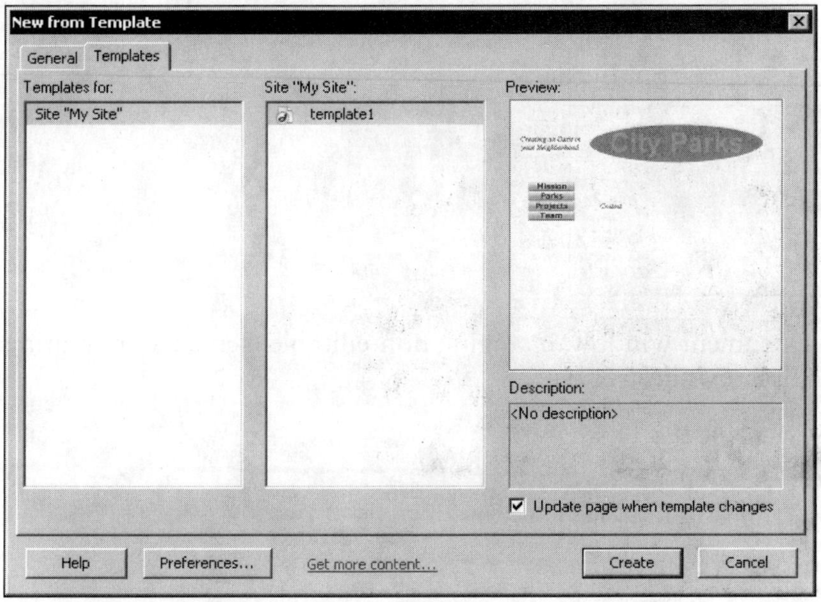

10. In the Templates for list, select the site that contains the template you want to use.
11. Select the template you want to use.
12. Make sure the option **Update page when template changes** is selected.

    With this option selected, Dreamweaver can update all template-based pages if you change the template later.

13. Click **Create** to create a new template-based page.

    The document opens in the Document window.

Edit a Template

You can edit a template at any time, even if you have created pages based on the template.

1. Choose **Window > Assets**.

   The Assets panel opens.

2. Click the **Templates** button on the left side of the panel.

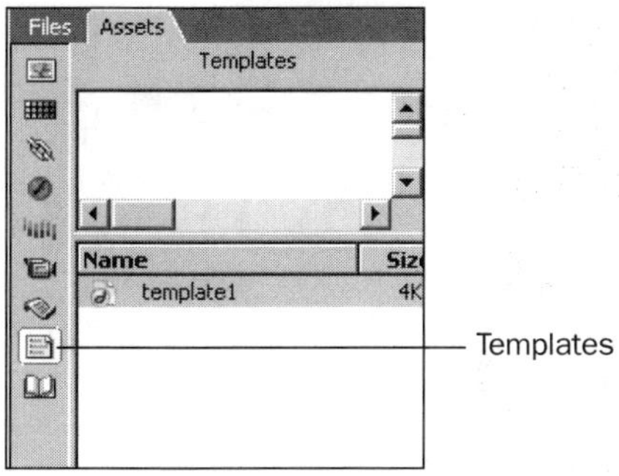

A list of the templates for your site appears in the lower pane. The upper pane displays a preview of the selected template. (You may need to scroll the preview pane to see this.)

3. Select the template you wish to edit and do one of the following:
   - Double-click the name of the template.
   - Click the **Edit** button at the bottom of the panel.

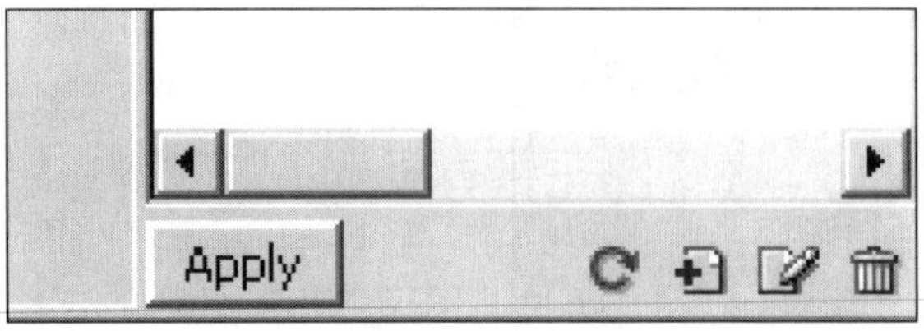

4. Edit the template in the Document window, changing non-editable elements or creating editable regions in the template as desired.
5. Save the edited template by choosing **File > Save**.

Delete a Template

1. Select the template in the Assets panel.
2. Click the **Delete** button (trash can icon) at the bottom of the panel and confirm that you want to delete the template.

   The template file is deleted from your site.

   Documents that were based on a template you have deleted retain the structure and editable regions that the template file had before you deleted it. To turn such a document into a normal HTML file without editable or locked regions, you must detach it from the template.

Detach from a Template

To remove the template structure and constraints from a document based on a template, you can *detach* the document from the template. Detaching a document from its template enables you to edit any element, including the regions that were previously locked.

1. To detach a document from a template, open the document.
2. Choose **Modify > Templates > Detach from Template.**

How to Use Libraries

You can use a Dreamweaver *library* to store page elements (such as images, text, sounds, or tables) that you want to reuse or update frequently throughout your Web site. When you insert a library item, Dreamweaver actually inserts a link to the library item. If you later need to make changes to a library item, such as changing some text or an image, updating the library item automatically updates each instance of the item in every page into which you've inserted it.

Create a Library Item

1. Select an element of a document (such as an image or text) to save as a library item.
2. Choose **Window > Assets**, click the **Library** button, and then click the **New Library Item** button at the bottom right of the Assets panel.

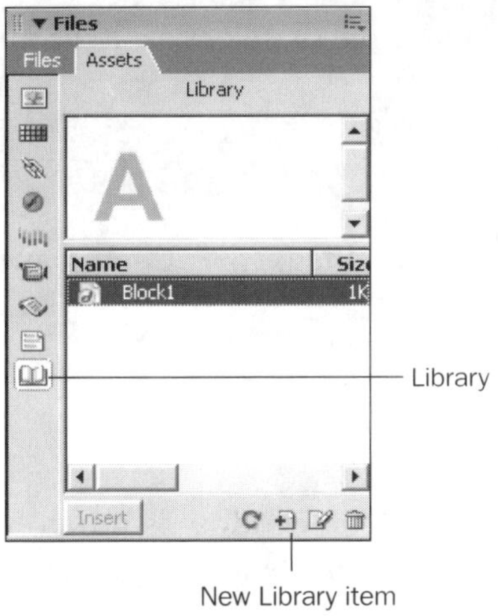

3. Enter a name for the new library item: If necessary, click **Untitled** to select it, type a name, and press **Enter** (Windows) or **Return** (Macintosh).

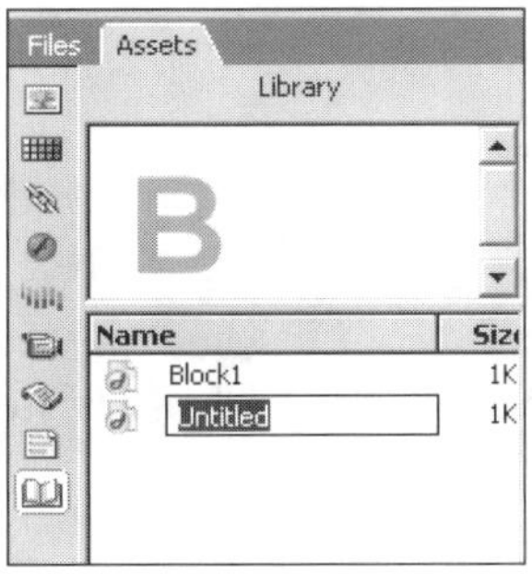

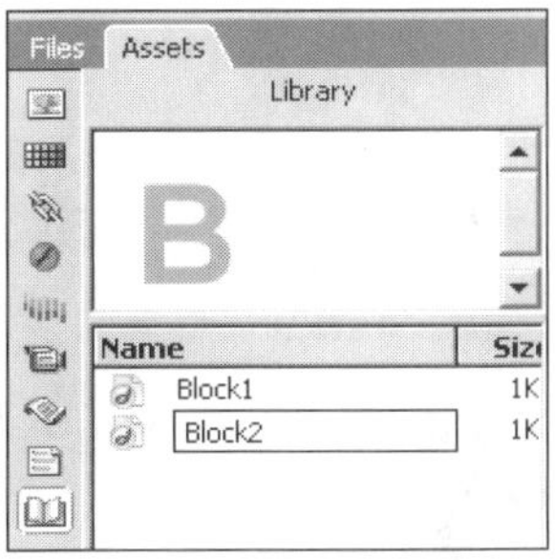

4. Each library item is saved as a separate file (with the file extension .lbi) in the Library folder of the site's local root folder.

Insert a Library Item

1. Position the insertion point in the Document window where you want to insert a library item.
2. Choose **Window > Assets** and click the **Library** button on the left side of the Assets panel.

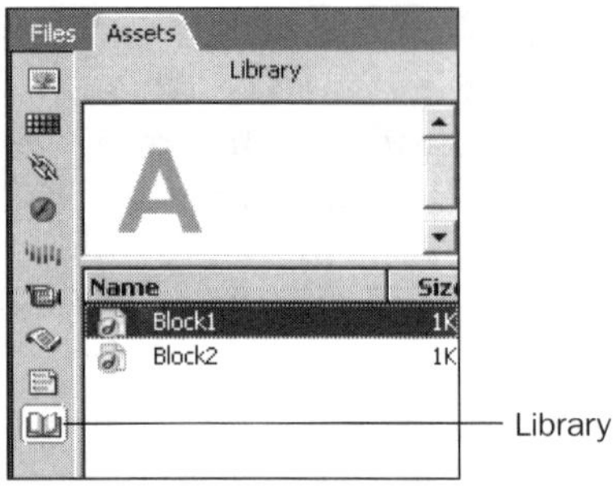

   The Assets panel opens and shows the Library category.

3. Drag a library item from the Assets panel to the Document window, or select an item and click the **Insert** button at the bottom of the panel.

Edit a Library Item

1. Choose **Window > Assets** and click the **Library** button on the left side of the Assets panel.

   The Library category of the Assets panel opens.

2. Select a library item.
3. Click the **Edit** button at the bottom of the Assets panel.

   Dreamweaver opens a new window for editing the library item. This window is much like a Document window. You can tell that it is a Library item by the .lbi filename extension in the document's tab. On the Macintosh, the background is also gray.

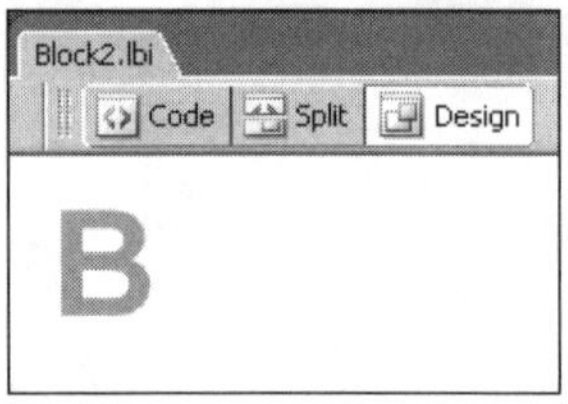

4. Edit the library item and then save your changes.

   The Update Library Items dialog box opens, with a list of the files that use the library item.

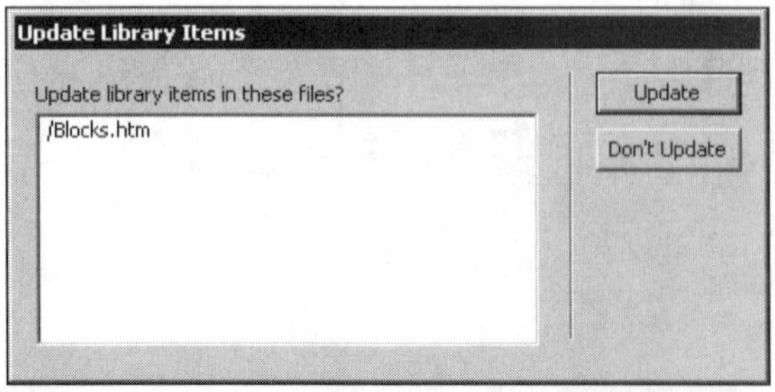

5. Click **Update** to replace the original library item with your edited version in the files that use the library item.

The Update Pages dialog box opens, with a report on the updating process.

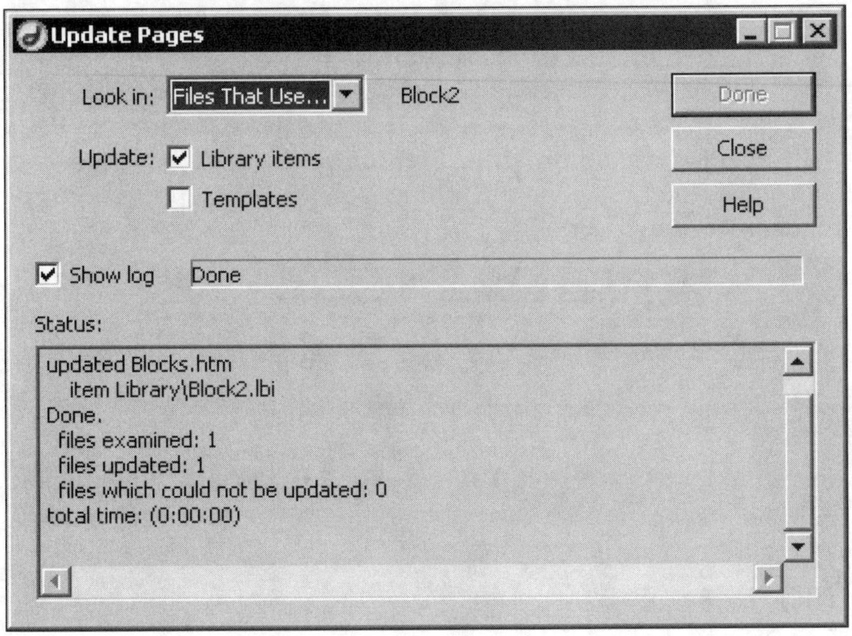

6. Click **Close**.

Update All Documents to Use Current Library Items

If you do not choose to update documents that use library items as you edit individual library items, you can later update all pages in the site to use the current version of all library items.

1. If necessary, open the library item you want to update documents with.
2. Choose **Modify > Library > Update Pages.**

   The Update Pages dialog box opens.

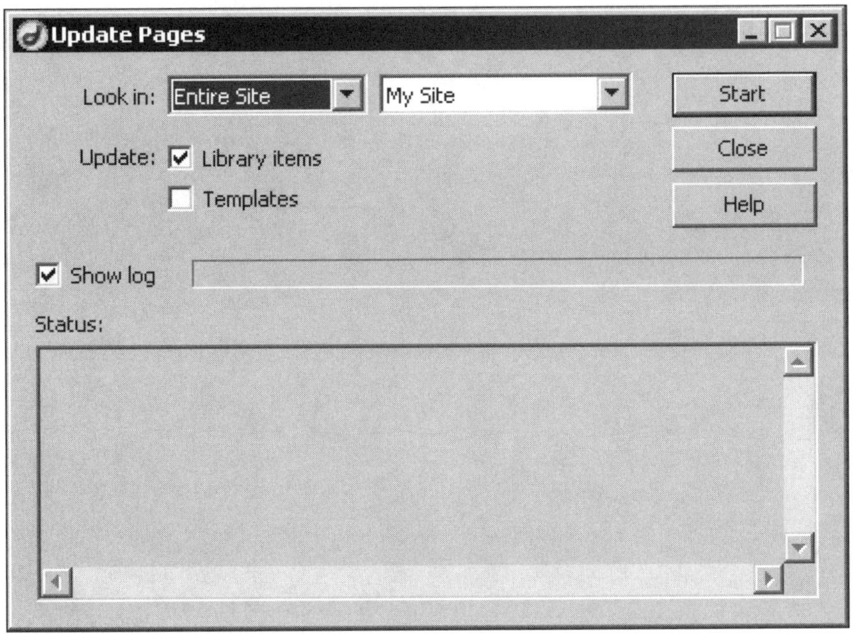

3. From the Look in pop-up menu, choose **Entire Site**, and then choose the site name from the adjacent pop-up menu.
4. Make sure **Library items** is selected in the Update section.
5. Click **Start**.

   Dreamweaver updates the documents and provides a report on the updating process. If you have updated documents at the time you edited library items, this report confirms that no additional updating was required.

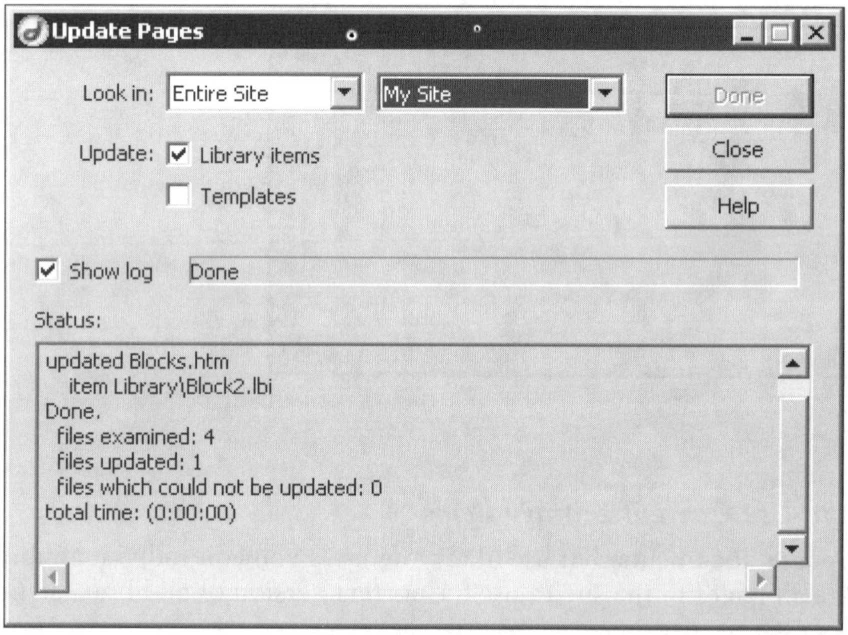

6. Click **Close**.

How to Check Files In and Out

When you're working on a collaborative team, you can use Dreamweaver to check files in and out from local and remote servers. Checking out a file is like declaring, "I'm working on this file now—don't touch it!" When a file is checked out, Dreamweaver displays a check mark next to the file's icon in the Files panel and also displays the name of the person who checked out the file. Checking in a file makes the file available on the remote server to other team members to check out and edit at their workstations.

Check Out Files

Use the Files panel to check out files on a remote server.

1. In the Files panel, select your local site from the Site menu.

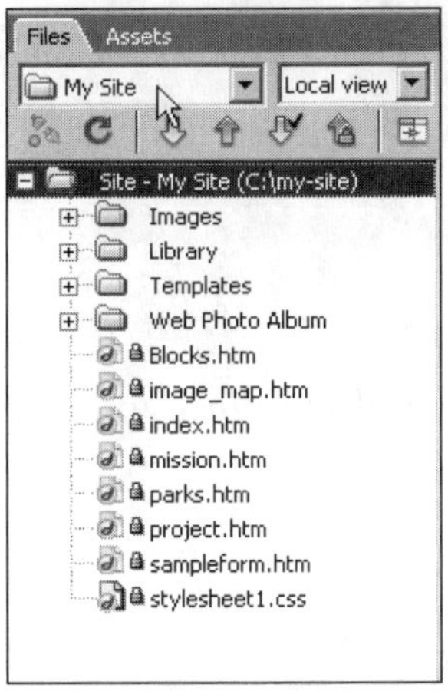

2. Click the **Expand/Collapse** button in the Files panel.

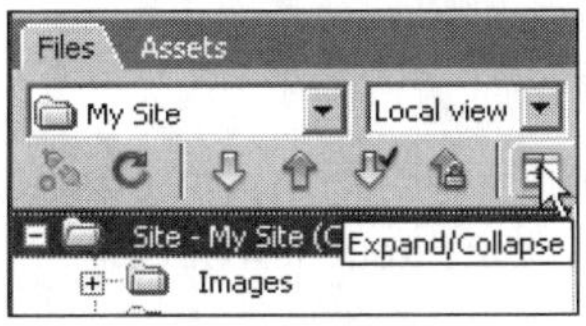

You can now see your remote site and local site panes side-by-side. You can also toggle between these two windows when the Files panel is collapsed.

3. Select one or more files in the Remote Site pane and click the **Check Out File(s)** button at the top of the Files panel.

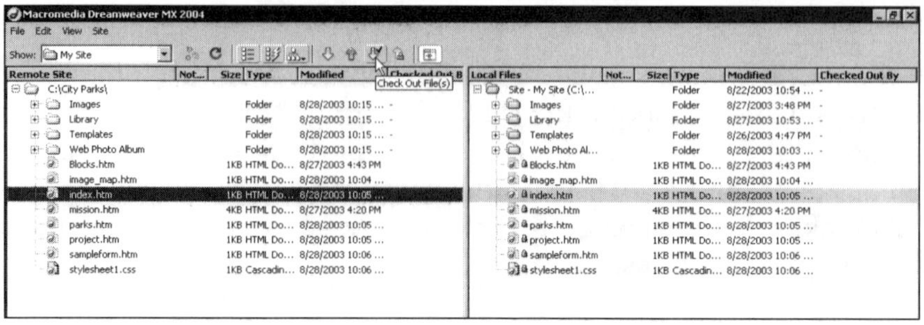

The Dependent Files dialog box appears.

4. To download dependent files along with the selected files, click **Yes** at the prompt. Otherwise, click **No**. (*Dependent files* are files that are used or displayed by one of your selected files.)

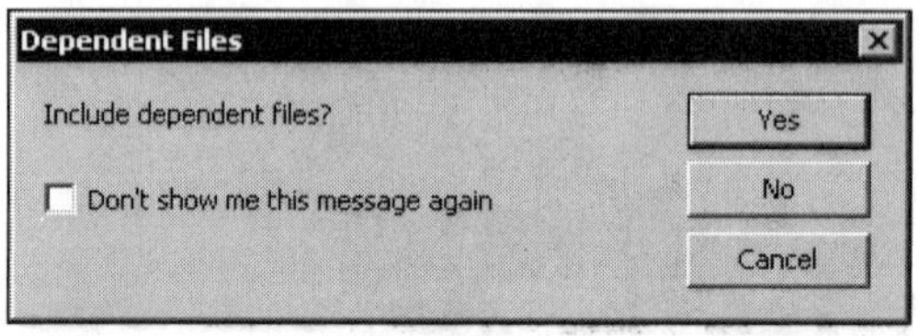

Dreamweaver displays a check mark beside each file you check out, along with your name.

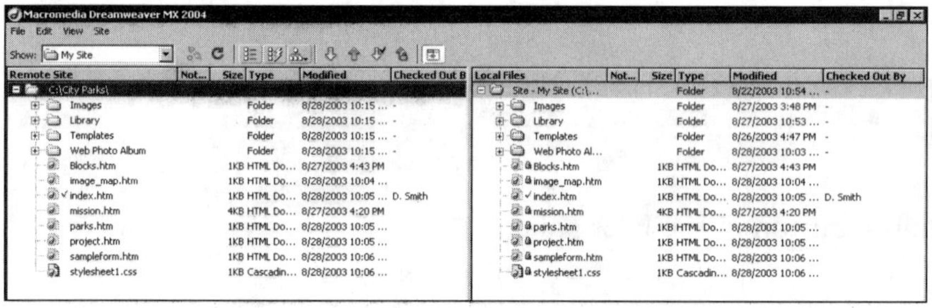

You can edit checked-out files on your workstation. When you finish working on checked-out files, remember to check them back in, so other team members can access them.

Check In Files

Use the Files panel to check in files to a remote server.

1. In the Files panel, select your local site from the Site menu.
2. Select one or more checked-out or new files in the Local Files pane of the Files panel.

3. Click the **Check In** button at the top of the Files panel.

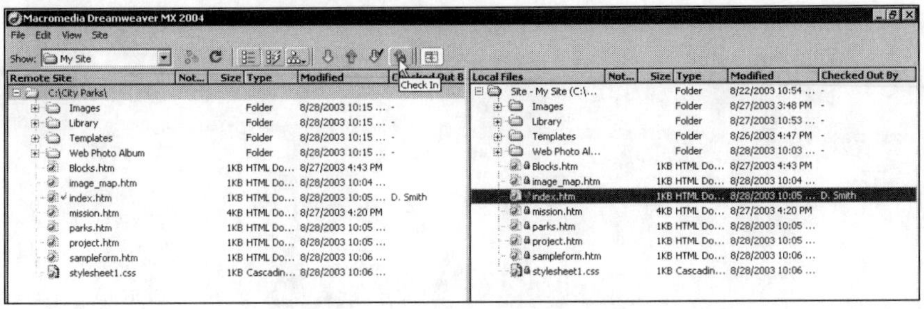

The Dependent Files dialog box appears.

4. To upload dependent files along with the selected files, click **Yes** at the prompt. Otherwise, click **No**.

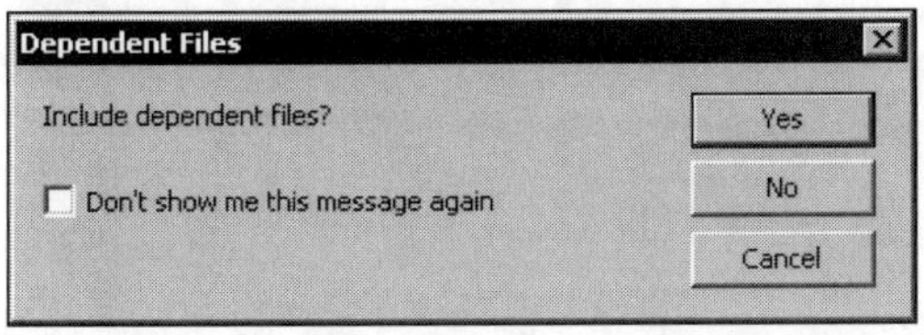

Dreamweaver displays a lock in the Local Files pane next to each file you check in, and clears the check mark that was displayed when you checked out the file.

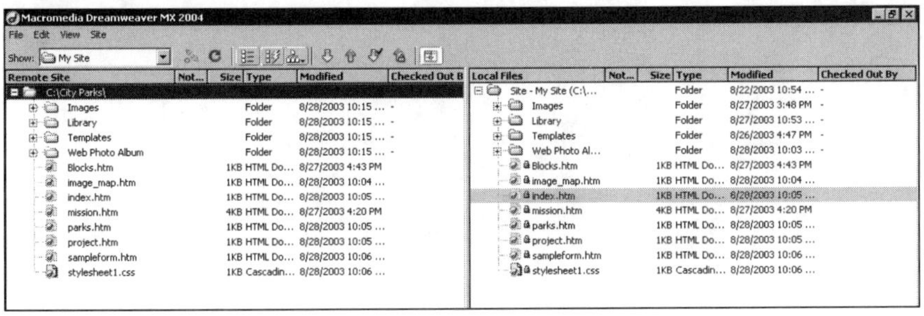

You can open any locked file in the Local Files pane to view it or print it. The lock reminds you that you cannot edit the file and save it, however, unless you first check it out.

5. Click the **Expand/Collapse** button to collapse the Files panel.

Unit 8: Redesigning a Client Web Site

Activity Guides

Activity 8.1: Defining Client Redesign Needs

Technical Features and Their Design Solutions

How to Make Web Sites Accessible

Activity 8.2: Writing a Design Document

Sample Design Document

Activity 8.4: Building Components of a Redesigned Client Site

CSS Styles Panel

How to Create Cascading Style Sheets

How to Create a Calendar

How to Create Forms

How to Create Image Maps

How to Create Rollover Images

How to Import Spreadsheet Tables

How to Create Pop-up Menus

How to Prepare Photographs

How to Create Animated Images

Technical Features and Their Design Solutions

Technical Feature	Design Solution
Pop-up menu	■ Display multiple links in a small amount of space ■ Provide navigation flexibility without long download times
Rollover image	■ Add highlighting or design effects with an image swap to draw user attention *Example:* Buttons that change appearance when the pointer rolls over them
Image map	■ Help set up navigation on a Web site *Example:* Geographic map with hotspots that link to sites about each country
Photo presentation	■ Add design elements to pictures to enhance the overall design of the site ■ Make changes to photograph presentation elements such as tone, color, and blending
Spreadsheet table	■ Quickly set up layout table of information such as a directory, large catalog, or schedule
Calendar	■ Quickly create an editable calendar *Examples:* Company calendars, list of community events.
Form	■ Interact and gather information from site visitors *Examples:* Feedback form, guest book, survey, or product order form
Cascading Style Sheets	■ Create a consistent design for all pages that easily updates multiple pages on a site ■ Use with templates for managing large sites
Animated image	■ Draw user attention to an area of the page ■ Add to overall message of the site *Examples:* Banner ads and cartoons

How to Make Web Sites Accessible

Alternate Text (Alt tags)

Alternate text for images is critical for many devices that assist disabled people to access the Web. The Property inspector in Dreamweaver has a field for entering alternative text (Alt tag) for an image, link, or button. The text can be descriptive and as long as necessary, but it should be as succinct as possible.

Cascading Style Sheet (CSS)

Developers use a CSS to separate content from presentation of their Web sites, which allow assisting devices easier access to the information provided in the content. Developers also use a CSS to create a consistent structure for text content, which aids interpretive devices (such as text-to-speech browsers).

Image Maps

Provide alternate text for hot spots in images to make them readable by interpretive devices.

Tables

Provide alternate text descriptions for tables, such as identifiers of row and column headings for data tables or longer descriptions for tables with textural information.

Templates and Library Objects

Designers can create a single, accessible template or a small set of templates as the basis of the entire site. Templates limit mistakes when multiple designers are working on a site. In addition, templates foster a consistent, easy-to-use site that keeps users oriented and has consistent common elements such as navigation bars.

Frames

Add descriptions of frames on the Property inspector. This alternate text provides additional information to Web browsers and readers when users are navigating each frame.

Device Independence

Use the Behaviors panel in Dreamweaver to create rollovers and other scripts that are triggered by logical events, such as onFocus and onBlur. Create scripts that combine mouse events with logical events to support a variety of users.

Sample Design Document

Coast Middle School Web Site

Project Overview

Site Challenges:

Navigation: The page is too long, so it requires users to scroll. There is too much information contained under too few topics. For example, the About Us section could be broken into Athletics, Activities, and Volunteer Opportunities.

Page Layout: Uses tables and anchor links that could be separated into multiple pages for people to get to all the information.

Colors: The colors do not work well together and the images do not draw the interest of the audience.

Accessibility: The main image does not have an Alt tag so a screen reader would not detect the image.

Possible Solutions:

Navigation: Split the page into multiple pages organized by topics, with a navigation structure on the home page.

Page Layout: Create a new logo to replace the small picture of a schoolhouse that repeats the name of the site.

Colors: Choose two or three unifying colors to create a consistent site.

Use technology structures such as templates and cascading style sheets that will make the pages consistent and easy to update.

Goals, Objectives, and Messages

The Coast Middle School needs a redesign of its Web site to make it easier for users to navigate and find information. The present site gives information about the school location, a map, a list of teachers, and a short description of the school and its activities. The school uses the site to inform parents and community members about the school. The school's mission is to build parental and community involvement with the school by informing them about volunteer activities and happenings around the school.

Audience

The intended audience of the site is parents, community members, school administrators, teachers, and students. They will go to the site for information about the school, its faculty, and its events, as well as to find more ways to be involved with the school.

Goals for Redesign

The redesign should include the following:

- Make the site easy to update so as to provide information about new school activities as well as changes in the faculty and staff.
- Incorporate the new logo.
- Give more detailed information about activities, athletics, organizations, and departments because these groups will be creating their own Web sites.
- Use a calendar to inform the community about events at the school.
- Give easy access to categories of information.
- Attract the audience to increase community and parental participation with the school.

Technical Specifications (Delivery Requirements)

Audience members will typically access this site, probably through a dial-up modem at 56K bps or a cable modem. They might use Netscape Navigator, Internet Explorer, or America Online. The site should optimize all images to load quickly while still being appealing.

Site Content

Home page:

- Logo for the Coast Middle School
- Title for the Coast Middle School
- Links to the following areas:
    - Academics: departments, schedules, class pages, library
    - Student Activities: athletics, clubs, organizations
    - School Information: news, calendar, handbook, volunteering
    - Faculty and Staff: teachers, administrators, staff
    - About Us: mission, directory, civics, contact info, maps, links

Sample content page:

- Text navigation bar
- Universal navigation to each of the following:
    - Academics
    - Student Activities
    - About Us
    - School Information
    - Faculty and Staff
- New Coast Middle School logo

Site Structure

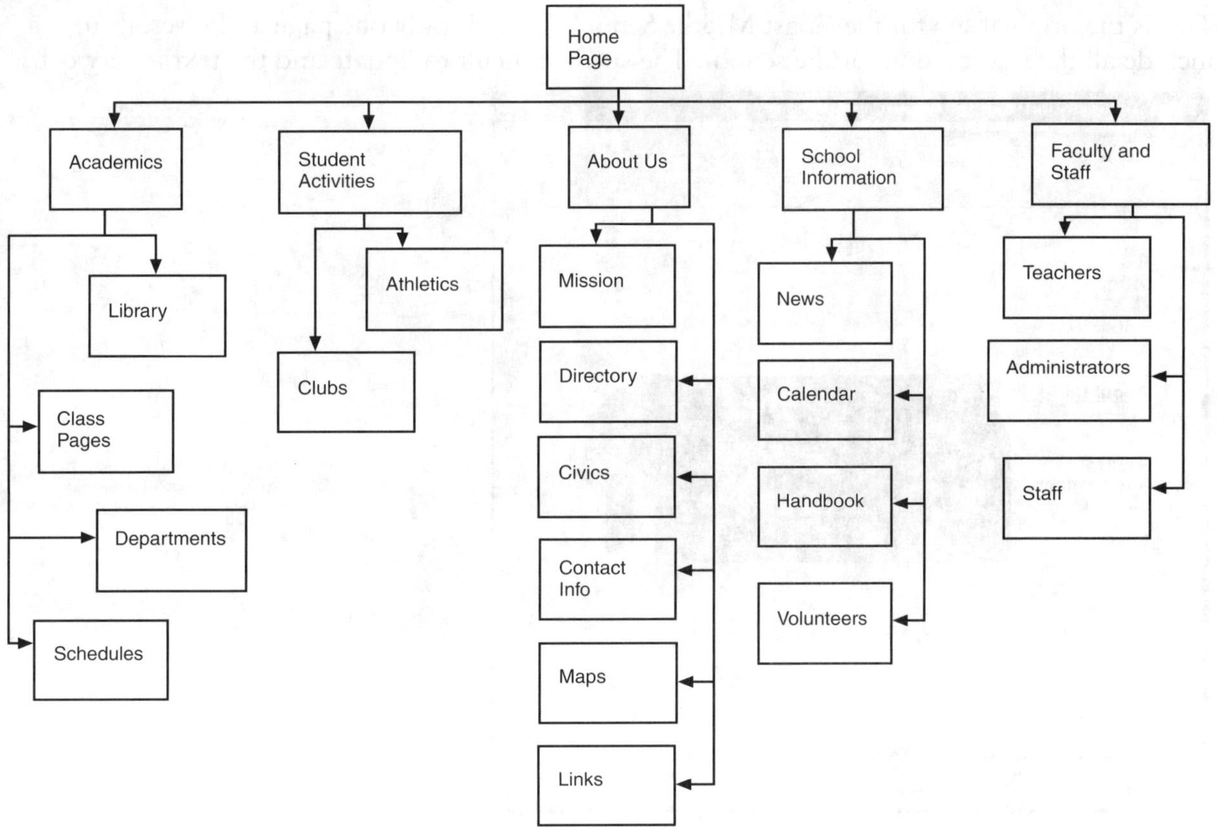

Visual Design

This is the original site for the Coast Middle School. There is only one page and it scrolls to include all the information for the school. The site is difficult to update and the text is very dense.

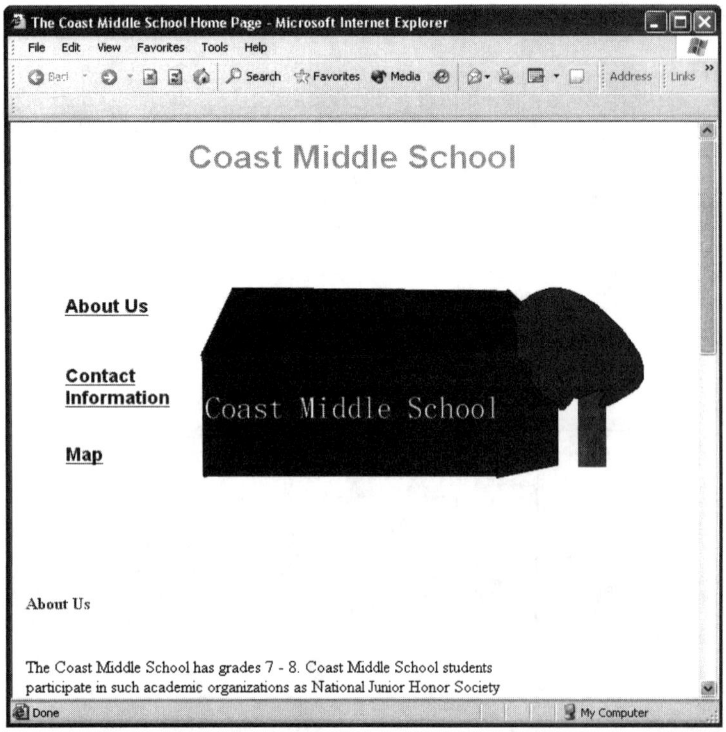

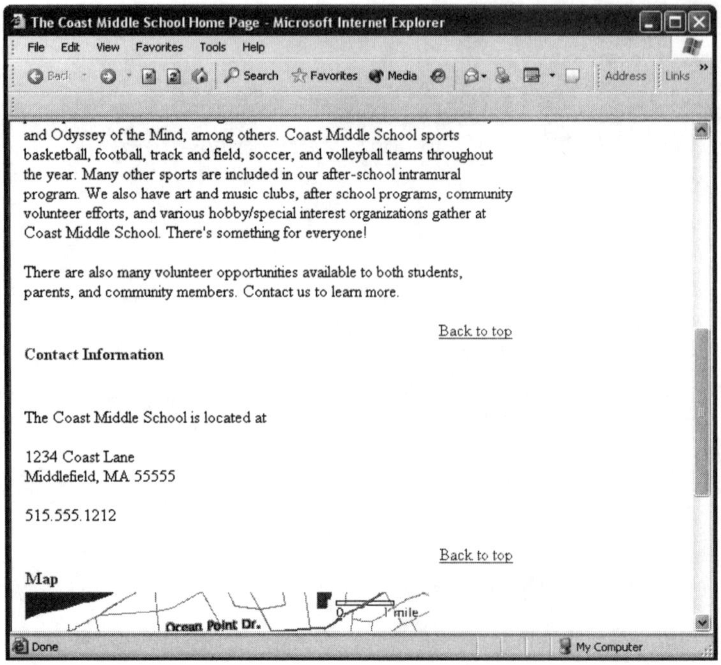

Color and Font Samples

Design A:

- The main blue color will be used for the navigation structure and as part of the logo.
- The pink color will be used for regular text on the page.
- The black and white colors will be used in the logo.

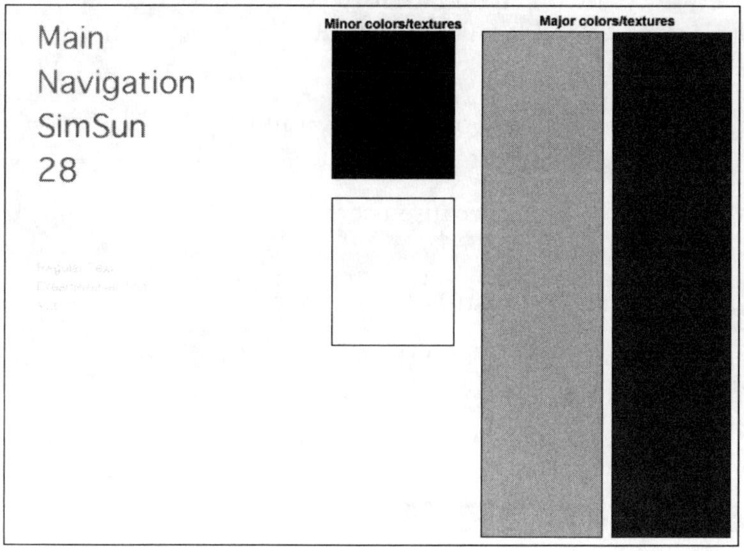

Design B:

- The main orange color will be used for the logo and to highlight any text.
- The gradient blue-black color will be used as a background for the navigation structure on all pages.
- The black and white colors will be any text on the page: white text on the blue-black background and black text on the white background.

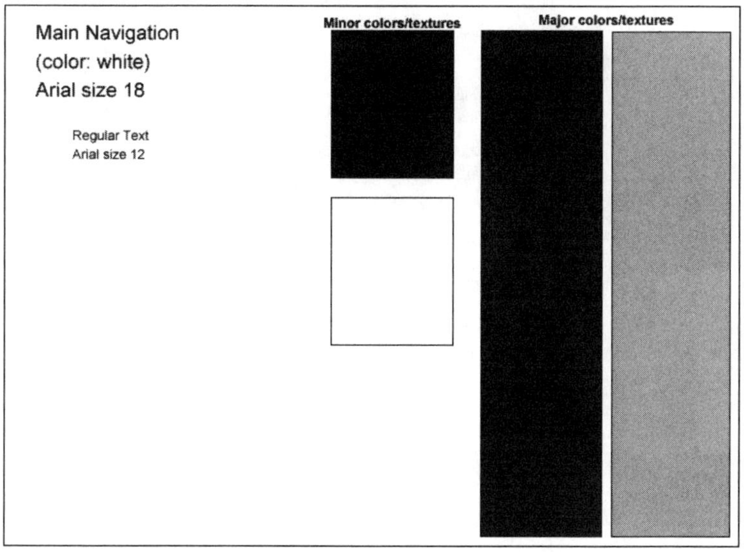

Sample Design Comps

Design A

This home page design uses pop-up menus to manage all the content and links for the main navigation. It uses the blue color for the navigation and a mix of blue and pink for the logo. The main text on the page is similar to the pink in the logo to draw the attention of the user. A content page would look exactly like the home page, with the same navigation bar across the top. For this design, the team would need to create one template for use throughout the site. This design unifies the site; however, it does make it difficult for users to know when they are on the home page versus a content page.

- *Consistency:* The site is consistent because it uses only three colors and uses the logo and footer on every page.
- *Ease of use:* Pop-up menus make the site easy to use because users can easily jump to specific information quickly.
- *Universal navigation:* A universal navigation is repeated on every page.
- *Layout:* The layout uses white space between the logo and the footer to focus user attention on the content in the middle of the page.

This design uses the logo and color choice to create a simple site that might appeal to multiple audiences.

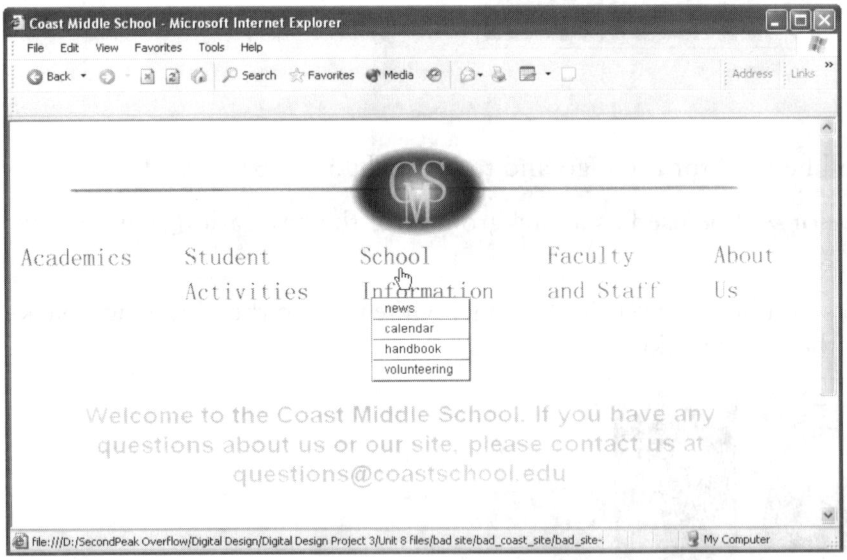

Design B

This design uses a large navigation menu for the home page instead of pop-up menus. Also, a school quiz is included to entice users to learn about the Coast Middle School. The main colors and logo are used as directed.

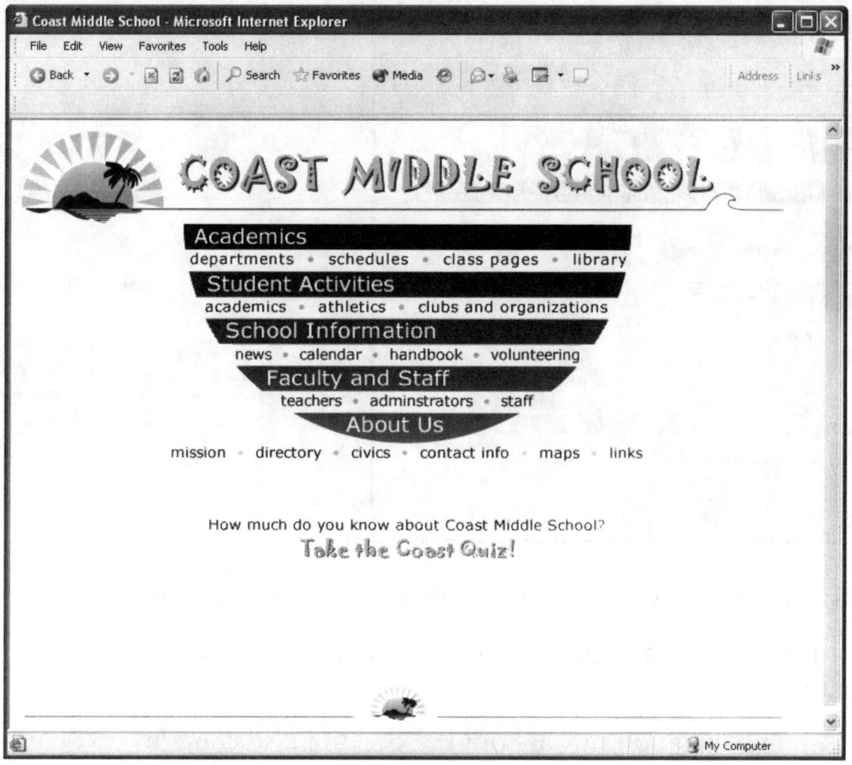

This sample content page is similar to the home page with the logo, but it contains a collapsed main navigation bar. Also, text links at the bottom of the page make the page more accessible. The site is unified by the logo and footer logo.

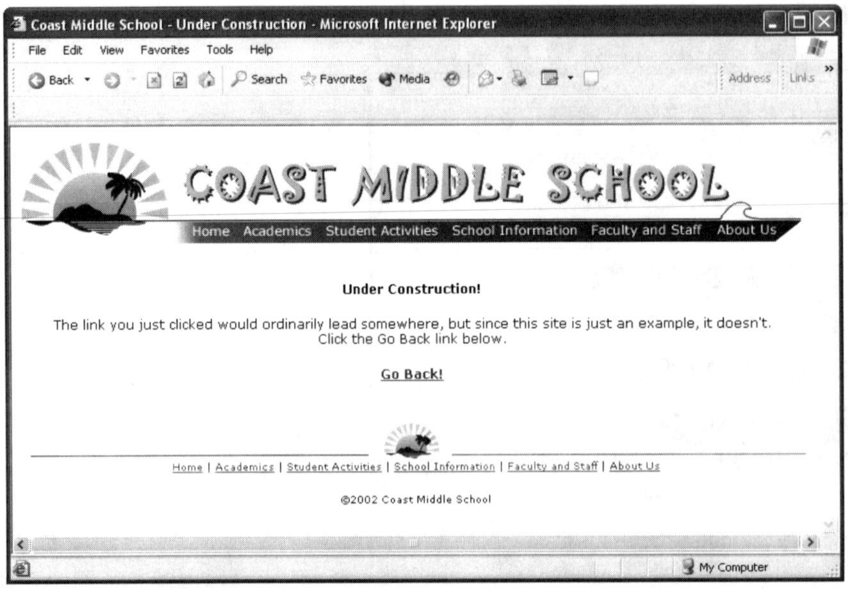

- *Consistency:* This site uses color consistently, and the logo appears on every page.
- *Universal navigation:* The navigation is a large menu on the home page and repeats in a simpler form on all content pages.
- *Ease of use:* The site has a main navigation throughout the site and also contains text navigation at the bottom for users who have turned off viewing of graphics.
- *Layout:* Layout focuses users on the white space between logo and footer.

This design uses fonts and color to make the site more fun and more representative of students in a middle school.

CSS Styles Panel

Use the CSS Styles panel to create, view, apply, or edit CSS styles for elements in a document.

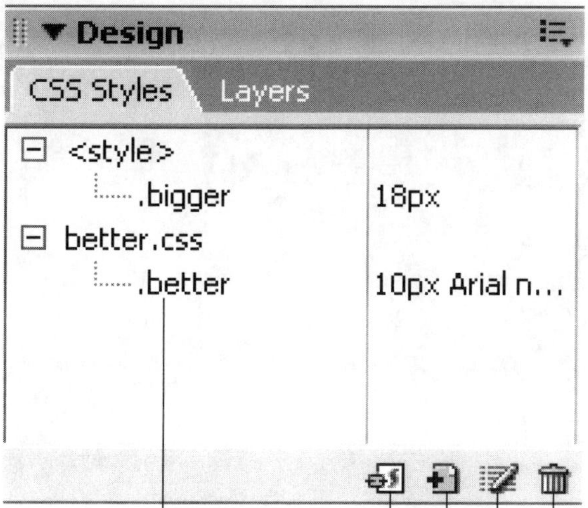

Select a style to apply it to selected text in your document. Select No CSS Style to remove a previously applied style.

Delete CSS Style: Delete the selected style, and remove the formatting from any element to which it was applied.

Edit Style Sheet: Make changes to styles in the current document or in an external style sheet.

New CSS Style: Create a new style.

Attach Style Sheet: Attach an external style sheet to your current document.

HOW TO CREATE CASCADING STYLE SHEETS

Cascading Style Sheets (CSS) are a collection of formatting rules which control the appearance of content on a Web page. With CSS styles you have flexibility and control of the exact page appearance, from precise positioning of layout to specific fonts and styles. CSS styles enable you to control many properties that cannot be controlled using HTML alone.

With CSS styles you can create consistent text design elements and easily update multiple pages on a site. You can use CSS styles in conjunction with Dreamweaver templates for managing large sites. *Internal style sheets* put all style information in the HEAD tag of a Dreamweaver document and the styles only apply to that page. *External style sheets* hold style information in a separate document that can be applied to multiple pages.

Create Internal Style Sheets

1. Open Dreamweaver.
2. Save and name the Dreamweaver document.
3. Choose **Window > CSS Styles**.

   The CSS Styles panel opens.

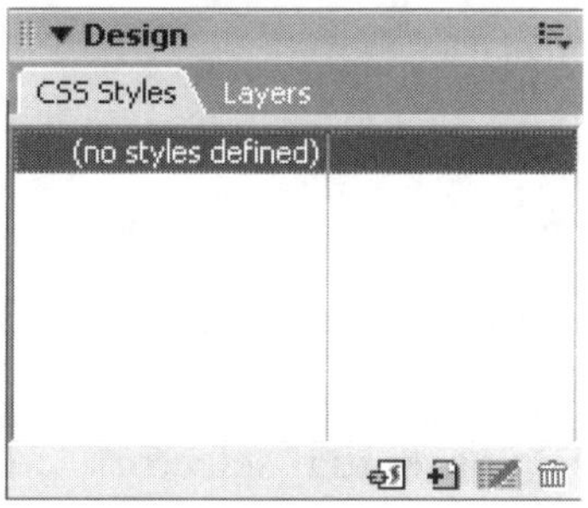

4. Click the **New CSS Style** button (+) at the bottom of the panel to create a new style.

   The New CSS Style dialog box opens.

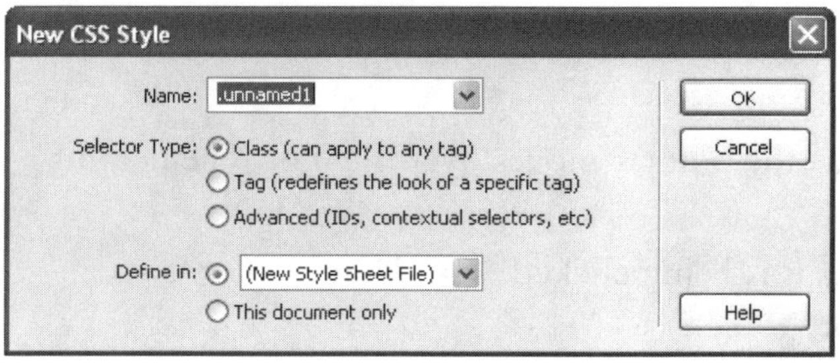

5. Choose the type of style you will create:
   - *Class.* Make your own HTML tag by naming a new style and defining its formatting.
     - In the New CSS Style dialog box, select **Class (can apply to any tag)** for Type.
     - For Name, type the name of your style.

Note: Names typically begin with a period and do not have spaces or special characters. Example: .boldredtext

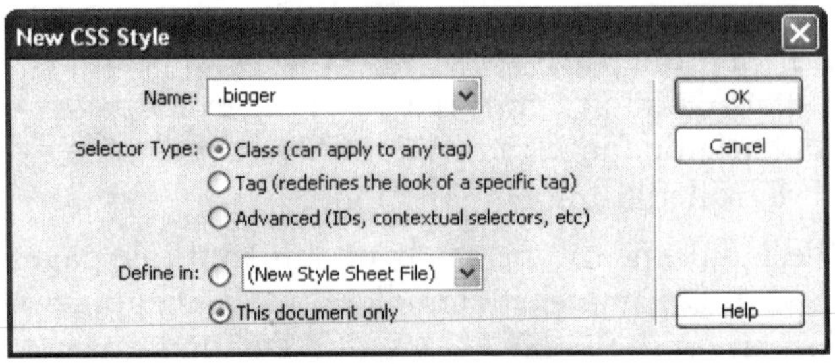

- *Tag.* Change the default format of any tag in a document.
  - In the New CSS Style dialog box, select **Tag (redefines the look of a specific tag)** for Type.
  - From the Tag pop-up menu, choose the type of tag to redefine (for example, h1 tag, body, or table).

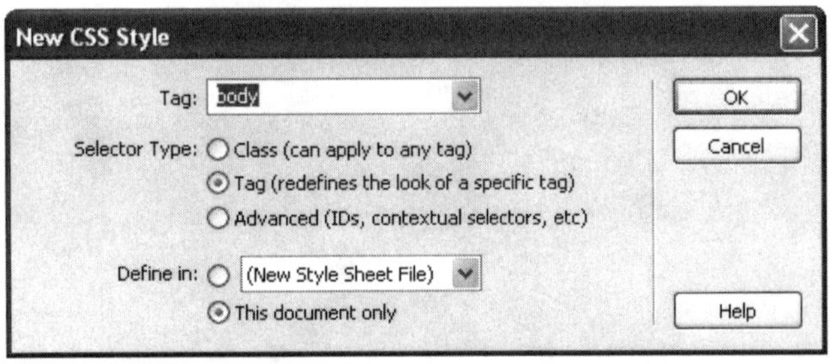

- *Advanced.* You can create styles for links that are active, visited, or covered by the pointer.
  - In the New CSS Style dialog box, select **Advanced (IDs, contextual selectors, etc.)** for Type.
  - From the Selector pop-up menu, choose the type of link you want to change.
    - *Link* controls the normal state of the link. The default color is blue.
    - *Visited* controls the link format after a user has clicked it. The default color is purple.
    - *Hover* controls the link format as the pointer moves over the link. The default color is red.
    - *Active* controls the link format as it is being clicked. The default color is red.

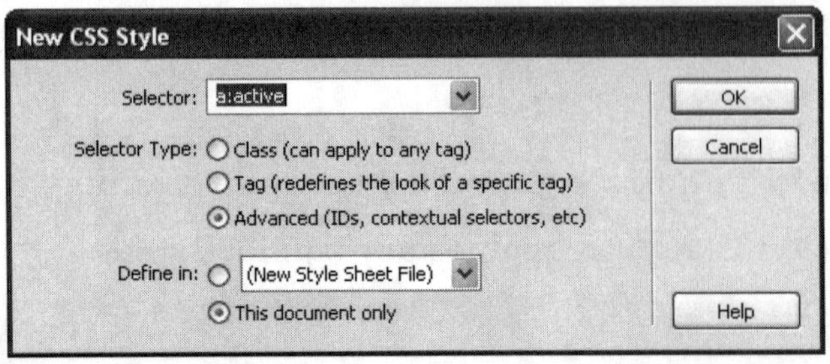

6. For Define in, select **This document Only**.
7. Click **OK**.

Format Styles

Whatever style type you choose, once you click OK, the CSS Style definition dialog box opens.

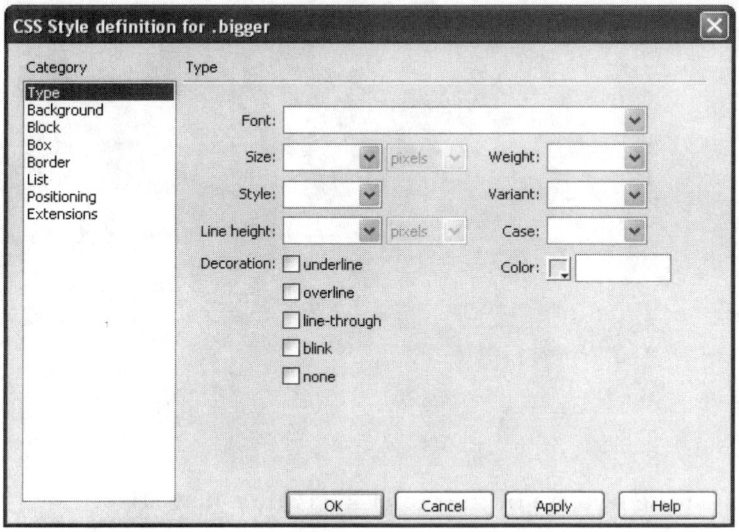

8. In the CSS Style definition dialog box, set any of the following formatting options. (For more details, choose **Help > Using Dreamweaver**.)
   - *Type* changes text properties such as font, size, and color.
   - *Background* controls background properties. For example, using color background or an image, or creating a fixed or scrolling background.
   - *Block* controls spacing and alignment of text and lines on the document.
   - *Box* changes the box that surrounds a block element. It affects properties such as height, width, padding, and margins.
   - *Border* changes the border properties around text such as thickness and color.
   - *List* controls list properties such as text type and bullet appearance.
   - *Positioning* defines text position on the screen.
   - *Extensions* controls page breaks and cursor visual appearance.
9. Click **OK** in the CSS Style definition dialog box.

Apply Styles

10. Once formatting is complete you will apply it differently, depending on the type of style you have defined (Class, Tag, or Advanced):
   - *Class.* Once completed, the new style appears in the CSS Styles panel. Apply the style by highlighting text you want to format and clicking the style name in the panel.
   - *Tag.* Since the tag has been redefined, you can apply the tag as you normally would from the Property inspector.

- *Advanced*. Since this style redefines links, there is no need to apply the style; it will be applied every time you create a link.

Create External Style Sheets

1. Open Dreamweaver.
2. Save and name the Dreamweaver document.
3. Choose **Window > CSS Styles**.

   The CSS Styles panel opens.

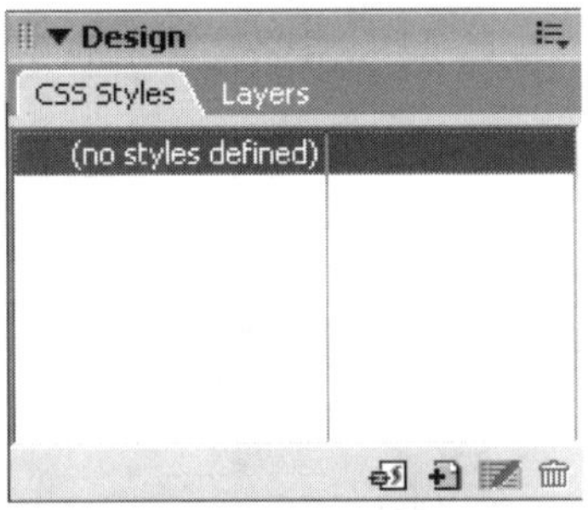

4. Click the **New CSS Style** button (+) at the bottom of the panel to create a new style.

   The New CSS Style dialog box opens.

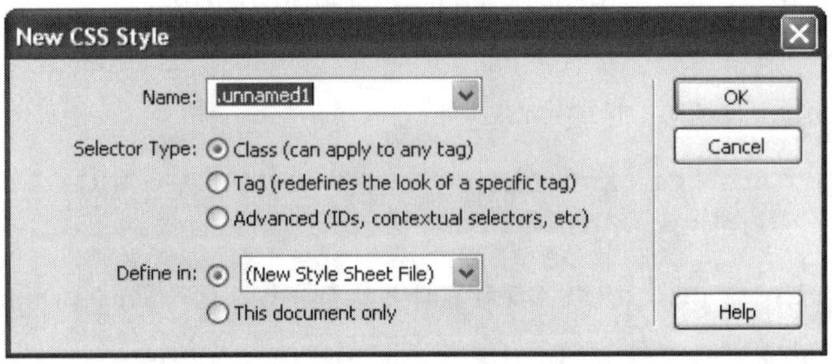

5. Choose the type of style you will create:
   - *Class*. Make your own HTML tag by naming a new style and defining its formatting.
     - In the New CSS Style dialog box, select **Class (can apply to any tag)** for Type.
     - For Name, type the name of your style.
6. In the New CSS Style dialog box, enter a name for the style sheet.

   Note: Names typically begin with a period and do not have spaces or special characters. Example: .boldredtext

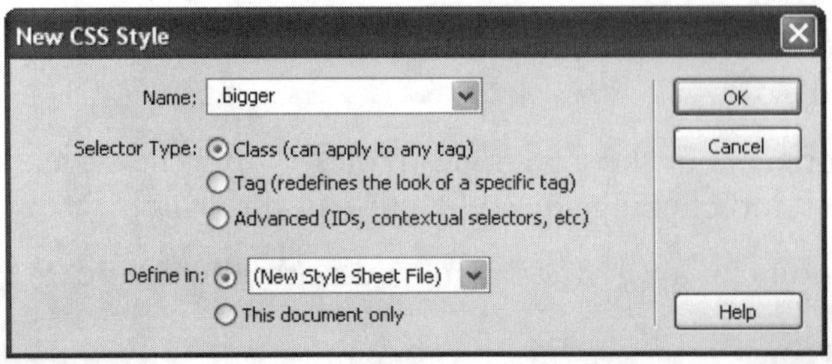

- *Tag.* Change the default format of any tag in a document.
  - In the New CSS Style dialog box, select **Tag (redefines the look of a specific tag)** for Type.
  - From the Tag pop-up menu, choose the type of tag to redefine (for example, H1 tag, body, or table).

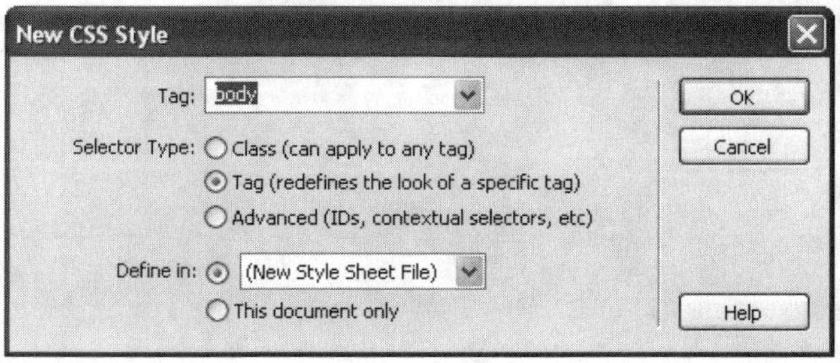

- *Advanced.* You can create styles for links that are active, visited, or covered by the pointer (hover).
  - In the New CSS Style dialog box, select **Advanced (IDs, contextual selectors, etc.)** for Type.
  - From the Selector pop-up menu, choose the type of link you want to change.
    - *Link* controls the normal state of the link. The default color is blue.
    - *Visited* controls the link format after a user has clicked it. The default color is purple.
    - *Hover* controls the link format as the pointer moves over the link. The default color is red.
    - *Active* controls the link format as it is being clicked. The default color is red.

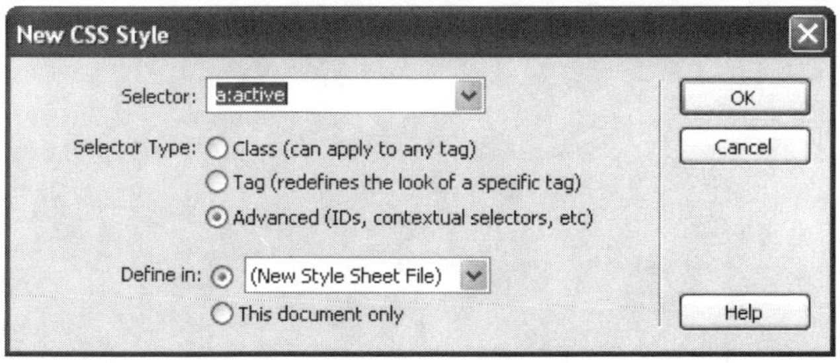

7. For Define In, select (**New Style Sheet File**).
8. Click **OK**.

The Save Style Sheet File As dialog box opens.

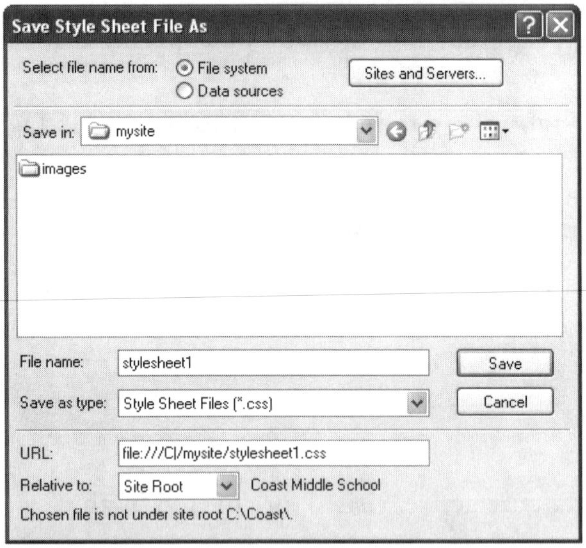

9. Name and save the style sheet in your local root folder.
10. Make sure **Site Root** (Windows) or **Site** (Macintosh) is selected in the Relative To box.
11. Click **Save.**
12. Use the CCS Style Definition dialog box to set the formats for the new style.

Attach External Style Sheets

1. Open a document.
2. Open the CSS Styles panel. (Choose **Window > CSS Styles**.)
3. Click the **Attach Style Sheet** button.

The Attach External Style Sheet dialog box opens.

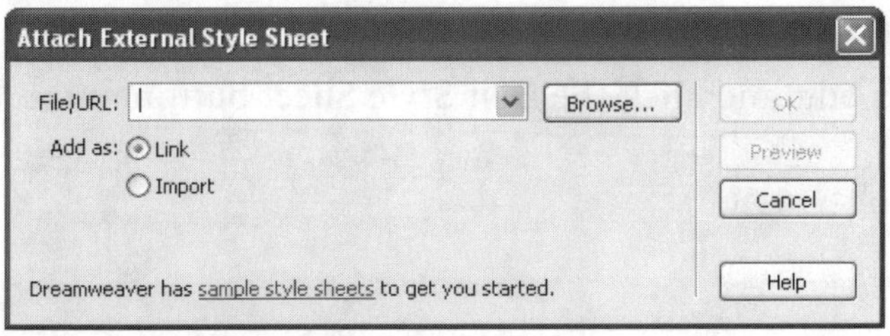

4. Click **Browse**, navigate to your saved style sheet, select it, and click **OK** (Windows) or **Choose** (Macintosh).

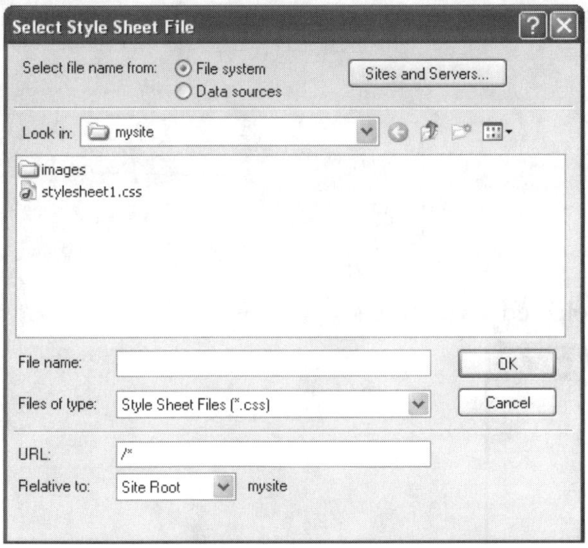

5. Click **OK** in the Attach External Style Sheet dialog box.

6. Dreamweaver attaches the style sheet to your document. On the Design panel, click the plus sign (Windows) or the right-pointing triangle (Macintosh) beside the style sheet to view the styles it contains.

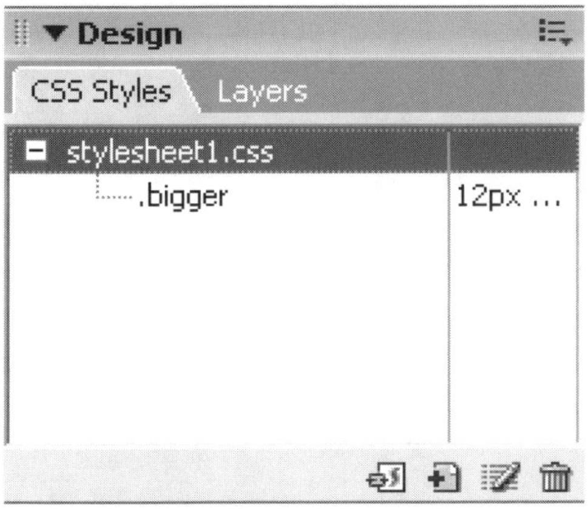

Edit Styles

1. To edit a style, select the style you want to edit and click the **Edit Style Sheet** button at the bottom of the panel.

The CSS Style Definition dialog box for the selected style opens.

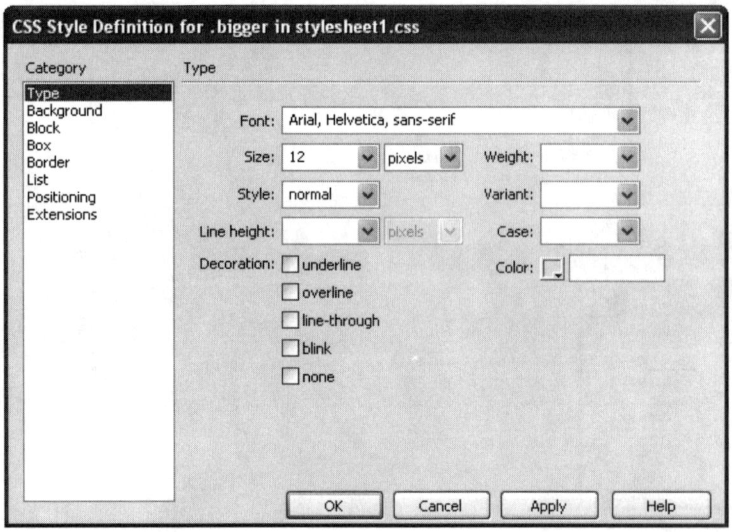

2. Make formatting changes in the CSS Style Definition dialog box. Then click **OK**. The changes will take effect immediately.

How to Create a Calendar

The Calendar extension for Dreamweaver is a quick way to create an editable calendar. Uses include company calendars and community event listings that can be updated and changed easily.

Create a Calendar

1. Download and install the Calendar extension from the Macromedia site: *www.macromedia.com/exchange/dreamweaver/*.

   Note: To download free extensions, you need to be a Macromedia member. Membership is free. You may need to click the Search Exchanges button and enter "Calendar" as the keyword for your search. Event Calendar 204 can be downloaded for free.

2. Open Dreamweaver.
3. Choose **Insert > Calendar**.

   The Insert Calendar dialog box opens.

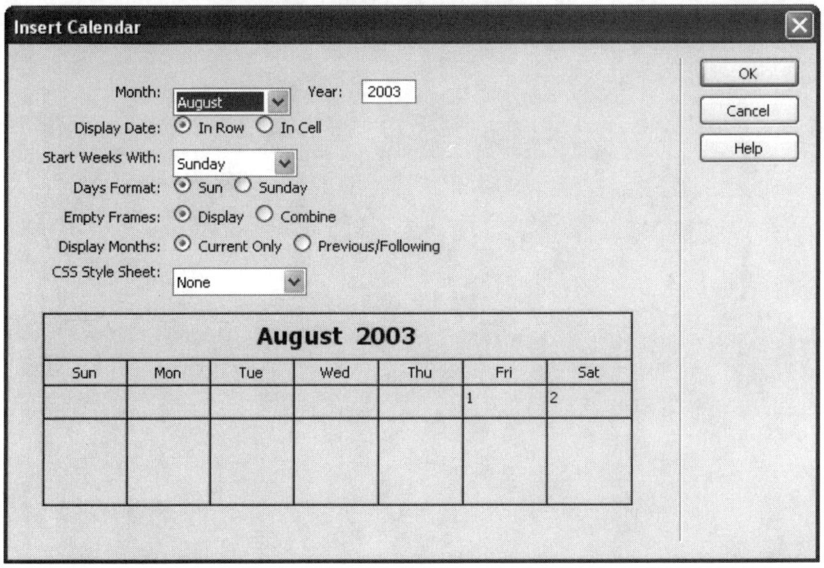

4. Set preferences as you choose in the Insert Calendar dialog box and click **OK**.

   The calendar month appears in the document.

5. To add information to a day, click in its cell and type.

How to Create Forms

Forms are used to interact with or gather information from site visitors. Forms can be used for site visitors to provide feedback, sign a guest book, take a survey, or place an order for merchandise. Dreamweaver lets you create a variety of form elements, such as text fields, password fields, radio buttons, check boxes, pop-up menus, and clickable images (such as a Submit button).

The Forms view on the Insert bar contains buttons for creating forms and inserting form elements.

Set Up the Form

The data gathered in forms is usually sent to a database on a server or through e-mail. To set up the form processing, contact your Web administrator. This guide will help you make the user interface of a form.

1. Open and save a page in Dreamweaver.
2. Change to the Forms view on the Insert bar.

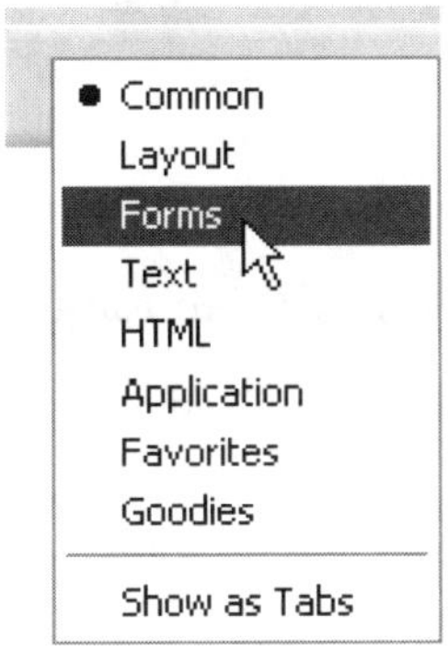

3. Place the insertion point on the page where you want to insert a form and click the **Form** button.

A blank form appears, with a red dotted outline. You place all form elements inside this outline.

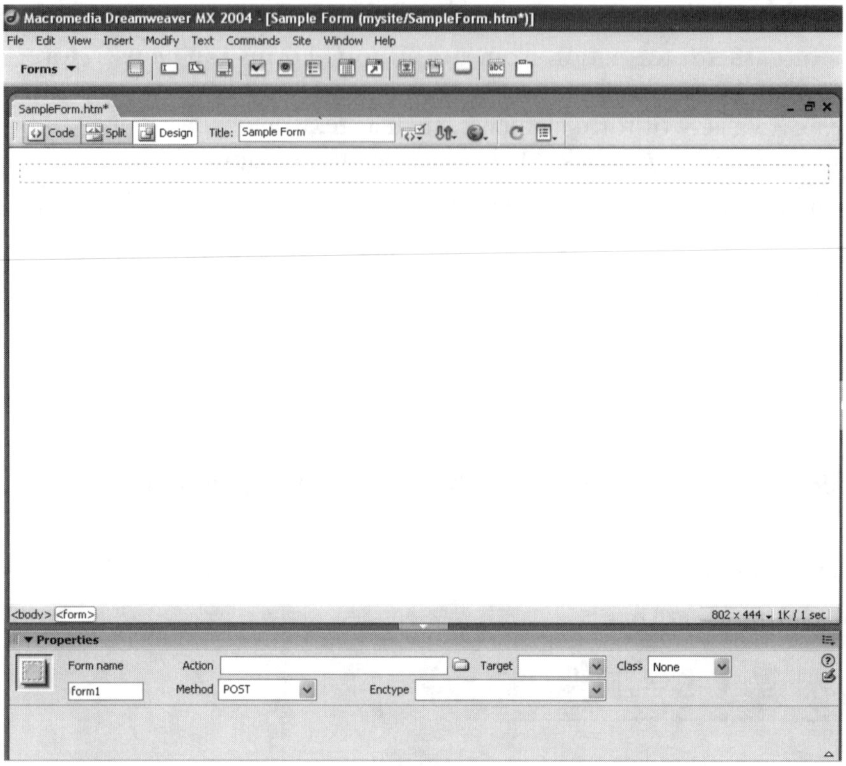

Form options appear on the Property inspector.

4. From the Method pop-up menu on the Property inspector, choose either **GET** or **POST**.
   - GET will append the form contents to the URL specified in the Action text box.
   - POST will send the form contents in the body of a message such as an e-mail.
5. In the Action text box, enter the URL or CGI script that will process the form. (Get this information from your Web administrator.)

Add Form Elements

Using the Forms view on the Insert bar, you can insert any combination of form elements within the red outline of the form. You can use tables to lay out these elements if you choose.

Using Form Fields

Form fields let users enter text into a form. There are three types of form fields:

- Text fields, in which a user enters a response
- File fields, in which a user enters the path of a file to upload to your server
- Hidden fields, which store information a user entered in another field

Text Fields

Text fields provide a space in which users can enter text.

1. Click the **Text Field** button on the Insert bar.

2. Enter a unique name for the text field in the Property inspector's TextField field. You may use any combination of letters, numbers, and an underscore (_).

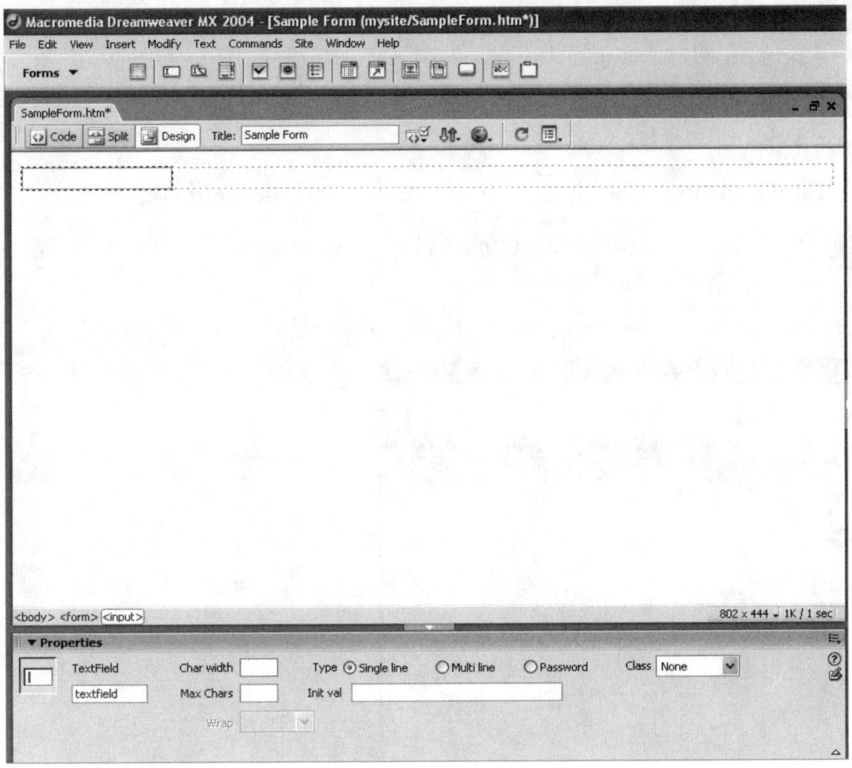

3. On the Property inspector, select one of the three types of text field:

- *Single line* text for short answers
- *Multi line* text for long answers such as the user's description of a problem with a purchased item
- *Password* text for passwords (in which asterisks appear in place of typed characters)

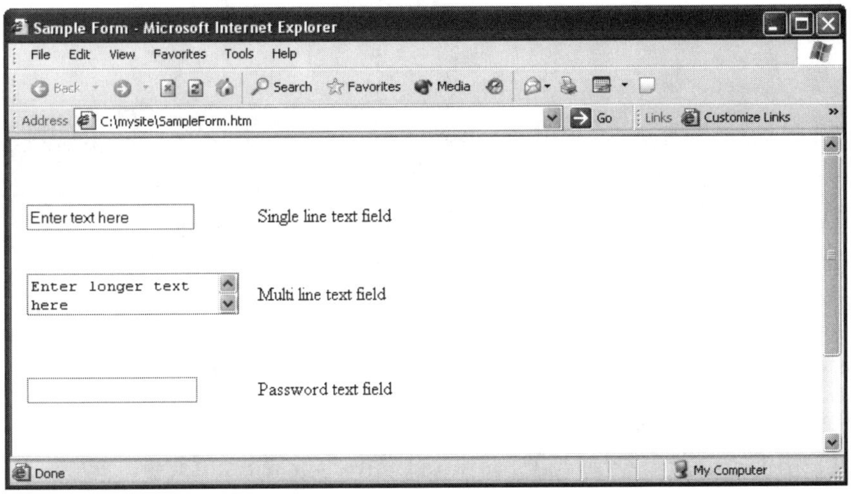

Note: You can also create a multiple-line text field by clicking the TextArea button on the Forms tab of the Insert bar. You can also use the Class menu on the Property inspector to apply CSS options.

File Fields

A file upload field lets users select a file on their computer (such as a word-processing document or graphics file) and upload it to your server. A file field looks like other text fields, except it also contains a Browse button. The user either types the path to the file they want to upload or uses the Browse button to locate and select the file.

1. Click the **File Field** button on the Insert bar.
2. In the Property inspector's FileField name field, enter a name for the file field object.
3. In the Char width field, specify the maximum number of characters users will see in the field.
4. In the Max chars field, specify the maximum number of characters the field will hold.

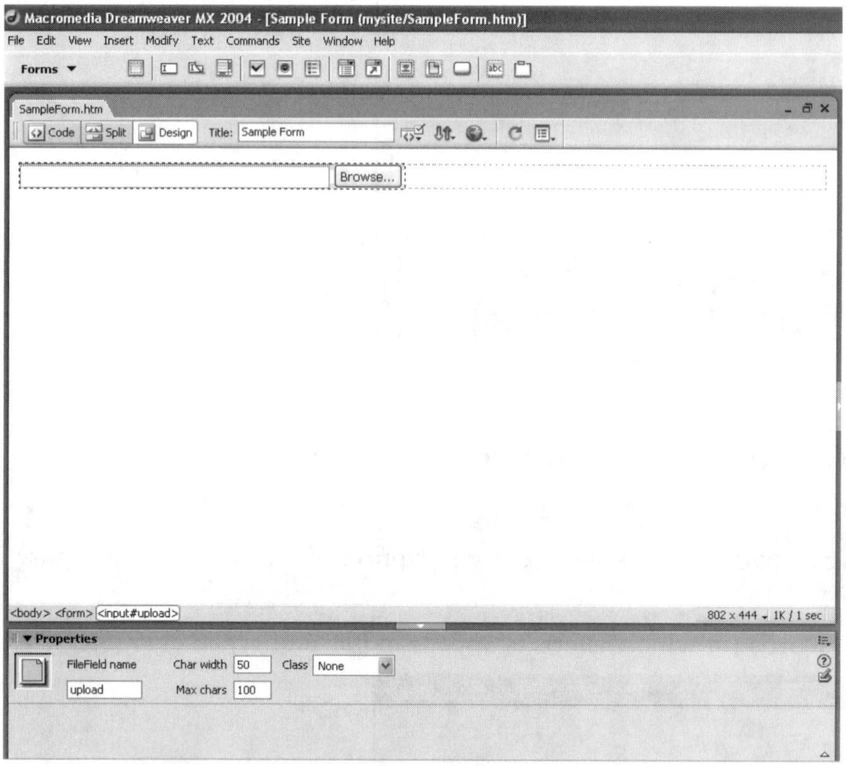

Note: Contact your Web administrator to confirm that anonymous file uploads are allowed before using the file field.

Note: You can also use the Class menu on the Property inspector to apply CSS options.

Hidden Fields

Hidden fields are text fields that you use to collect information about users (information a user entered in another field). The information is sent back to your server when the form is submitted.

1. Click the **Hidden Field** button on the Insert bar.
2. In the Property inspector's HiddenField field, type a unique name for the field.
3. In the Value field, type the value you want to assign the field.

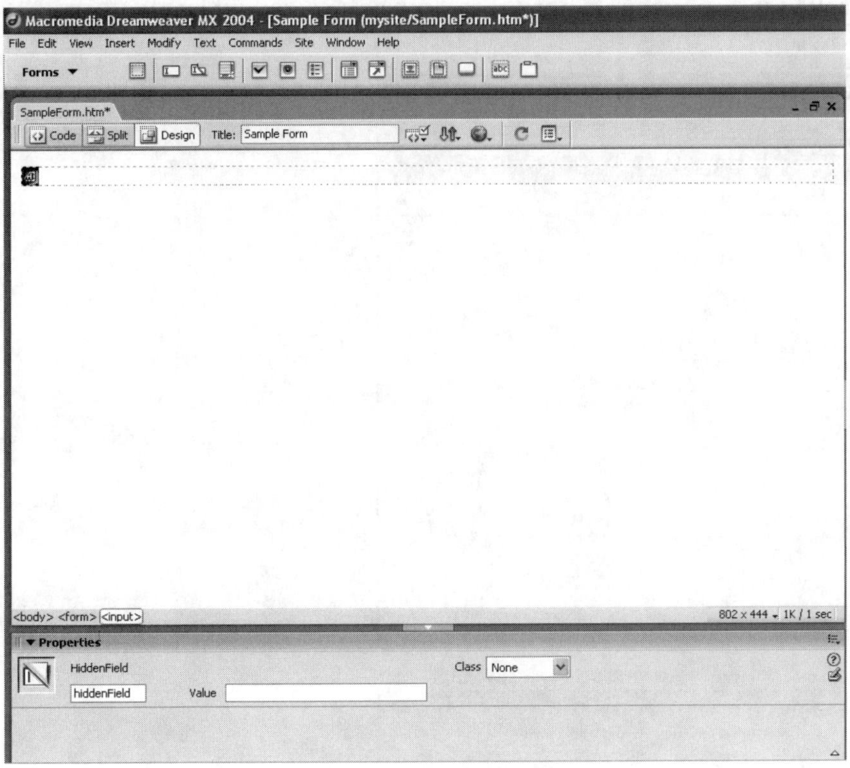

Note: You can also use the Class menu on the Property inspector to apply CSS options.

Using Check Boxes and Radio Buttons

Users click a check box or radio button to make a choice. With check boxes, users can select one or more options from a group of options. With radio buttons, users can select only one option from a group of options.

Check Boxes

1. Click the **Checkbox** button on the Insert bar.
2. In the Property inspector's CheckBox name field, enter a unique, descriptive name for the check box.
3. In the Checked value field, type a value for the check box. (For example, in a survey you might set a value of 4 for strongly agree and a value of 1 for strongly disagree.)

4. For Initial state, click **Checked** if you want an option to appear selected when the form first loads in the user's browser.

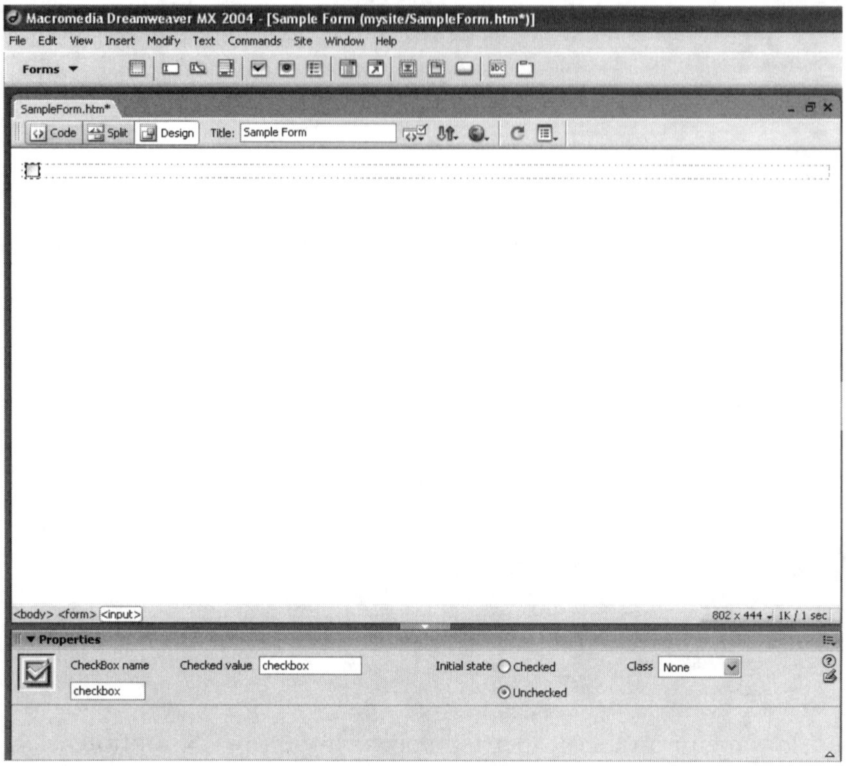

Note: You can also use the Class menu on the Property inspector to apply CSS options.

Radio Buttons and Radio Groups

Radio buttons are typically used in groups.

1. Click the **Radio Group** button on the Insert bar to insert a group.

   The Radio Group dialog box opens.

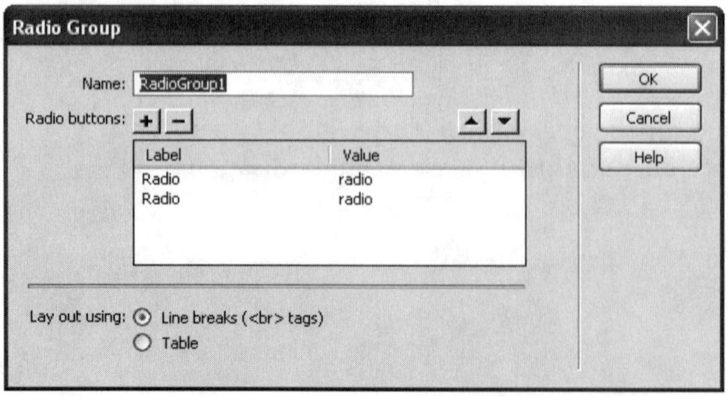

2. Enter a name in the Name text box.
3. Click the plus (+) button to add a radio button to the group.
4. Enter a label and (if you want) a checked value for each button.

5. Click the up or down arrows to reorder the buttons.
6. Click OK.

   When you insert a single radio button, you can use the Property inspector to enter a checked value, but you must create a separate label. If you insert a group of radio buttons individually, you must give each one the same name to create a group.

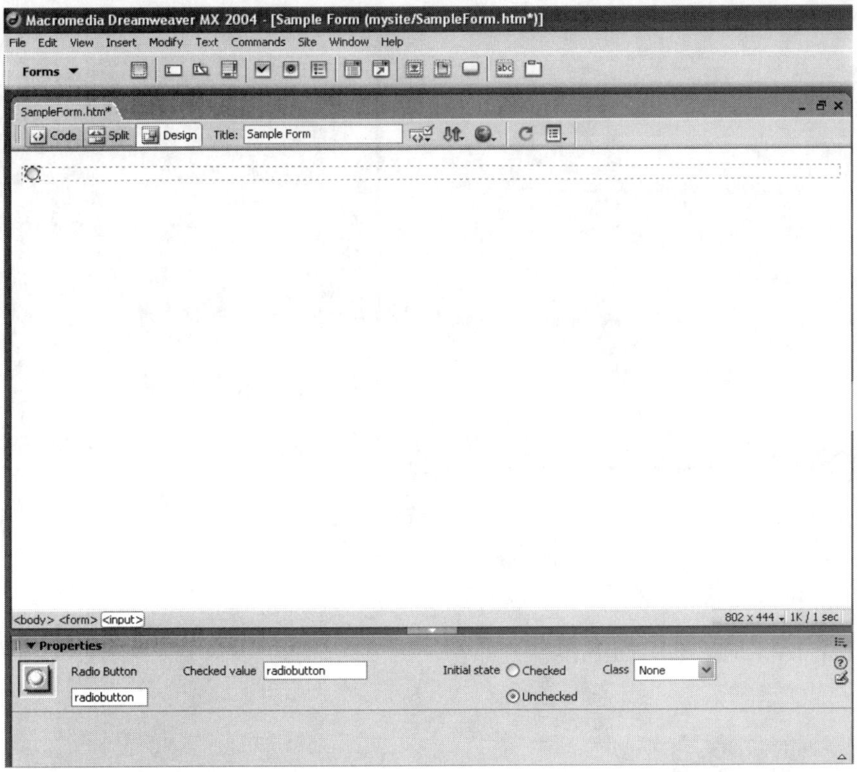

Note: You can also use the Class menu on the Property inspector to apply CSS options.

Using Lists and Menus (List/Menu)

Lists and menus allow users to select options from a list or pop-up menu. Scrolling lists enable you to display multiple options in a confined space. You can allow the user to select multiple items. Users can select only one item from a pop-up menu.

Scrolling Lists

1. Click the **List/Menu** button on the Insert bar.
2. On the Property inspector, enter a unique name for the list in the List/Menu field.
3. For Type, select **List**.
4. In the Height field, enter the number of items the list will display.

   If this number is less than the total number of items in the list, a scroll bar will be displayed.

5. If you want to allow the user to select more than one item in the list, select **Allow multiple** for Selections.

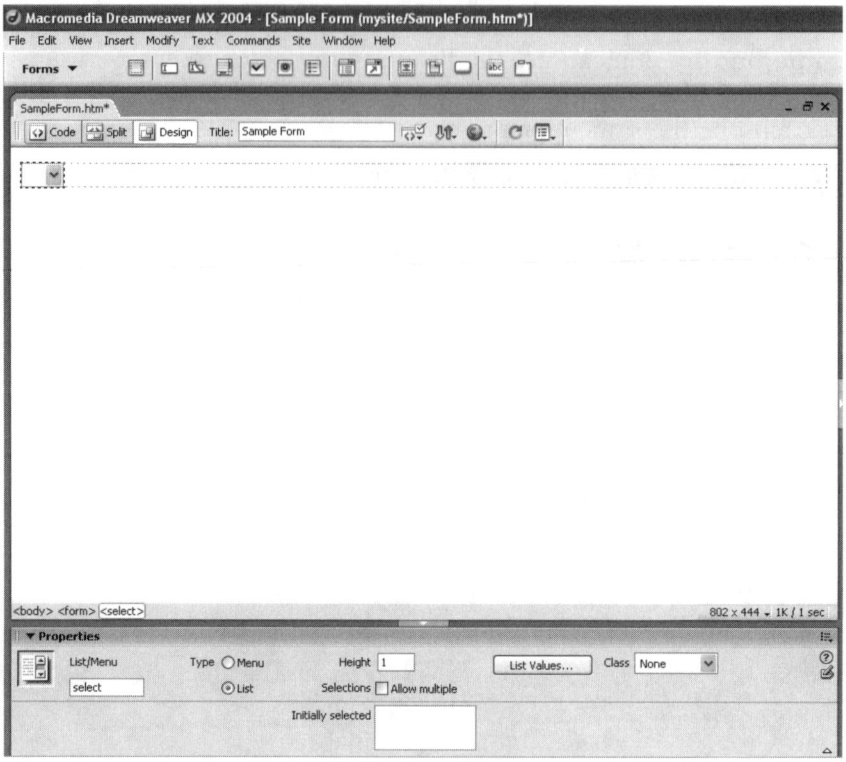

6. Click the **List Values** button to add the list items.

   The List Values dialog box opens.

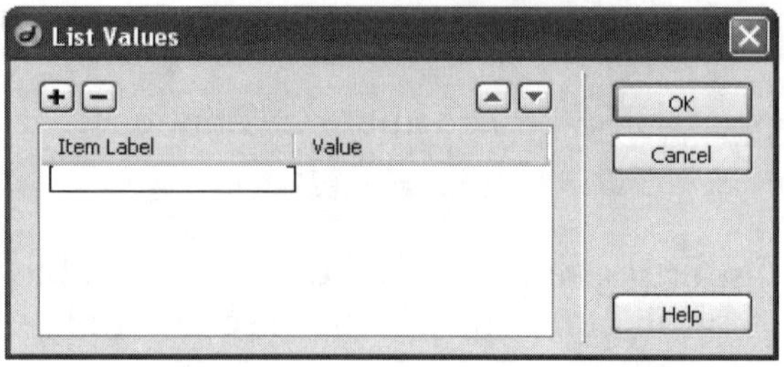

7. With the insertion point in the Item Label field, enter the text you want to appear in the list.
8. In the Value field, enter data you want sent to the server when a user selects the item.
9. To add another item to the list, click the plus (+) button.
10. When you finish, click **OK** to close the List Values dialog box.
11. To have one of the items in the list be selected by default, select that item in the Initially selected field on the Property inspector.

    Note: You can also use the Class menu on the Property inspector to apply CSS options.

Pop-up Menus

1. Click the **List/Menu** button on the Insert bar.
2. On the Property inspector, enter a unique name for the list in the List/Menu field.

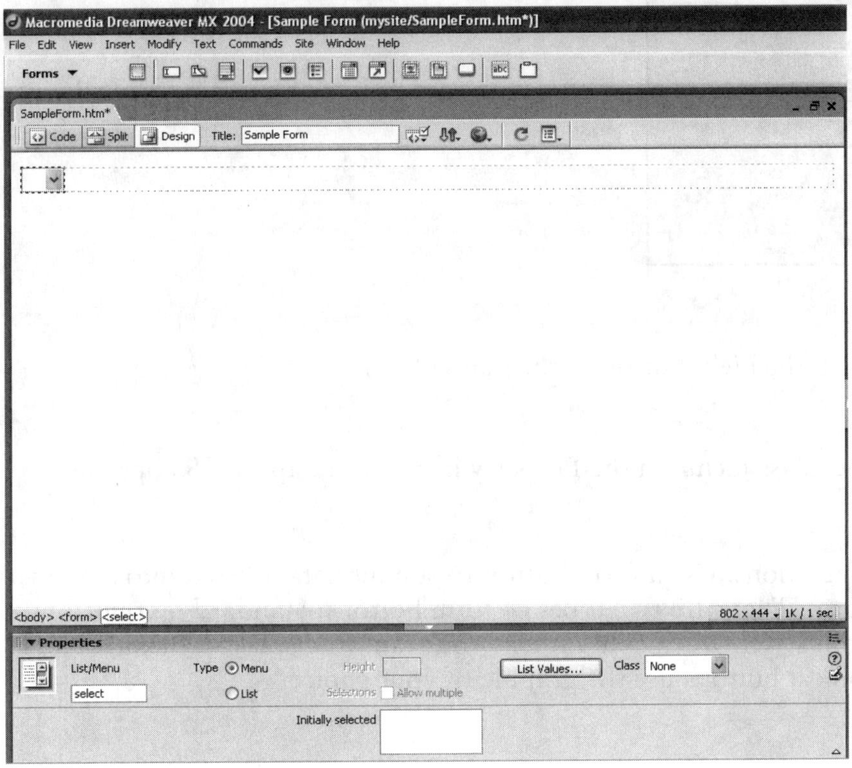

3. For Type, select **Menu**.
4. Click the **List Values** button to add the menu items.

   The List Values dialog box opens.
5. With the insertion point in the Item Label field, enter the text you want to appear in the menu.
6. In the Value field, enter data you want sent to the server when a user selects the item.
7. To add another item to the menu, click the plus (+) button.
8. When you finish, click **OK** to close the List Values dialog box.
9. To have one of the items in the menu be selected by default, select that item in the Initially selected field on the Property inspector.

   Note: You can also use the Class menu on the Property inspector to apply CSS options.

Jump Menus

A jump menu is a pop-up menu with options that link to documents or files. You can create links to documents in your Web site or other Web sites, e-mail links, links to graphics, or links to any file type that can be opened in a browser.

1. Click the **Jump Menu** button on the Insert bar.

The Insert Jump Menu dialog box opens.

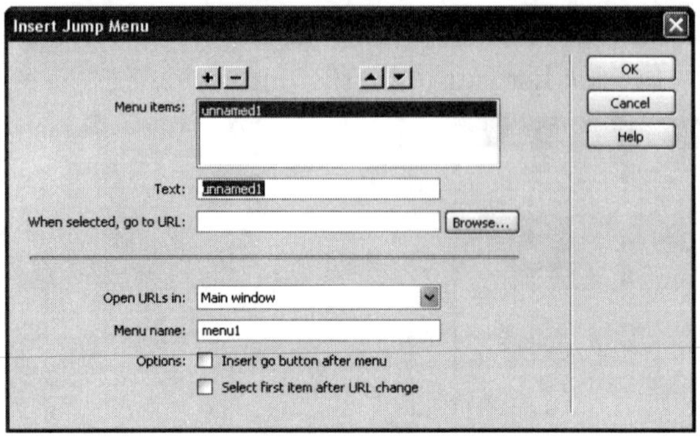

2. Complete the dialog box.

   For more information, click the **Help** button in the dialog box.

3. Click **OK**.

   Note: You can also use the Class menu on the Property inspector to apply CSS options.

Using Form Buttons

Form buttons control form operations. Use a form button to submit data entered into a form to the server or to reset the form. There are two types of form buttons: Standard text buttons are the browser's default button style, which contain text you want to display (typically Submit, Send, or Reset); graphical buttons use the graphic of your choice.

Standard Text Buttons

1. Click the **Button** button on the Insert bar.

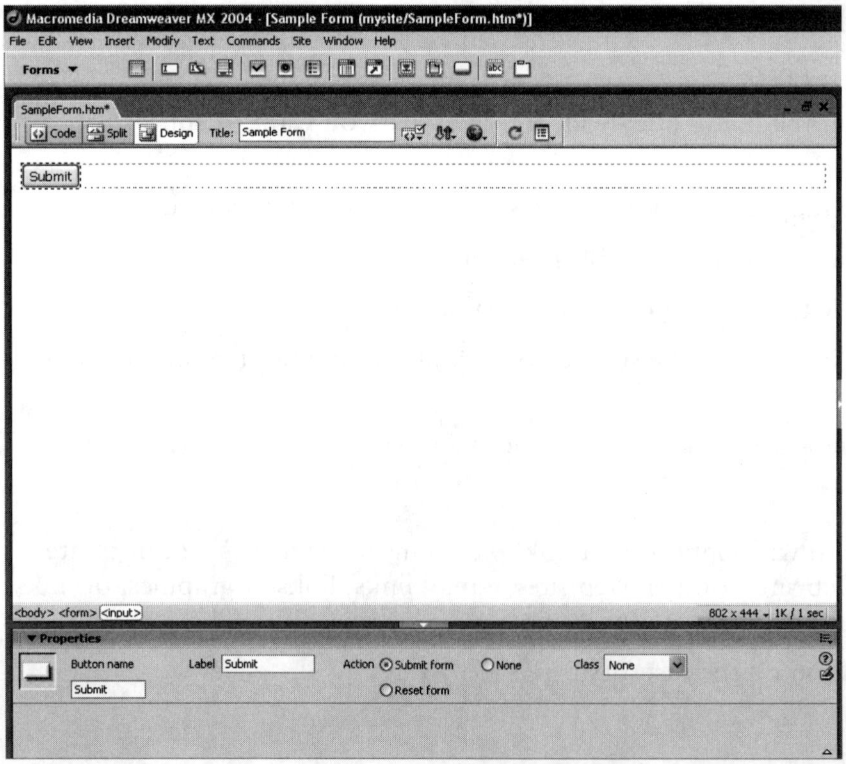

2. Enter a name for the button in the Property inspector's Button name field

   Note: There are two reserved names: "Submit," which submits the form data for processing, and "Reset," which resets all the form fields to their original values.

3. In the Property inspector's Label field, enter the text you want to appear on the button.

4. Select the type of Action.

   Note: You can also use the Class menu to apply CSS options to the button.

Graphical Submit Buttons

You can use images as submit button icons. Using an image to perform tasks other than submitting data requires attaching a behavior to the form object using the Behaviors panel.

1. Click the **Image Field** button on the Insert bar.
   The Select Image Source dialog box appears.

2. Locate and select the image to use as the submit button icon, and then click **OK** (Windows or **Choose** (Macintosh).

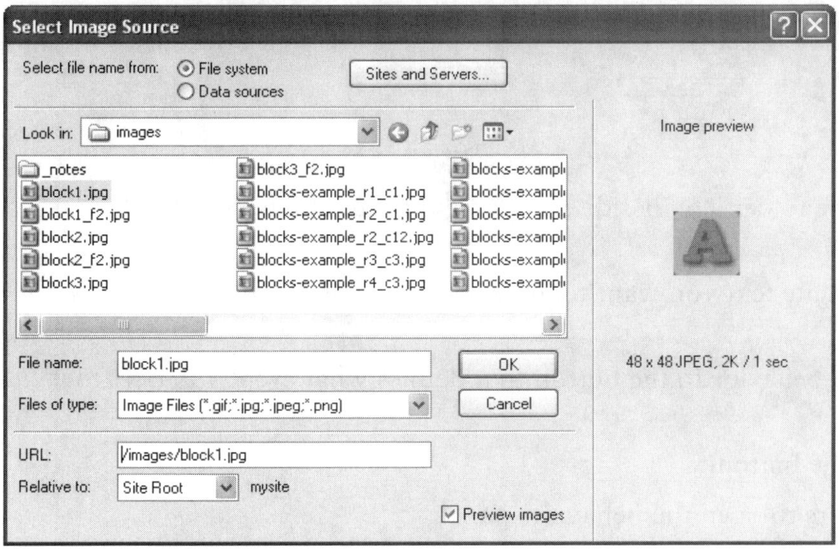

3. On the Property inspector, enter a unique name for the image in the ImageField field.

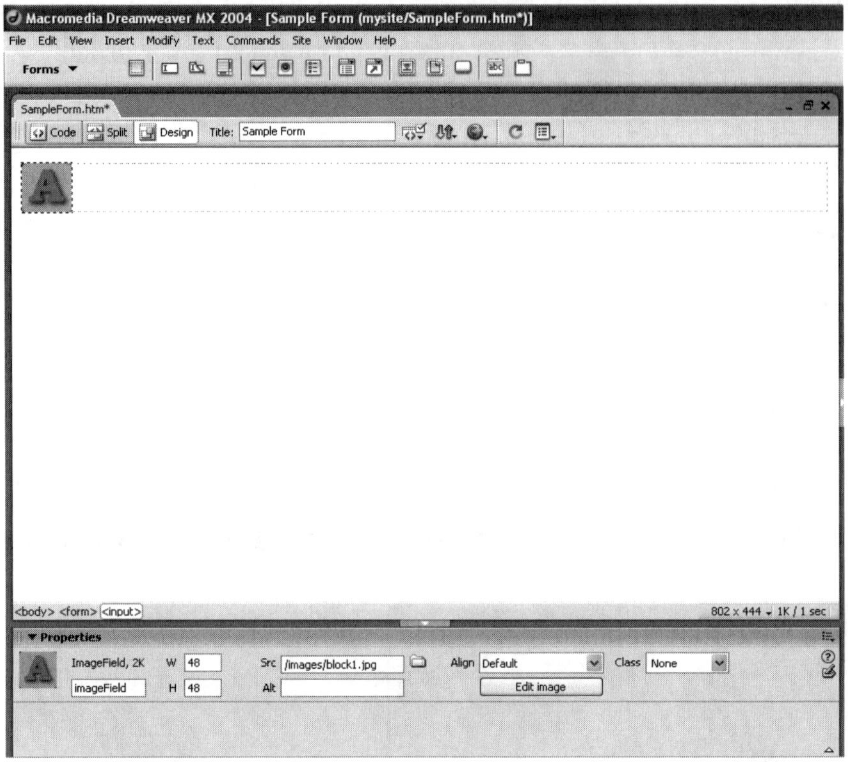

Note: You can also click the folder icon beside the Src field to select a new image for the button.

4. In the Alt field, enter alternate text you want to appear in place of the image for text-only browsers.

   The next step is to apply a behavior to the button that defines what event will occur when the button is clicked.

5. Click the image to select the button.
6. Choose Window >Behaviors to open the Behaviors panel.
7. Click the Add behavior button (the plus sign) on the Behaviors panel, and select a behavior button.

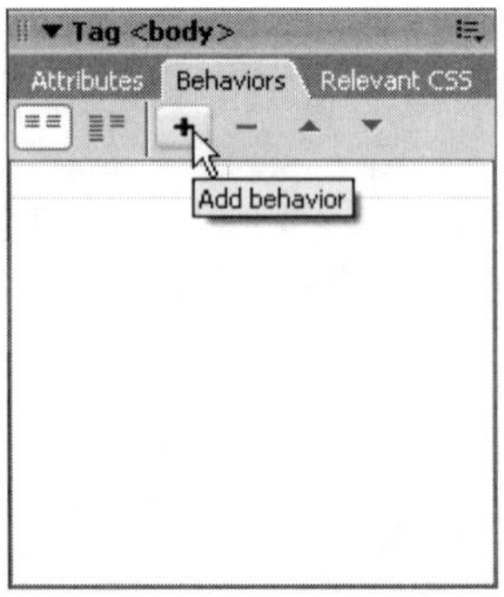

Note: If the behavior you want to apply is not available, click the Add behavior button, choose Show Events For, and select a later browser.

How to Create Image Maps

An *image map* is an image that has been divided into regions, or hotspots. When a hotspot on your site page is clicked by a viewer, an action occurs, such as opening another Web page. You can use an image map to create a graphic navigation element on a Web site. An example is a geographic map that links each country on the map to another page in your site or an external Web site containing information about that country.

Create an Image Map

1. Open Dreamweaver and open the document in which you want to create an image map.
2. Make sure the **Common view** is selected on the Insert bar.

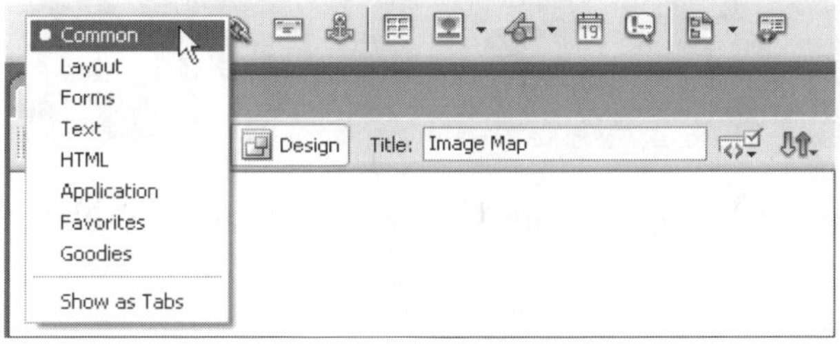

3. Click the small arrow on the **Images** button and click **Image**.

   The Select Image Source dialog box opens.

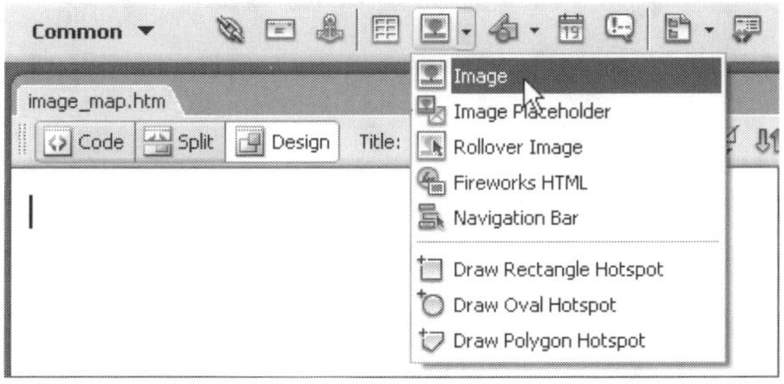

4. Locate an image for the image map, select it, and click **OK** (Windows) or **Choose** (Macintosh).
5. Select the image, if necessary. On the Property inspector, enter a name for the map in the Map text box. (See figure on the next page.)

   Note: Naming conventions for image maps follow the same rules as filenames: no spaces or special characters.

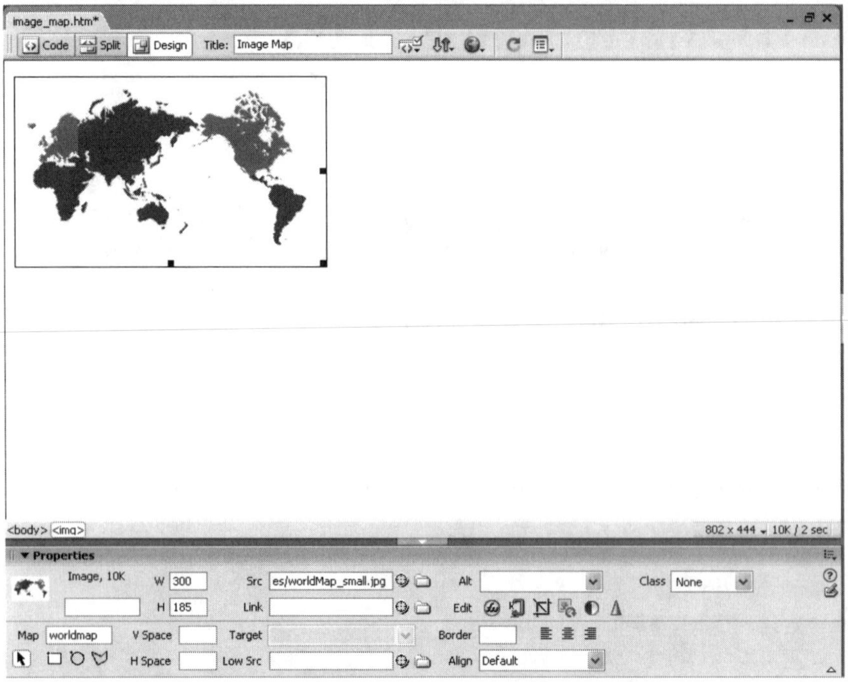

6. Select one of the hotspot tools located below the Map name and draw a rectangle, circle, or polygon around a part of the image.

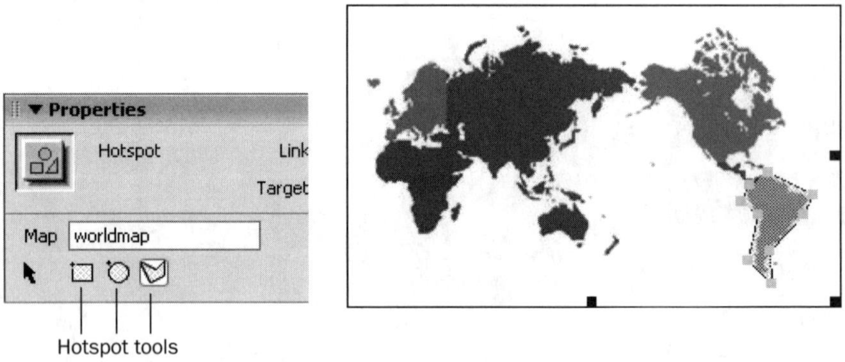

7. On the Property inspector, do the following:
   - Add a link to a page in your site or to an external URL.
   - Type a descriptive phrase for the link destination in the Alt text box.

8. Repeat steps 6 and 7 to add other hotspots on the image map.
9. Save the page.
10. Choose **File > Preview in Browser** and choose a browser from the submenu to preview the page and test the link.

How to Create Rollover Images

A *rollover* is an image that changes when the pointer moves across it. A rollover actually consists of two images: the primary image (the image displayed when the page first loads) and the rollover image (the image that appears when the pointer moves over the primary image).

Rollover images add highlighting or design effects by drawing user attention when the images are swapped. For example, buttons that highlight or change color when the pointer passes over them are rollover images.

Create a Rollover Image

1. Open Dreamweaver and open the document in which you want to create an image rollover.
2. Make sure the **Common** view is selected on the Insert bar. Click the small arrow on the **Images** button and click **Rollover Image**.

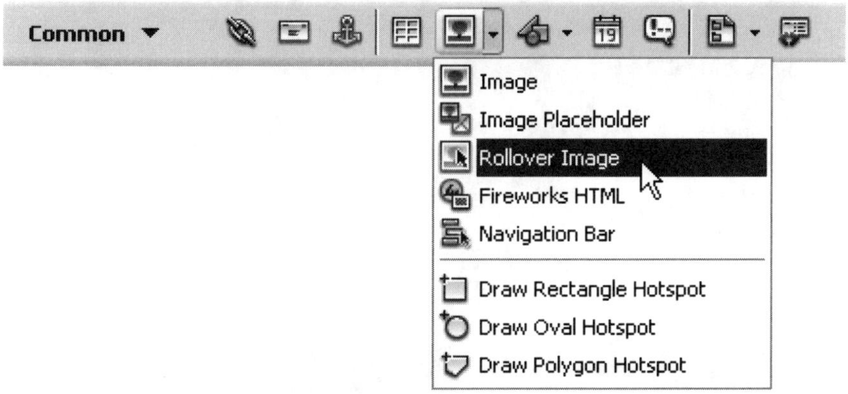

3. The Insert Rollover Image dialog box opens.

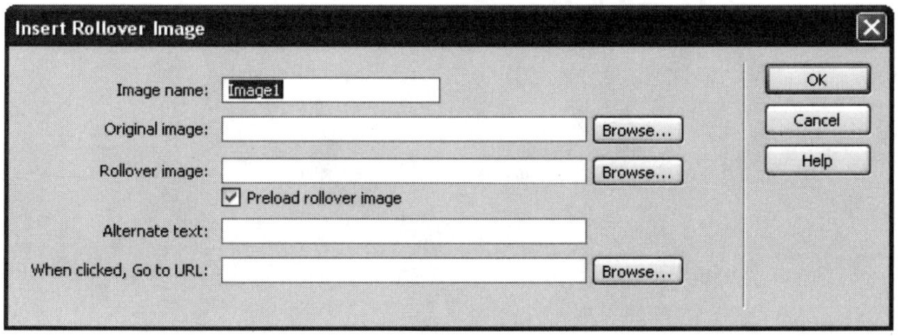

4. Use the Insert Rollover Image dialog box to set up your rollover.
   - *Image Name*: Type a name for the rollover image.
   - *Original image*: Click **Browse** and select the image that will be displayed when the page loads. Click OK (Windows) or Choose (Macintosh).

- *Rollover image*: Click **Browse** and select the image that will display when the pointer rolls over the original image.
- *Alternate text*: Type the text you want to appear as the alternate text for the image.
- *When clicked, Go to URL*: Click **Browse** and select the file (or enter the path to the file) that will open when the image is clicked. Click **OK** (Windows) or **Choose** (Macintosh).

5. Click **OK** to close the dialog box.
6. Save the page.
7. Choose **File > Preview in Browser** and choose a browser from the submenu to preview the page and test the link.

How to Import Spreadsheet Tables

You can import a spreadsheet table created in a program such as Microsoft Excel into your Dreamweaver page. Save the spreadsheet file in tab-delimited (txt) or comma-separated-values format (csv). These tables are a quick way for setting up the layout for a catalog or directory of information.

Save the Spreadsheet in TXT or CSV Format

1. Open the spreadsheet file in the program in which you created it, such as Microsoft Excel.
2. Choose **File > Save As.**
3. For the file format, choose either **Text (Tab delimited)** or **CSV (Comma delimited)** from the Save as type (Windows) or Format (Macintosh) drop-down menu to save the spreadsheet as a data file.
4. Save and close the spreadsheet program.

Insert the Spreadsheet into a Dreamweaver Document

5. Open Dreamweaver and open the document into which you want to insert the spreadsheet table.
6. Change to the **Layout** view on the Insert bar and click the **Tabular Data** button.

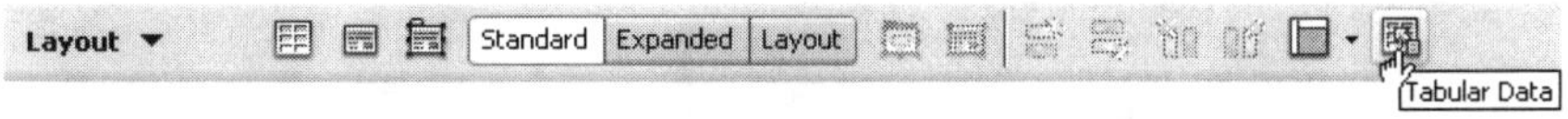

The Import Tabular Data dialog box opens.

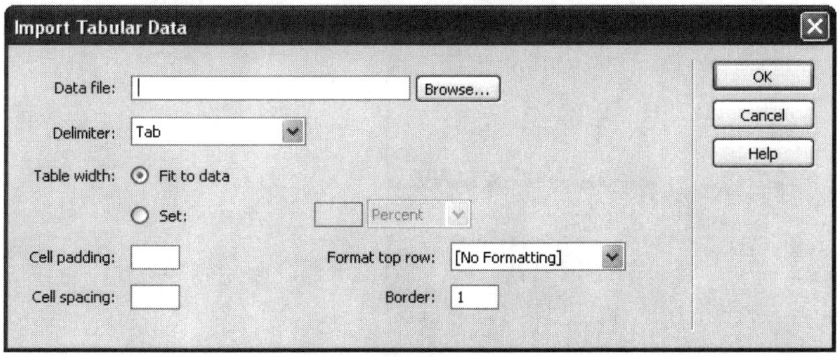

7. In the dialog box, click **Browse** and select the spreadsheet file. Click **Open**.

8. On the Delimiter pop-up menu, choose **Tab** if you saved the spreadsheet file in tab-delimited format or choose **Comma** if you saved the file in CSV format.

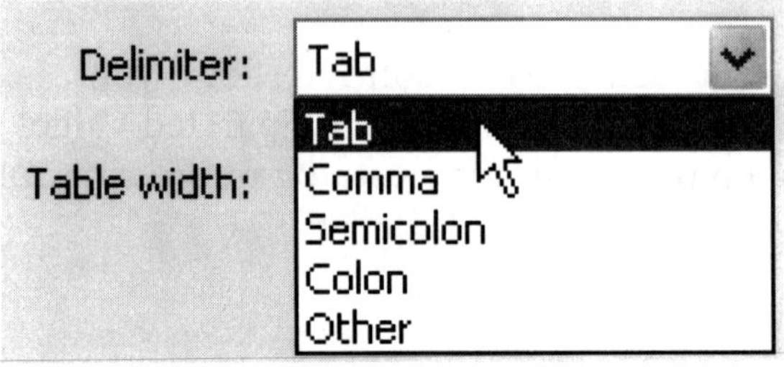

9. Click **OK** to close the Insert Tabular Data dialog box.

Format Data Tables

10. To format the imported table, select the table in the Dreamweaver document and use the Property inspector to set formatting options, or choose either **Format Table** or **Sort Table** from the **Commands** menu.

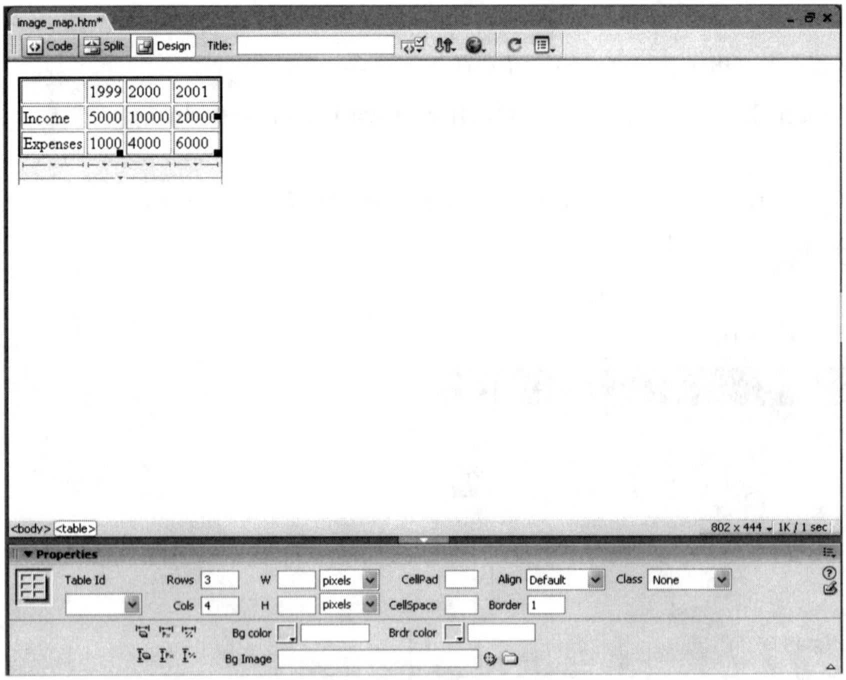

How to Create Pop-up Menus

Pop-up menus are menus that are displayed in a browser when the user moves the pointer over or clicks a trigger image. Pop-up menu items can have URL links attached to them for navigation.

Pop-up menus enable you to display multiple links within a small space. They provide navigation flexibility without long download times. You can define the appearance of the pop-up menu so that it matches the overall look and feel of your Web site. A pop-up menu is similar to a table: each menu item is like a table cell. You can customize the menu by choosing from a selection of font types, cell colors, and background image styles.

Create Pop-up Menu Entries

1. Open Macromedia Fireworks MX 2004.
2. Open or create the image that will trigger the pop-up menu.

   Note: The trigger image may be a text object or a graphic. Be sure to set the canvas dimensions to account for the size of the pop-up menu; you can trim the canvas after you build the menu to adjust the size.
3. Click the trigger image to select it.
4. Choose **Edit > Insert > Slice** to insert a slice over the trigger image.

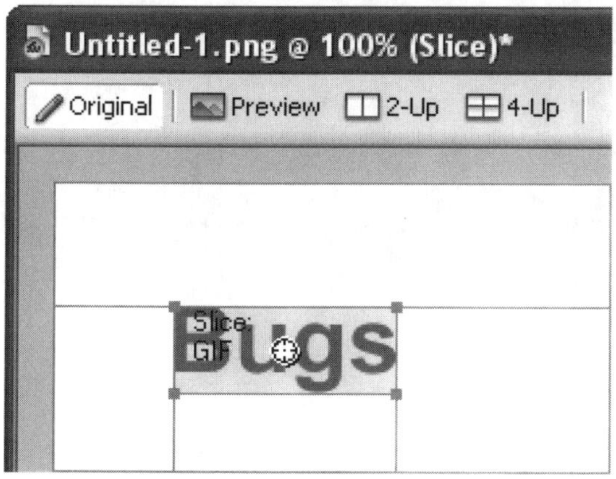

When a slice is selected, a circle with cross hairs appears in the center of the slice. This is called a *behavior handle*.

5. Click the behavior handle and choose **Add Pop-up Menu** from the context menu.

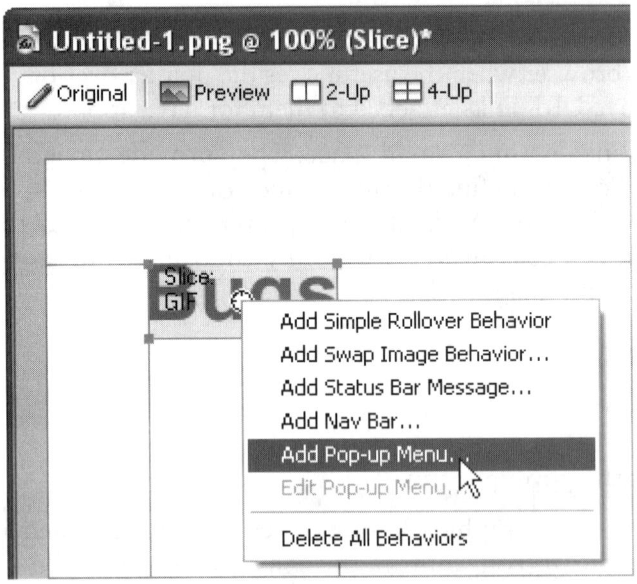

The Pop-up Menu Editor opens.

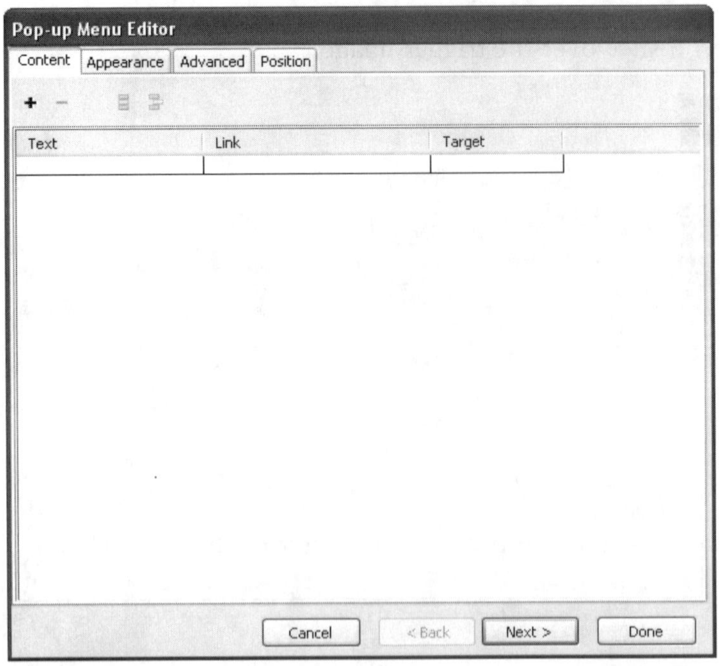

6. On the Content tab of the Pop-up Menu Editor, double-click to place the insertion point in the first Text box. Enter the text for a menu item. Press **Tab** to move to the Link box, and enter the name of the file it links to.

7. To add a new menu item, click the **Add Menu** (+) button and repeat step 6.

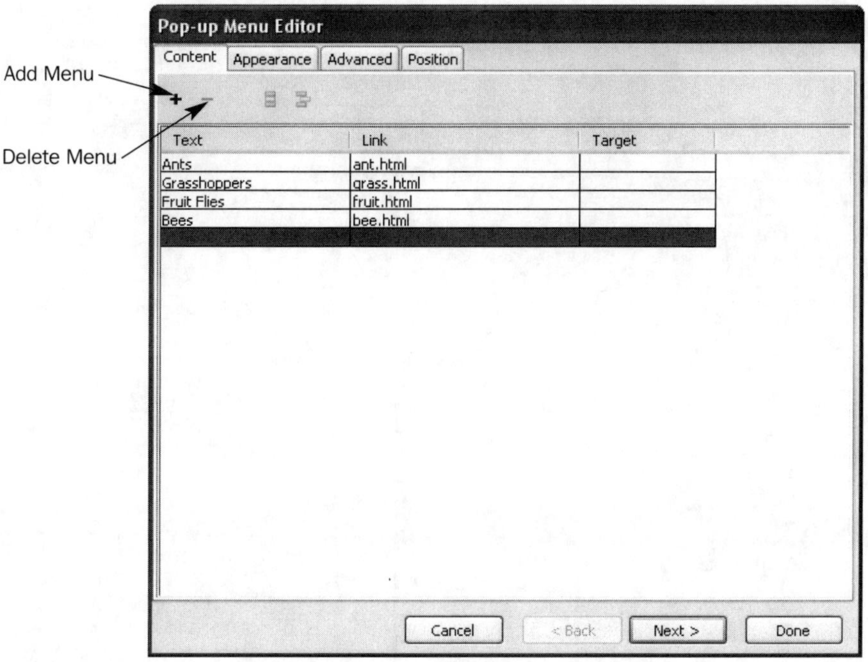

8. To delete a menu item, select the item and click the **Delete Menu** (–) button.
9. After you have entered all the menu items, click **Next** or click the **Appearance** tab.

Set the Appearance of a Pop-up Menu

On the Appearance sheet of the Pop-up Menu Editor, you can format the text, apply graphic styles to the Over and Up states, and choose vertical or horizontal orientation for the pop-up menu.

10. Select either **HTML** or **Image** for Cells.

    Note: *HTML* sets the menu's appearance using only HTML code; this setting produces pages with smaller file sizes. *Image* gives you a selection of graphic image styles to use as the cell background; this setting produces pages with larger file sizes.

11. Select **Vertical Menu** or **Horizontal Menu** from the Orientation pop-up menu near the top of the Appearance sheet.

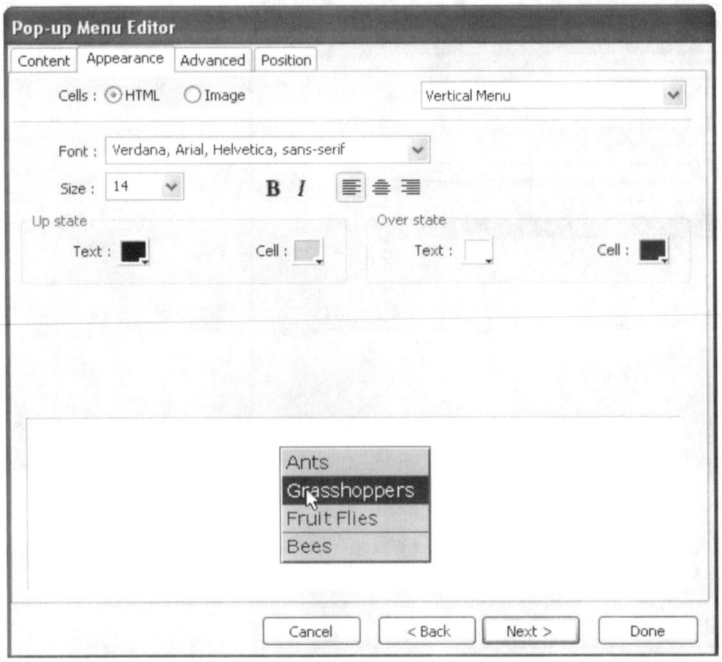

Settings you choose immediately appear in the preview menu near the bottom of the Appearance sheet.

12. Select font type, font size, and text styles for your menu item.
13. Select text and background (Cell) colors for the Up state and the Over state. These states are similar to button states. The Up state of a menu item is its default appearance in the menu. The Over state is the appearance of the menu item when the pointer passes over it.
14. If Image is selected as the cell type, choose a graphical style for the Up state and the Over state.

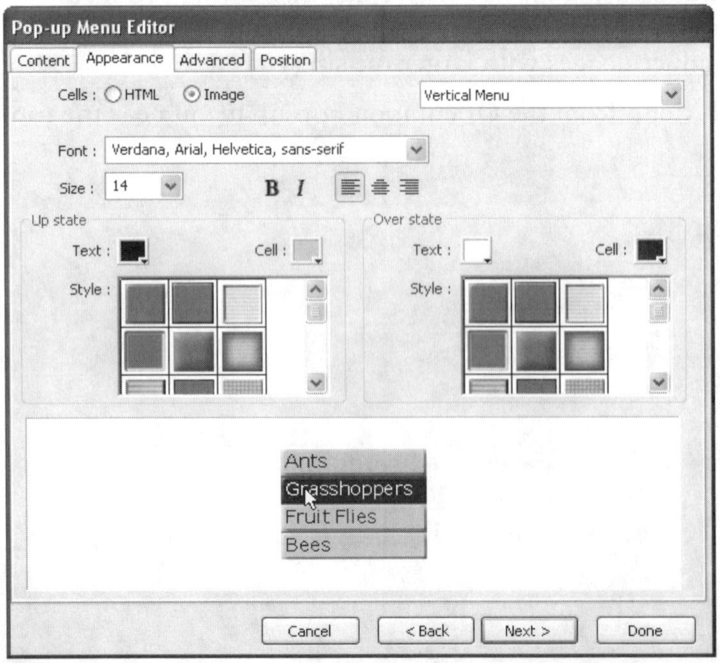

15. Click **Next** or click the **Advanced** tab if you want to make changes to cell or border attributes.

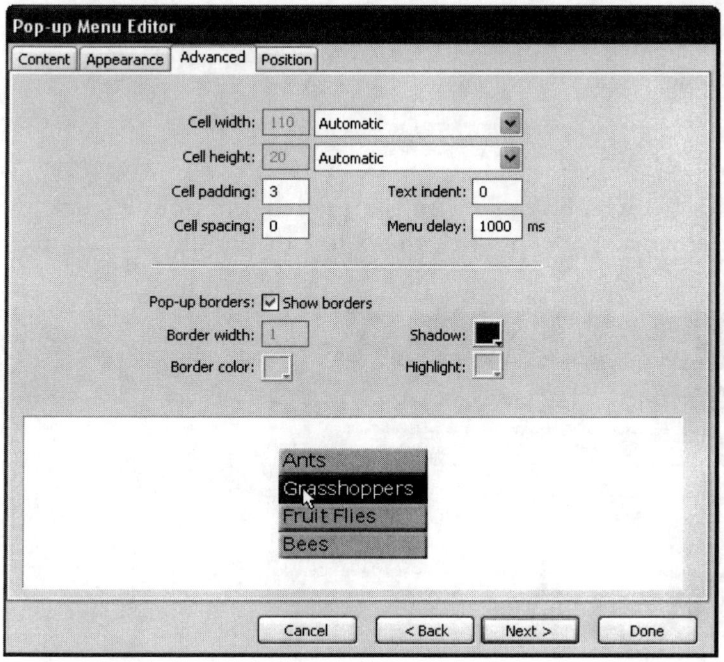

Set the Position of a Pop-up Menu

16. Click **Next** or click the **Position** tab in the Pop-up Menu Editor.

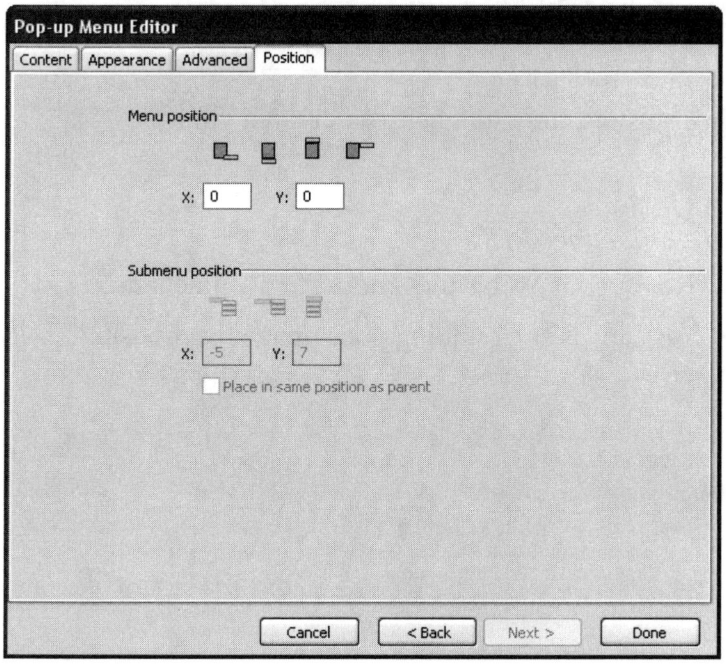

17. Click a Menu position button to position the pop-up menu relative to the trigger slice.

Note: Alternatively, you can enter X and Y coordinates. Coordinates of 0, 0 align the upper left corner of the pop-up menu with the upper left corner of the trigger slice.

18. Click **Done**.
19. To preview your pop-up menu, choose **File > Preview in Browser** and choose a browser from the submenu.

Edit a Pop-up Menu

1. To edit a pop-up menu, select the slice to which your menu is attached and double-click the pop-up menu's blue outline in the workspace, or click the behavior handle and choose **Edit Pop-up Menu**.

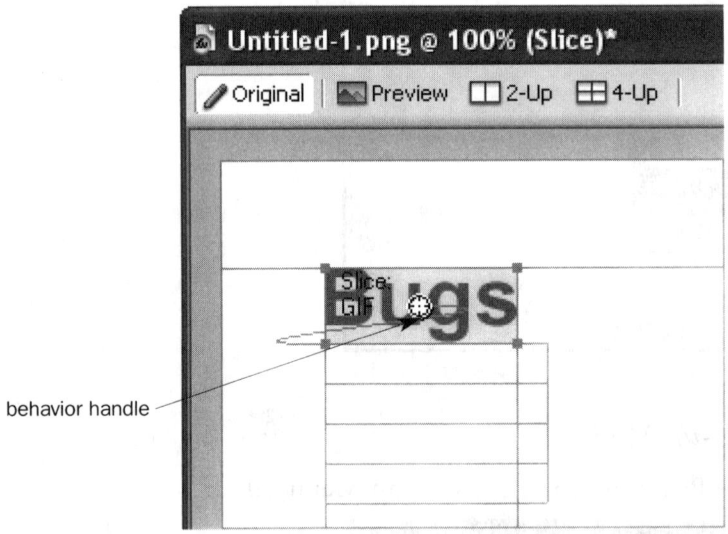

   The Pop-up Menu Editor opens.

2. Set options in the Pop-up Menu Editor just as you did when you created your pop-up menu.

Export a Pop-up Menu for Use in Dreamweaver MX

To save the pop-up menu so it will be active on your Web site, export the document as HTML.

1. While still in Fireworks, trim any excess canvas surrounding your image by choosing **Modify > Canvas > Trim Canvas.**
2. Save the file.
3. Choose **File > Export.**

   The Export dialog box opens.

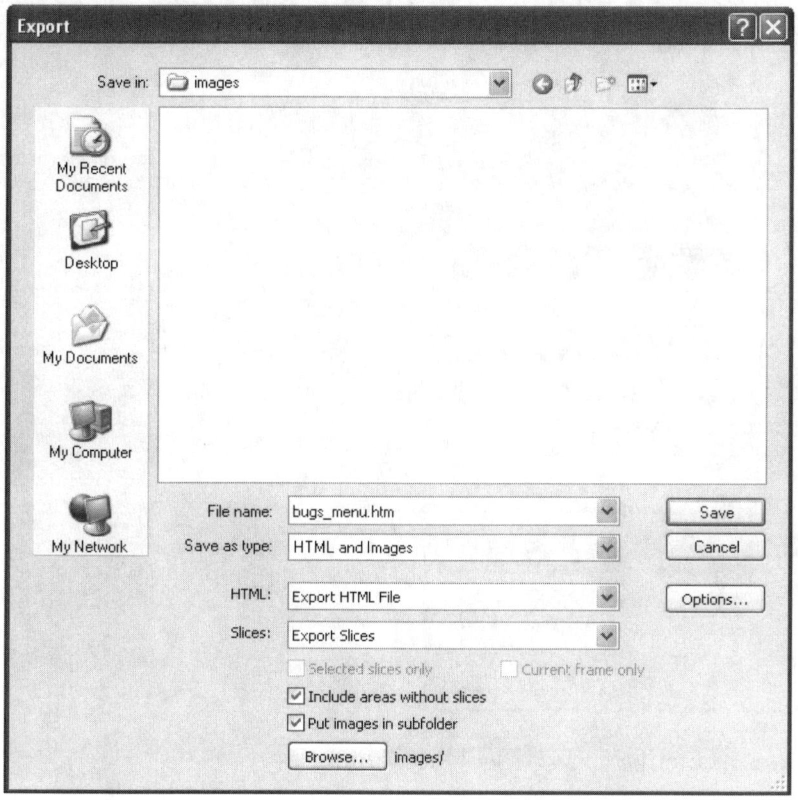

4. Navigate to the appropriate folder in your local root folder, such as Images.
5. Give the pop-up menu a short, descriptive name.
6. Select **HTML and Images** from the Save as type (Windows) or Save As (Macintosh) menu.
7. Click the check box for **Put images in subfolder**.

   Note: Putting all the exported image files in a subfolder is a good way to manage those files.

8. Click **Save**.

Import a Pop-up Menu into Dreamweaver MX 2004

1. Open Dreamweaver.
2. Open the document into which you want to import the pop-up menu.
3. Position the cursor where you want the pop-up menu to appear.

4. Make sure the Common view is selected on the Insert bar. Click the arrow on the **Images** button, and then click **Fireworks HTML**.

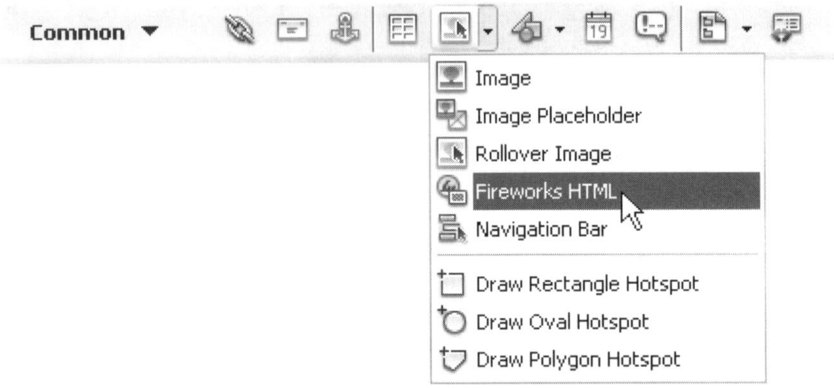

The Insert Fireworks HTML dialog box opens.

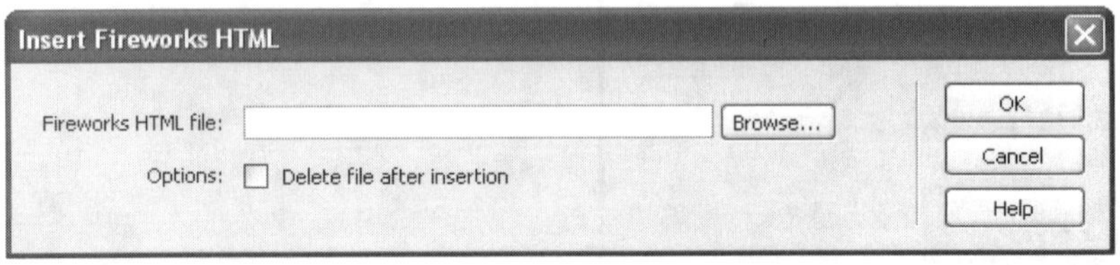

5. Click **Browse** and select the pop-up menu HTML file. Click **Open**.

   Note: The Images subfolder contains the sliced images for your pop-up menu.

6. Click **OK**.

   The pop-up menu is inserted into your Dreamweaver document.

7. Save your page, and then choose **File > Preview in Browser** and choose a browser from the submenu to test the menu and links for the menu items.

How to Prepare Photographs

Presenting photos on a Web page can be challenging in that pictures have to work well with text, colors, and design of the site. In Macromedia Fireworks MX 2004, you can adjust the tone of photographs or mask them with shapes that work better with the overall design of the site.

Masking Photographs

Masks are bitmap or vector images placed on top of a photograph that leave visible only the part of the photograph that is inside the masking image. You can use masks to create cutout effects or transparency effects on photos.

Create a Bitmap Mask

1. Open Fireworks and open the photograph to be masked.

2. Select a bitmap drawing tool such as the Brush, Pencil, Rectangle, or Ellipse and draw a masking region on the photo.

3. Choose **Edit > Cut** to move the bitmap mask to the clipboard.
4. Select the photograph and choose **Edit > Paste as Mask.**

Only that portion of the photograph in the area outlined by the bitmap mask is visible.

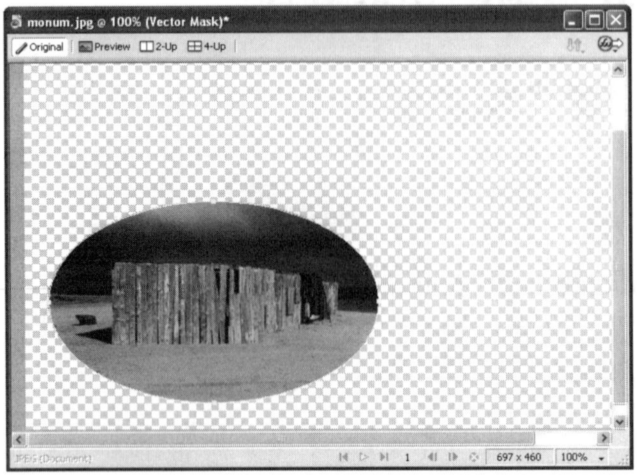

5. Click the image thumbnail on the Layers panel.

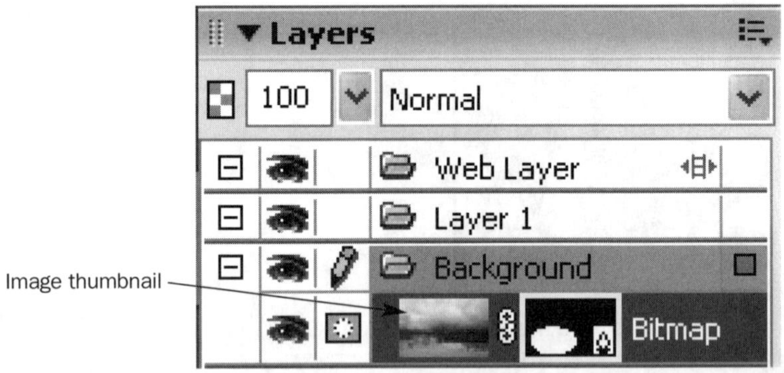

A light blue handle appears in the image. You can use this handle to adjust the position of the image within the mask.

6. Drag the image center point to rearrange the position of the image under the mask.

7. Save and export the image as a JPEG or GIF file.

Feather and Add Effects to Masks

1. Select the bitmap mask thumbnail in the Layers panel.

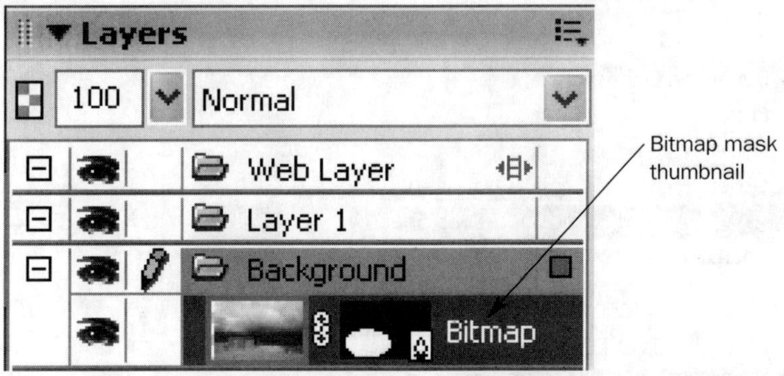

2. In the Fill section of the Property inspector, select **Feather** from the Edge menu and increase the amount of Feather. (Either type a higher number in the text box to the right of the Edge menu or click the down arrow and drag the slider.)

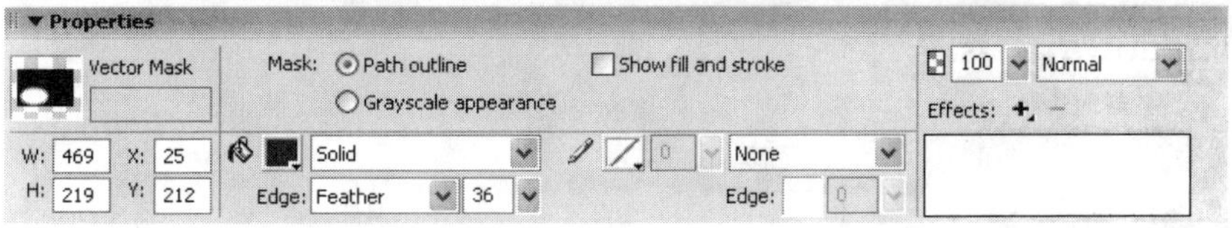

The edge of the mask is feathered. You can see the feathering better if you deselect the image.

3. To add a Glow, select the image thumbnail (not the mask) on the Layers panel.

4. On the Property inspector, click the **Add effects** (+) button and choose **Shadow and Glow > Inner Glow** from the pop-up menu.

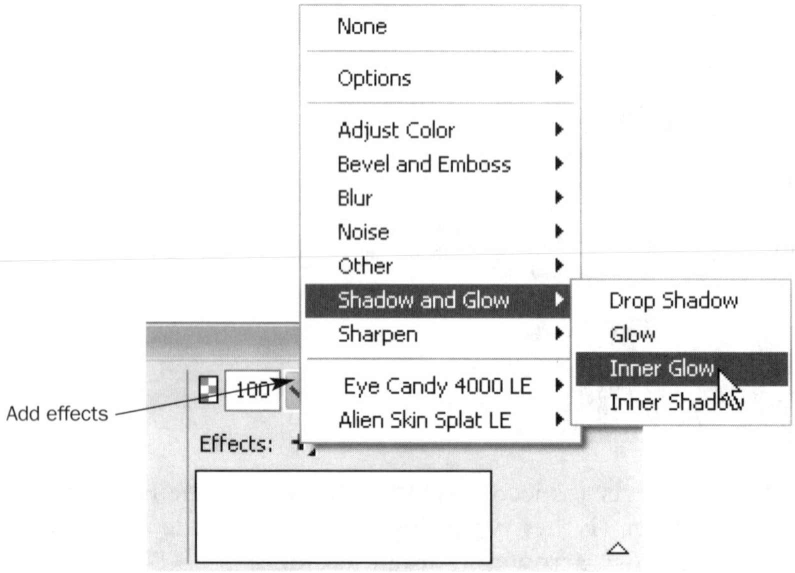

The Inner Glow pop-up window opens.

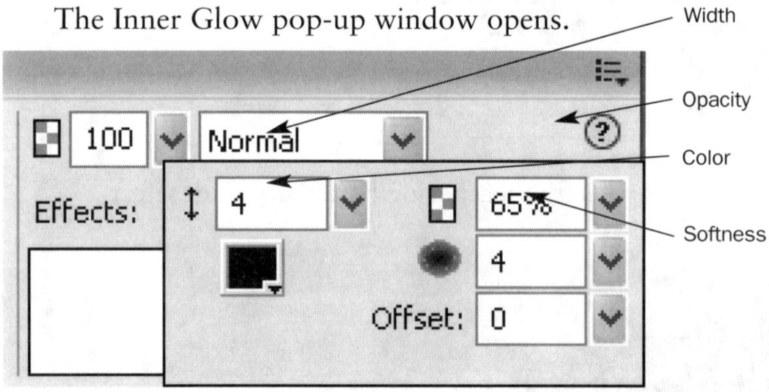

5. Increase the Offset and Width of the glow until you can see it in the masked image.
6. Adjust the Softness, Opacity, and Color until you achieve the desired effect.
7. When you finish, click outside the window or press **Enter** (Windows) or **Return** (Macintosh) to close it.
8. Save and export the image as a JPEG or GIF file.

Create a Text Mask

1. Open Fireworks and open the photo to be masked.
2. Create text to become the mask for the Image.

3. Adjust the text size and font and choose **Edit > Cut** to move the text to the Clipboard.
4. Select the photo and choose **Edit > Paste as Mask**.

   The image appears only in the area outlined by the text mask.

5. Click the image thumbnail in the Layers panel.

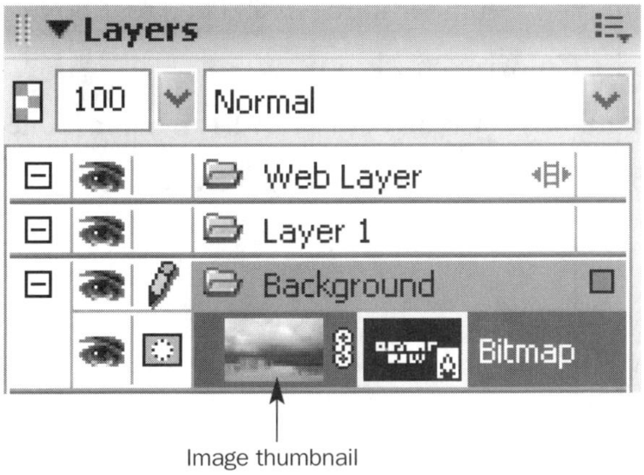

A light blue handle appears in the center of the image.

6. Drag the image center point to rearrange the position of the image under the mask.
7. Save and export the image as a JPEG or GIF file.

Adjust the Color Tone of Photos

1. Select the bitmap image for color adjustments.
2. Choose **Filters > Adjust Color > Hue/Saturation**.

   The Hue/Saturation dialog box opens.

3. Make sure the **Preview** check box is selected.
4. Drag the Hue, Saturation, and Lightness sliders to create the desired color feel for the photo.

   Note: As an alternative to dragging a slider, you can type a number in the associated text box.
5. To adjust the general color of the photo, select the **Colorize** check box.
6. To give an auburn tint to the photo, choose **Commands > Creative > Convert to Sepia Tone**.
7. To make the photo black and white, choose **Commands > Creative > Convert to Grayscale**.

HOW TO CREATE ANIMATED IMAGES

Animated Images

You can use animated images to emphasize aspects of your site or site message. Animation draws viewer attention. The challenge is to use animations sparingly, so they don't distract viewers. Animations are often used in banner ads and cartoons.

You make animations in Fireworks by creating symbols and changing their properties over time to create the illusion of motion. A symbol is like an actor whose movements you direct. The action of each symbol is stored on a frame. When you play all the frames together in a sequence, you get motion.

You can apply different settings to the symbol to gradually change the content of successive frames. You can make a symbol appear to move across the canvas, fade in or out, get bigger or smaller, or rotate.

To begin, you can create a new animation symbol or you can convert an existing object to an animation symbol.

Create an Animation Symbol

1. Open Fireworks.
2. Create a new blank document.
3. Choose **Edit > Insert > New Symbol.**

   The Symbol Properties dialog box opens.

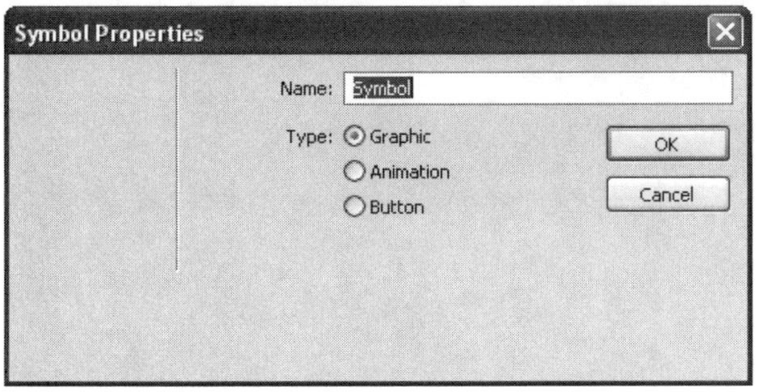

4. Enter a name for the new symbol.
5. For Type, select **Animation** and click **OK.**

   The Symbol Editor opens.

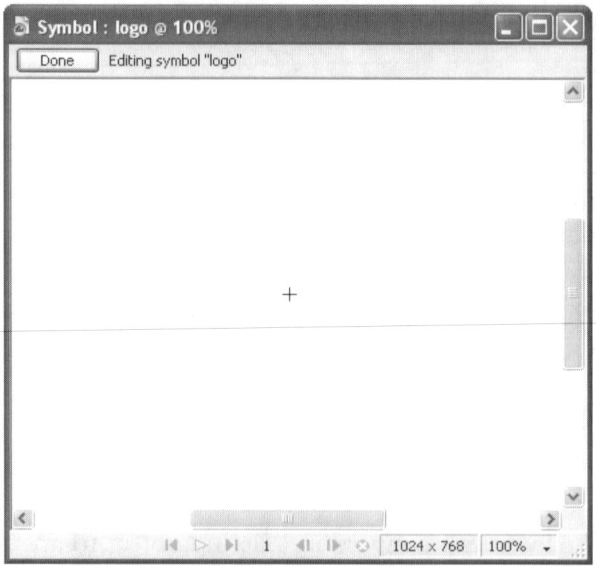

6. In the Symbol Editor, use the drawing and text tools to create a new object.
7. Click Done (Windows) or the Close button (Macintosh) to close the Symbol Editor.

Edit Animation Properties

1. Select the animation symbol on the canvas.
2. Choose **Modify > Animation > Settings**.

   The Animate dialog box opens.

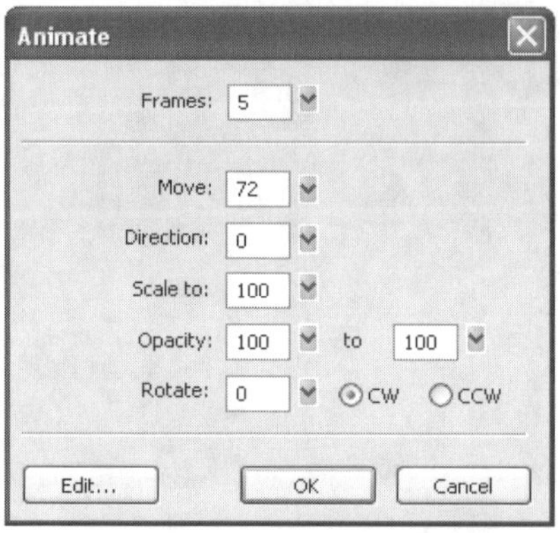

3. Enter the desired settings.
   - *Frames* is the number of frames you want to include in the animation.
   - *Move* is the distance (in pixels) that you want the object to move.
   - *Direction* is the direction (in degrees) in which you want the object to move.
   - *Scale to* is the percent change in size from start to finish.
   - *Opacity* is the degree of fading in or out from start to finish.
   - *Rotate* is the degree of rotation from start to finish. You can rotate clockwise (CW) or counterclockwise (CCW).
4. Click **OK**. If you entered more than one frame, click **OK** again to add new frames to the animation.

5. You can also select an animation symbol and change animation settings on the Property inspector.

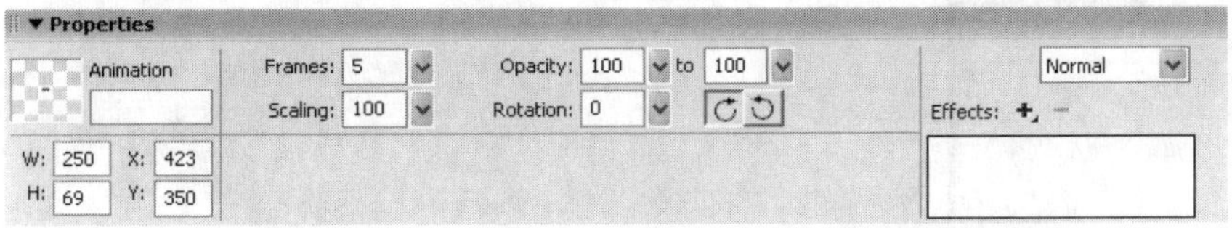

6. To change Movement and Direction settings manually, select the animation symbol on the canvas.

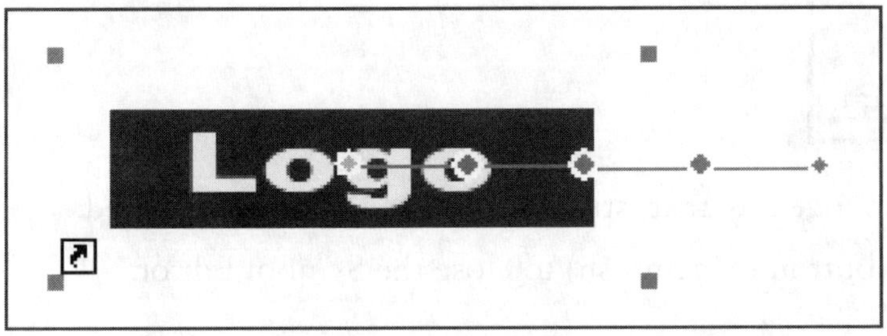

A motion path is attached to the symbol. The dot in the center of the symbol indicates the starting point of the animation; this dot is called the *start handle*. The red dot at the other end shows the end point; this dot is called the *end handle*. The blue dots in between represent frames.

7. To change the movement or direction of the motion, drag either the start or end handles to a new location.

Convert an Existing Object to an Animation Symbol

1. Select the object.
2. Choose **Modify > Animation > Animate Selection.**

   The Animate dialog box opens.

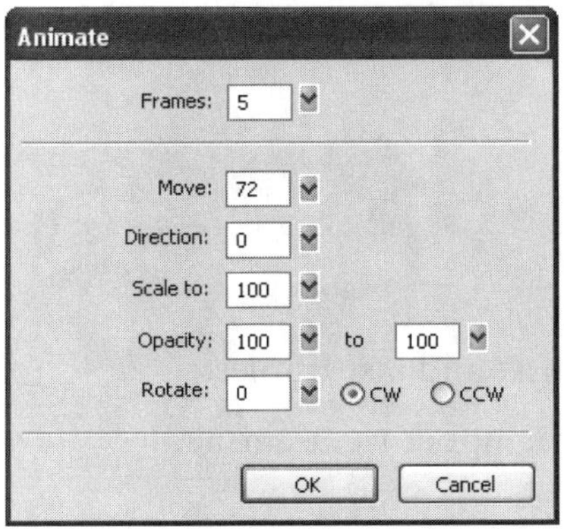

3. Enter the desired settings.

Edit Symbol Graphics

1. To change the graphic attributes of an animation symbol, select the symbol and choose **Modify > Symbol > Edit Symbol.**

The Symbol Editor opens.

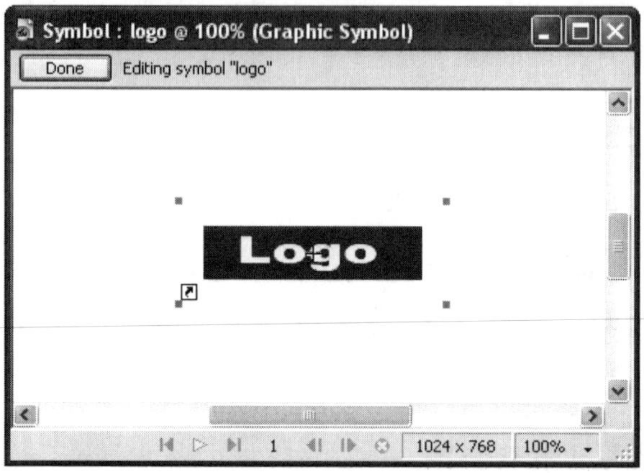

2. Modify the animation symbol and change any text, strokes, fills, and effects as desired.
3. Click Done (Windows) or the Close button (Macintosh) to close the Symbol Editor.

Change the Speed of an Animation

Each stage of your animation is in a different frame. You can see the contents of each frame using the Frames panel.

The frame delay determines how long the current frame is displayed when you play the animation. It is specified in hundredths of a second. For example, a setting of 50 displays the frame for a half a second. To slow the speed of an animation, increase the frame delay.

1. Select the animation symbol and choose **Window > Frames** to open the Frames panel.

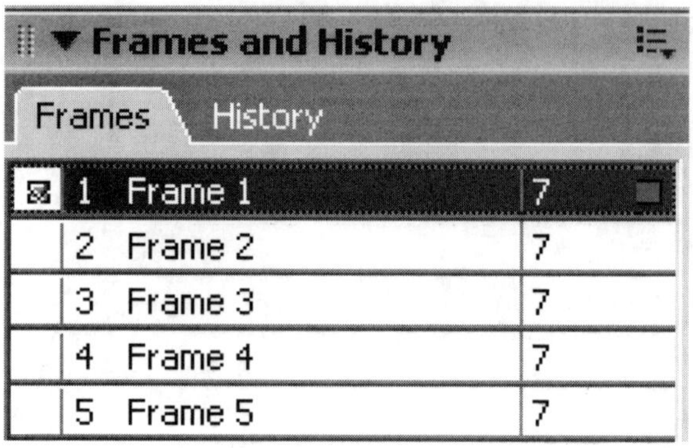

2. Select one or more frames in the Frames panel.

   Note: To select a contiguous range of frames, Shift-click the first and last frames.

3. Choose **Properties** from the Frames panel Options menu in the upper right corner.

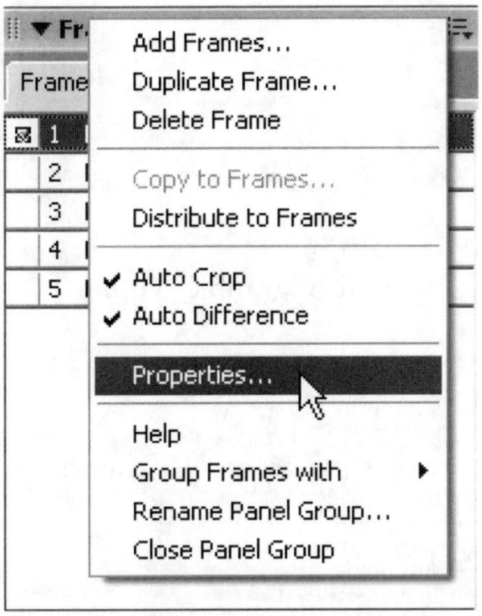

The Frame Properties pop-up window opens.

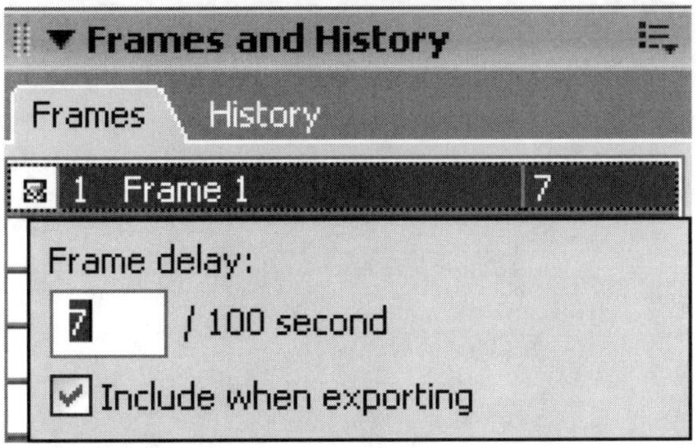

4. Enter a value for the frame delay.
5. Press **Enter** (Windows) or **Return** (Macintosh) or click outside the panel to close the pop-up window.

Tweening

Tweening is a traditional animation term that describes the process in which a lead animator draws only the frames containing major changes while assistants draw the frames in between.

In Fireworks, tweening blends two or more instances of the same graphic symbol, creating interim instances between the frames.

1. Select two or more instances of the same graphic symbol on the canvas.
2. Choose **Modify > Symbol > Tween Instances.**

The Tween Instances dialog box opens.

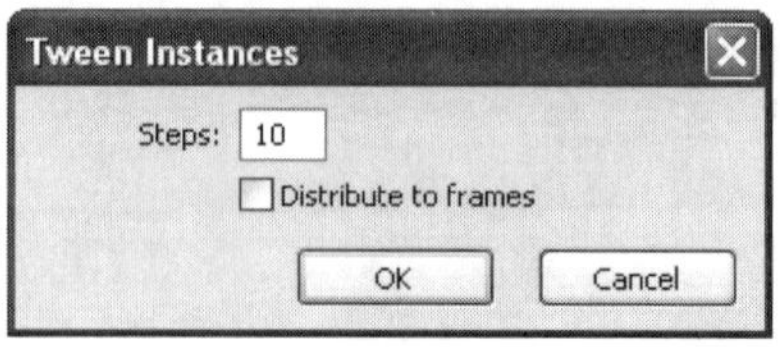

3. Enter the number of tween steps to be inserted between the original pair of graphic symbols.
4. Select **Distribute to frames** and click **OK**.

Preview an Animation

You can preview an animation while you are working on it to check its progress. Use the frame controls that appear at the bottom of the document window.

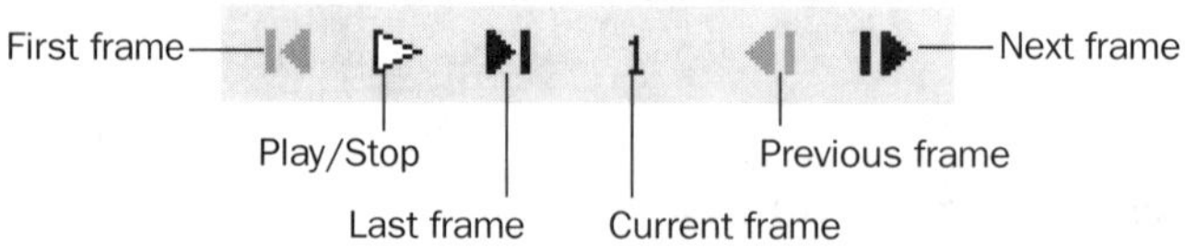

To preview an animation in a Web browser, choose **File > Preview in Browser**, and choose a browser from the submenu.

Export an Animated Image

1. Select the animation symbol.
2. Choose **Window > Optimize** to open the Optimize panel.

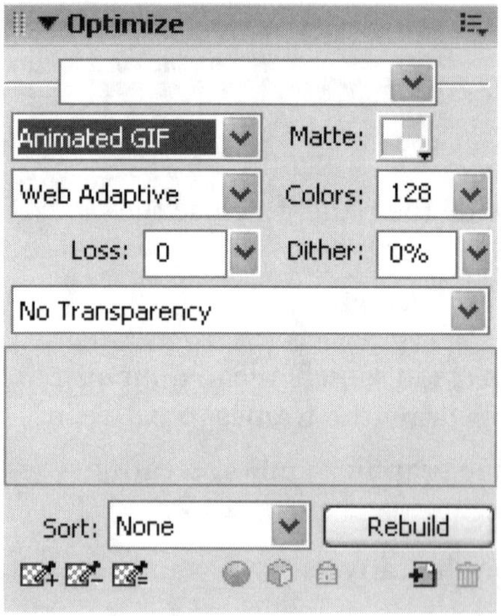

3. In the Optimize panel, choose **Animated GIF** as the Export file format.
4. Choose **File > Export**.
5. The Export dialog box opens.

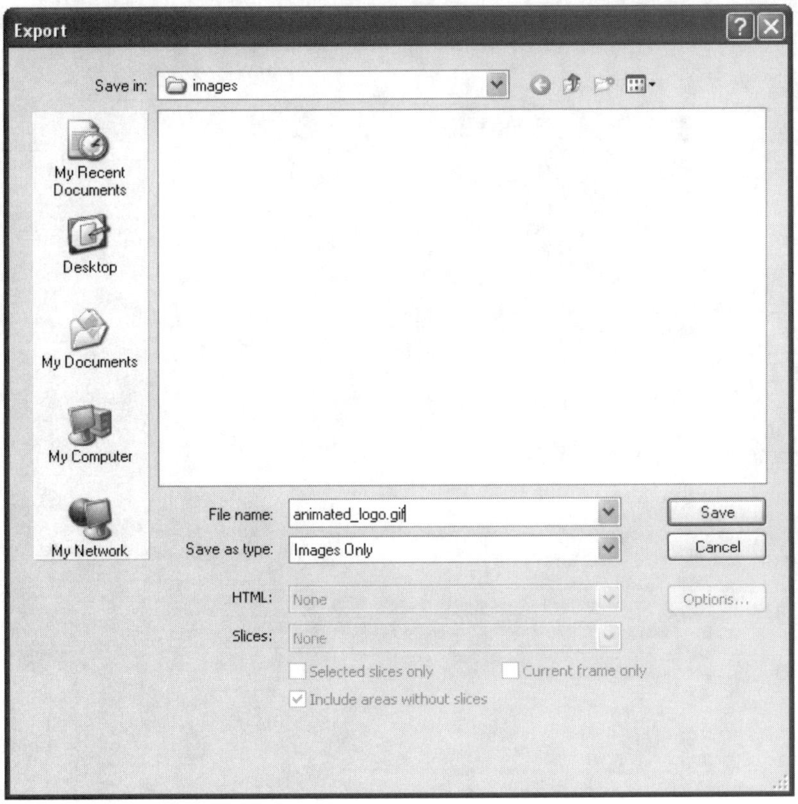

6. Enter a name for the file, locate the folder in which you wish to save it, and click **Save**.

   You can insert the exported animated GIF into a Dreamweaver document.

Unit 9: Enhancing User Experience on the Web

Activity Guides

Activity 9.1: Introduction to Macromedia Flash MX 2004

The Macromedia Flash MX Workspace
How to Create an Animated Face
Symbols, Instances, and the Library
How to Create Motion and Shape Tweens
How to Import Sound and Video
How to Create a Button Symbol

Activity 9.2: Examining Macromedia Flash on the Web

Analyzing Macromedia Flash on the Web

Activity 9.3: Creating Effects and Film Techniques with Macromedia Flash MX 2004

How to Apply Colors and Gradients
How to Create Transitions with Motion Tweens
How to Use Filmmaking Techniques

Activity 9.5: Creating a Storyboard for a Digital Narrative

Sample Narrative Summary and Storyboard

Activity 9.6: Building a Digital Narrative

How to Organize Movie Content

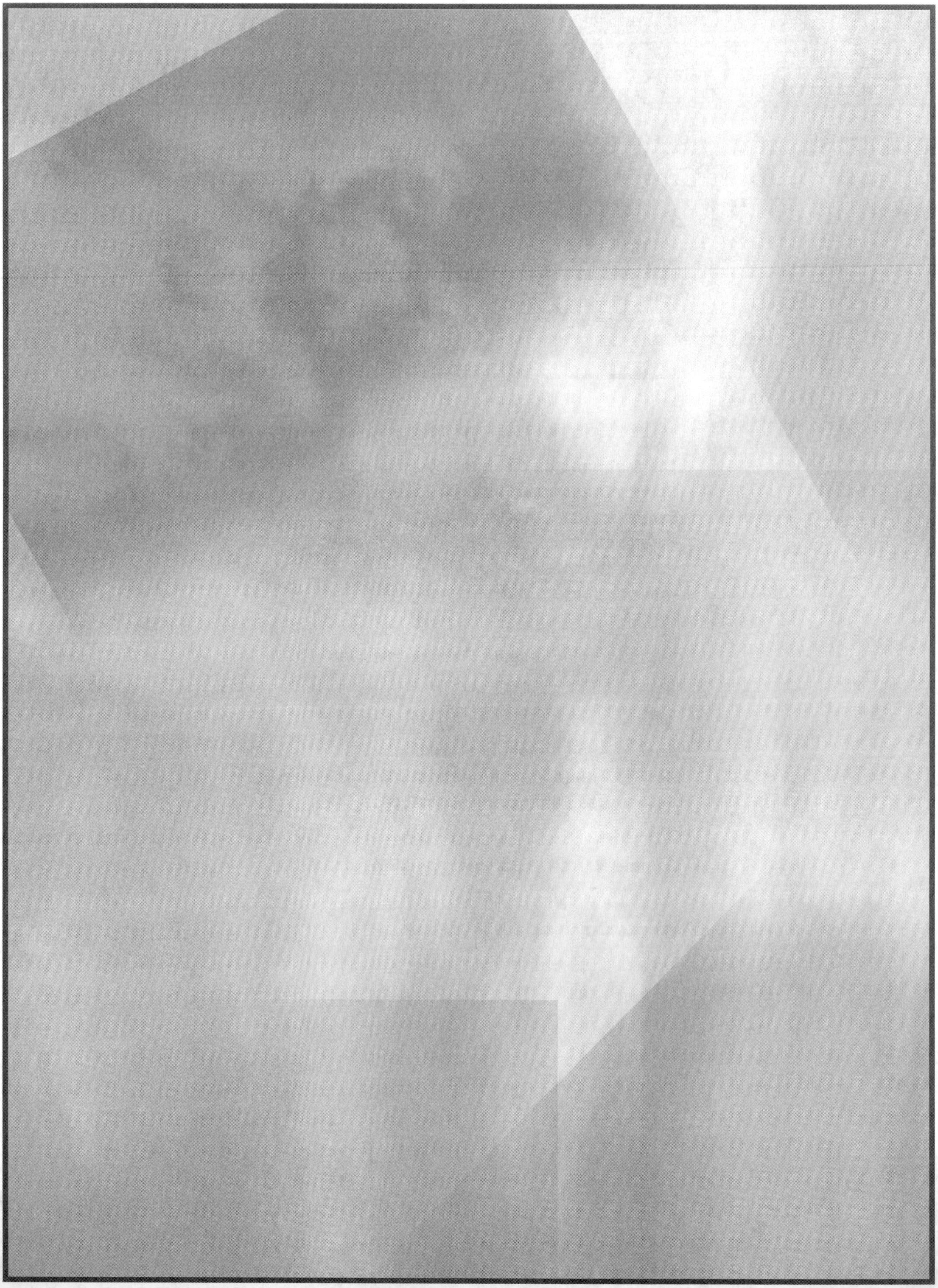

THE MACROMEDIA FLASH WORKSPACE

Stage

The *Stage* is the white area of the workspace. Objects you place on the Stage will appear in your movie. The light gray area around the Stage is called the *work area*. Nothing in the work area will appear in your finished movie, but you can place objects there until you want them to appear on the Stage.

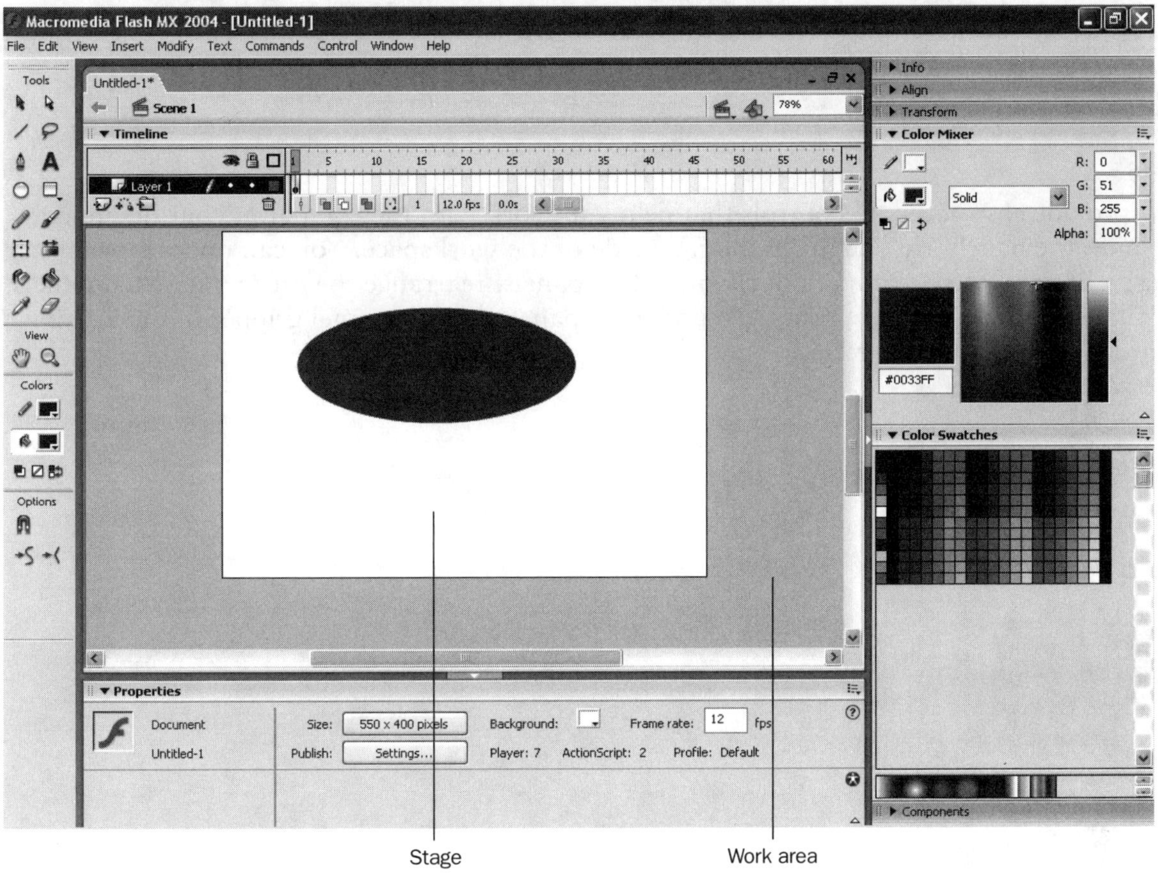

Timeline and Layers

The *Timeline* is where you control the images and sounds in your Macromedia Flash MX 2004 document. The Timeline is divided into frames. You can add content to the frames in the Timeline.

Current frame, frame rate, and elapsed time are all shown at the bottom of the Timeline. The *playhead*, represented by a red rectangle with a long red line, shows the current frame that you are viewing in the Timeline. You can click and drag the playhead back and forth in the Timeline to quickly view all or any part of your animation.

Layers provide a way to organize the elements of your movie. You can arrange content from front to back by placing it on separate layers. This allows you to place objects in front of or behind one another. The layer controls appear on the left side of the Timeline. Each layer has an option for hiding or showing the layer, locking it, and displaying its contents as outlines.

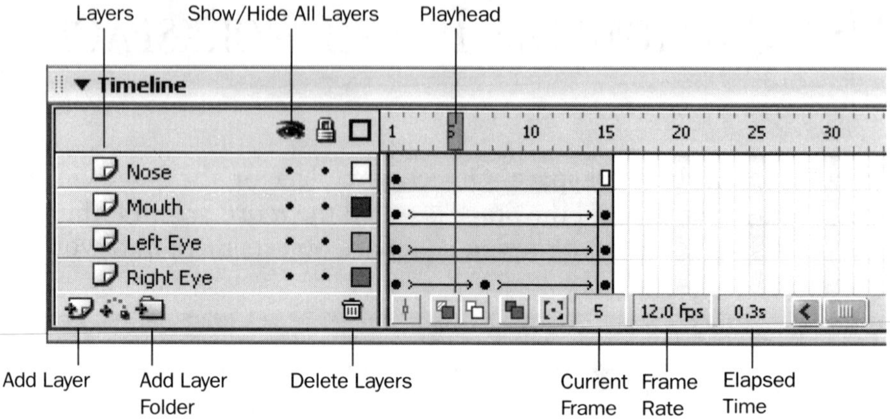

Panels

Panels provide easy access to controls that help you work with the content in your document. By default, the panels are docked to the right side of the workspace. You can undock panel groups, add panels to a group, undock individual panels, rearrange the order of docked panels, and collapse and close panel groups. To undock a panel, drag the panel gripper in the upper left corner of the panel's title bar.

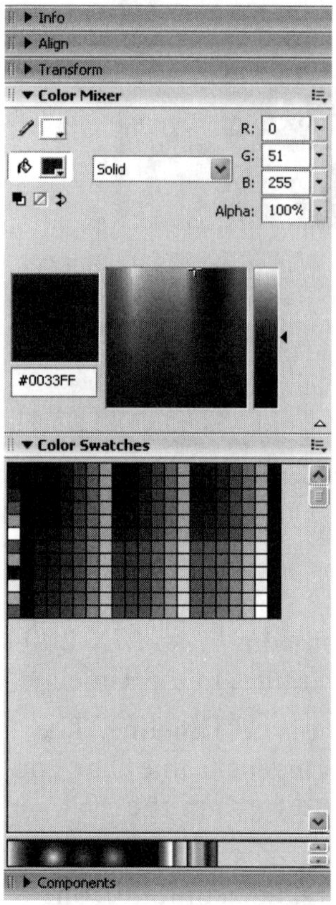

Toolbar

The Flash *toolbar* is divided into labeled sections for easy tool selection. The Options section of the toolbar lets you modify a tool you have selected. If the toolbar is not visible, you can display it by choosing **Window > Tools**. To select a tool, just click it. (You can also use the shortcut key shown in parentheses in the Tooltip that appears when you rest the pointer over a tool for a few seconds.)

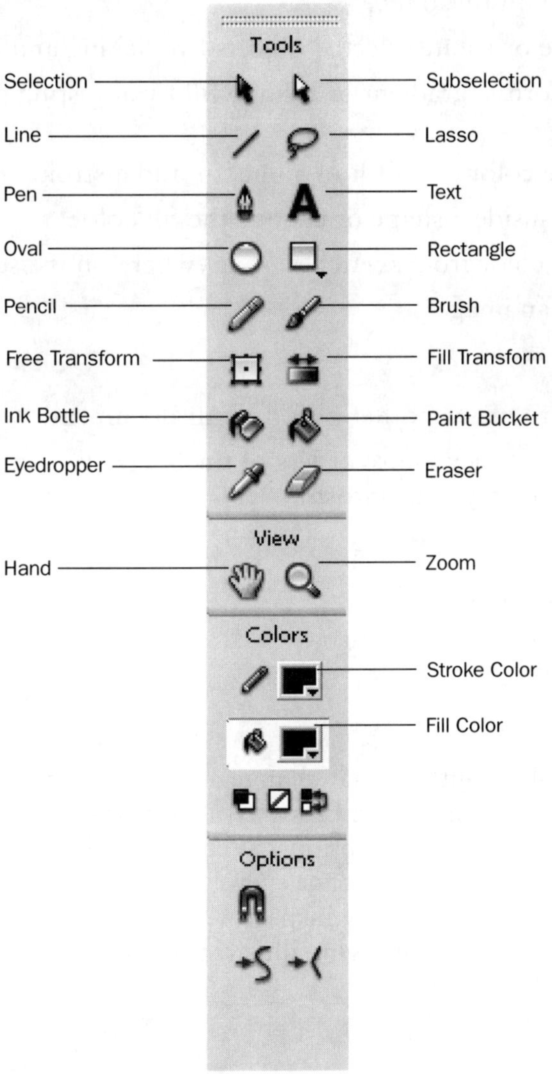

Drawing tools

Selection tool (black arrow): Click an object to select it. Drag a selected object to move it.

Subselection tool (white arrow): Select and move points of an object or edit paths between adjacent points.

Line tool: Draw straight lines.

Lasso tool: Click and drag to select an area.

Pen tool: Create straight or curved lines. You can also create Bezier curves.

Oval tool: Create circles and ovals composed of fills and strokes, just fills, or just strokes.

Rectangle tool: Create rectangles or squares composed of fills and strokes, just fills, or just strokes.

Pencil tool: Create lines in any of three modes—straighten, smooth, or ink.

Brush tool: Create shapes with fills only.

Free Transform tool: Resize or rotate selected objects by clicking and dragging.

Fill Transform tool: Transform a gradient or bitmap fill by adjusting the size, direction, or center of the fill.

Ink Bottle tool: Change the color or width of a line, or add a stroke to a shape.

Paint Bucket tool: Add fill inside a shape or change the fill color.

Eyedropper tool: Sample a color from swatches or anywhere on the screen.

Eraser tool: Erase parts of an image.

View tools

Hand tool: Drag the Stage to view another part of your document.

Zoom tool: Zoom in or out to view more or less of the Stage. To zoom out, hold down the **Alt** key (Windows) or the **Option** key (Macintosh).

Color tools

Stroke Color: Set the stroke color.

Fill Color: Set the fill color.

Property Inspector

The Property inspector displays options that change according to the current object or tool selection. When you open a document, the Property inspector displays document properties. When you choose a tool, it displays tool options. When you select a vector object, it displays options such as stroke and fill. You can change these and other options directly from the Property inspector. By default, the Property inspector is visible; you can hide or show it by choosing **Window > Properties**. The following illustrations show the properties for a text object and a rectangle shape, respectively.

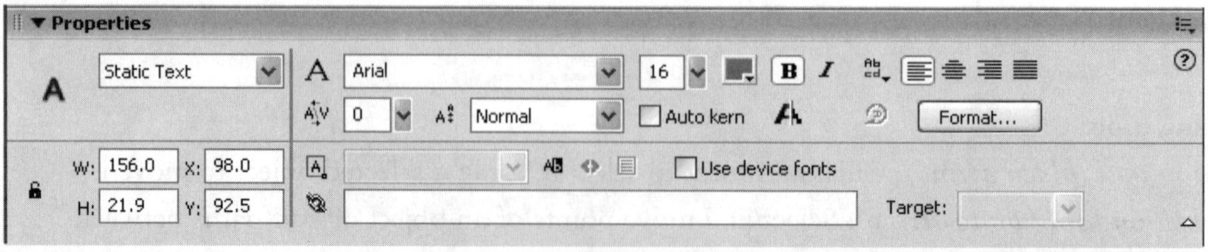

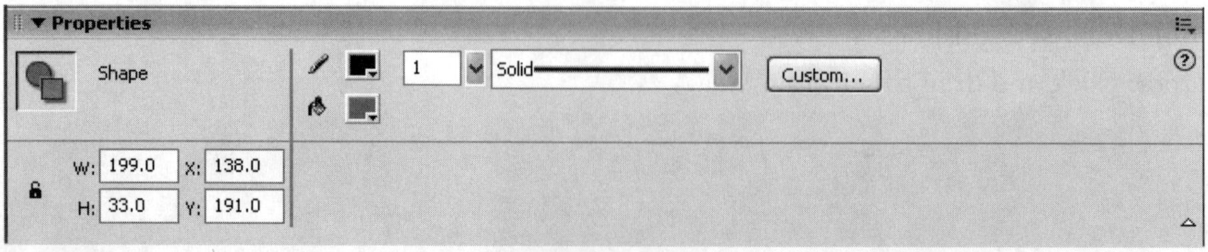

How to Create an Animated Face

This activity walks you step by step through the process of creating a simple Macromedia Flash MX 2004 animation. You will use many basic Flash techniques, including drawing tools, motion and shape tweens, button symbols, and basic ActionScript to provide user controls. You will also import a sound file to provide a musical soundtrack while the movie plays. After you have tested your movie, you will publish it for playback by others, either through a browser or directly with the Flash player.

Draw Facial Features

Draw the Right Eye

1. Start Flash, and choose **File > New** to open a blank new document.

   The New Document dialog box opens.

2. Select Flash Document and click **OK.**

   The new document contains one layer and one empty keyframe.

3. Select the **Oval** tool and draw a small circle to represent the right eye on a face.

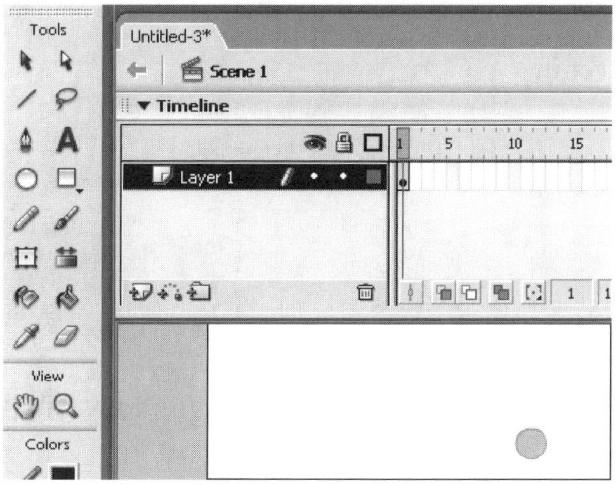

4. Select the **Selection** tool and double-click the circle to select it.

5. To change the outline color of the eye, click the **Stroke color** box in the Property inspector and select a new color. To change the fill color, use the **Fill color** box.

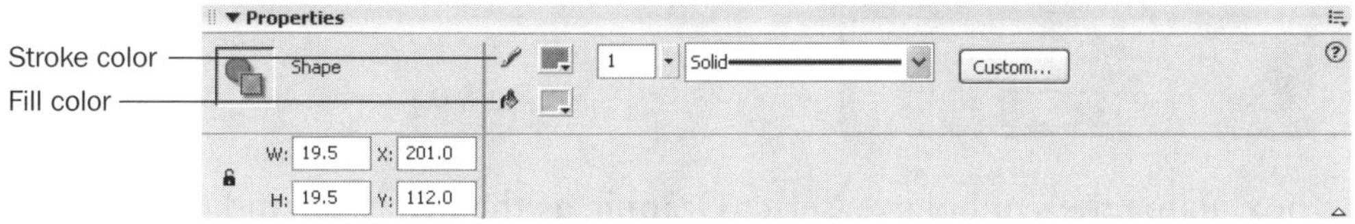

6. In the Timeline, double-click the layer name, **Layer 1**.

   This selects the layer name so that you can rename it.

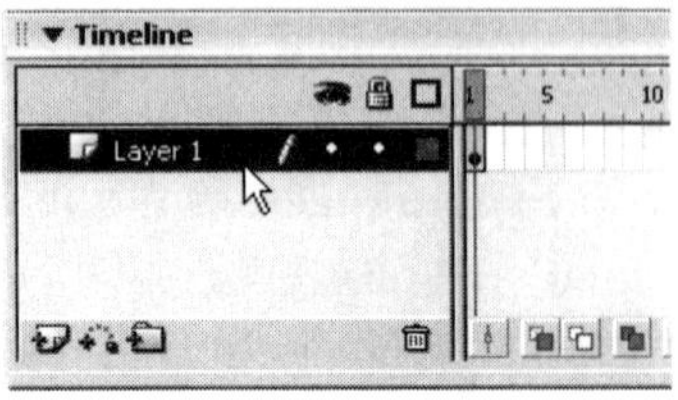

7. Rename the layer **Right Eye** and press **Enter** (Windows) or **Return** (Macintosh).

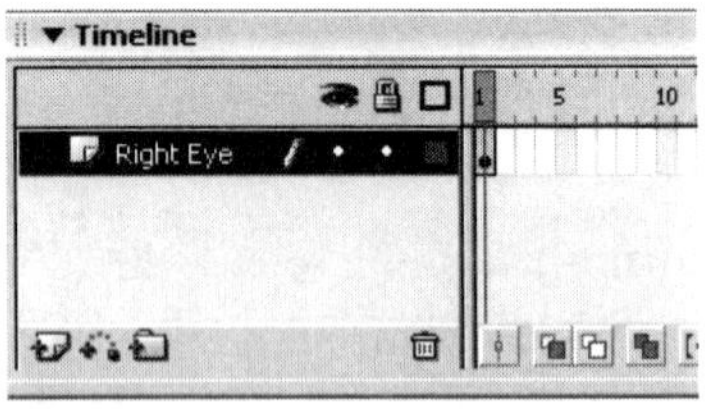

Save the Eye Graphic as a Symbol in the Library

Instead of creating two eyes separately, convert the right eye from a shape to a graphic symbol. This adds the eye to the library so you can use it over and over. This will also reduce the size of your finished movie.

8. In the Right Eye layer, click frame **1** to select it.

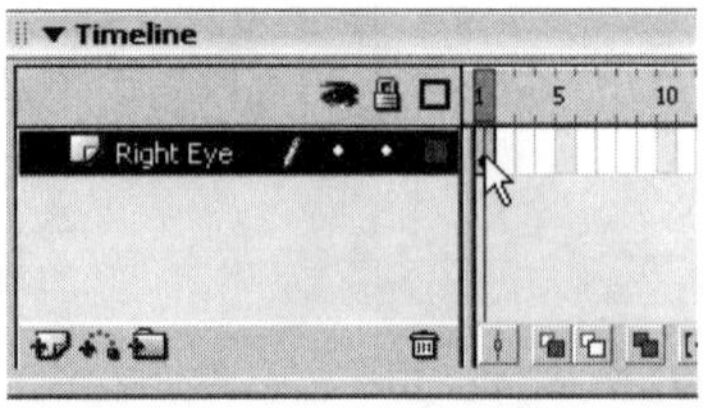

   This automatically selects the contents of frame 1.

   Note: If the right eye is not completely selected, double-click the eye on the Stage with the **Selection** tool to select it.

9. Choose **Modify > Convert to Symbol.**

   The Convert to Symbol dialog box opens.

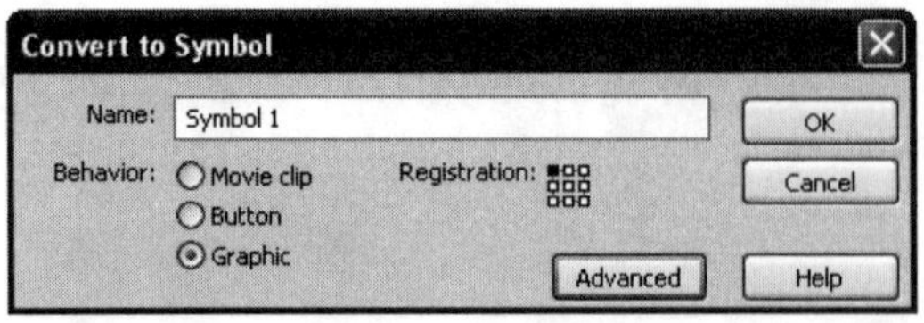

10. In the dialog box, name the symbol **eye**, select **Graphic** as the behavior, and click **OK**.

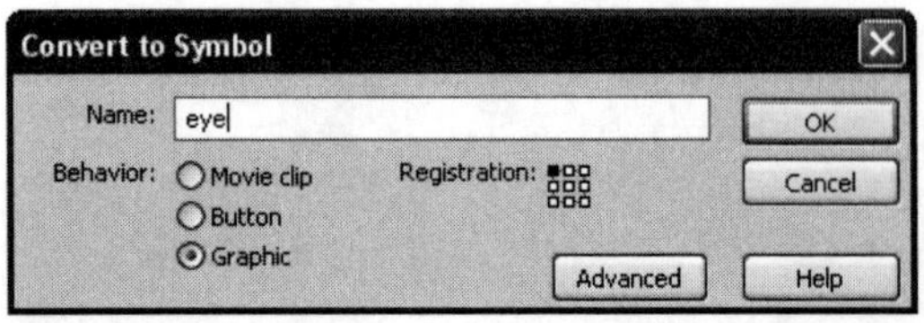

The eye on the Stage is now just an instance (copy) of the master eye symbol, which is stored in the library. The eye now has a single blue selection border and can be selected with a single click.

11. Choose **Window > Library** to see that your symbol has been added to the Library panel.

    Note: You must select the eye symbol in the library to see the graphic in the preview window, as shown in the following illustration.

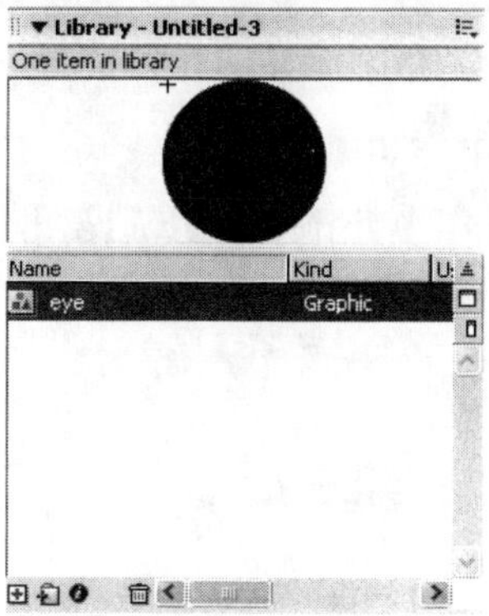

You can now reuse the eye symbol as many times as you want without redrawing it.

Reuse the Eye Symbol to Create the Left Eye

12. Click the **Insert Layer** button in the lower left corner of the Timeline to insert a new layer.

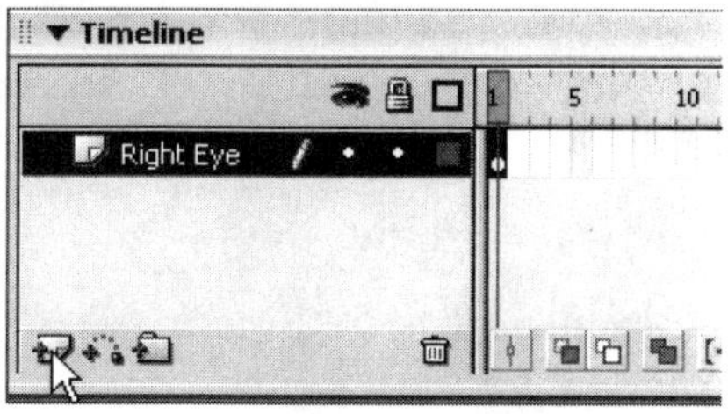

13. Double-click the layer name and change the name to **Left Eye**.
14. In the Left Eye layer, select frame **1**.
15. Select the eye symbol in the Library panel and drag the symbol onto the Stage.

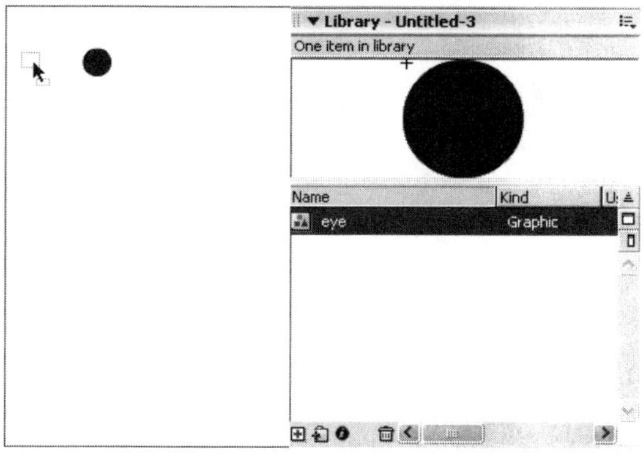

You now have a second instance of the eye on the Stage. Using instances from the library keeps the file size of your movie smaller than copying and pasting. Smaller movies load faster in a browser.

Draw the Nose

16. Insert a new layer and name it **Nose**.
17. Select frame **1** in the Nose layer.
18. Select the **Line** tool and draw two lines that form an angle to represent a nose.
19. To adjust the angle after you've drawn it, use the Subselection tool (white arrow) to drag one end of the line. (You might try dragging one end of a line with the Selection tool to see the difference between the two tools.)

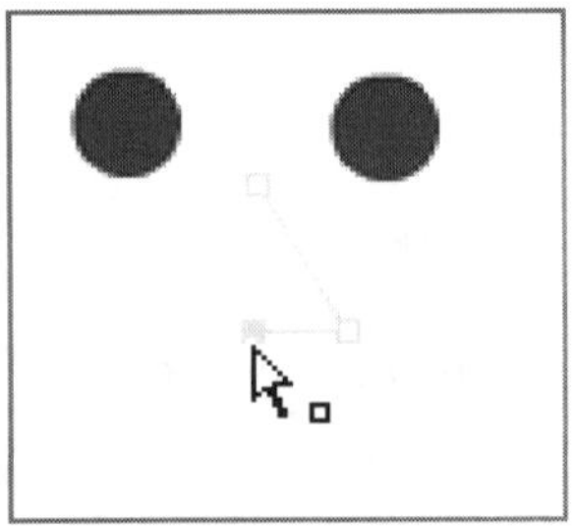

Add Frames to Make a Three-second Movie

A Flash movie typically plays 12 frames per second. To keep the nose on the Stage for 3 seconds, for example, you need to insert frames in the nose layer up to frame 36.

20. Select frame **36** in the Nose layer and choose **Insert > Timeline > Frame**.

    Flash inserts frames through frame 36. Observe that the playhead (the red rectangle at the top of the Timeline) is on frame 36 and that the nose is visible, but the eyes have disappeared. At the bottom of the Timeline, you can see that this movie is currently 36 frames, is set to play at 12 frames per second, and will play for 2.9 seconds.

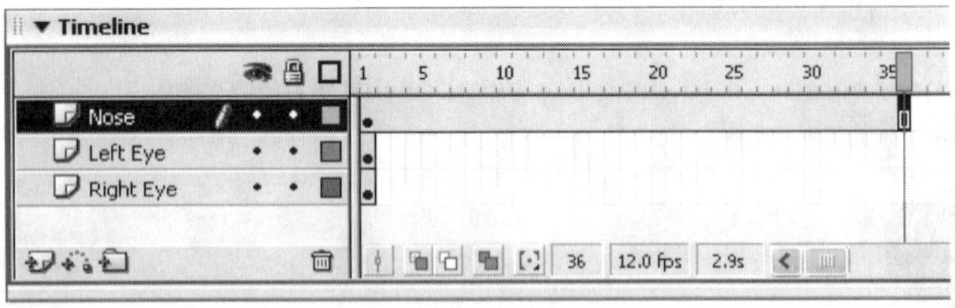

    Note: The keyboard shortcut for inserting a frame is **F5**.

21. Drag the playhead to various frames.

    The nose remains visible in frames 1 through 36, but the eyes appear only in frame 1.

22. To see your movie, drag the playhead to frame 1, then choose **Control > Play**.

    At this point, not much is happening beyond frame 1.

Draw the Mouth

23. Insert a new layer and name it **Mouth**.
24. Select frame **1** of the Mouth layer.
25. Draw a mouth in frame 1:
    - Use the **Line** tool to draw a straight line.

    - Select the **Selection** tool and click on the Stage away from the line to deselect it.

    - Move the pointer toward the middle of the line. When a curve appears next to the pointer, drag the middle of the line downward to create a smile.

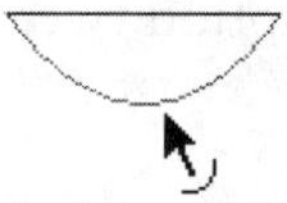

    - When you release the mouse button, only the smile remains.

Animate the Facial Features

Use Motion Tweens to Animate the Eyes

Because you created the eyes using a graphic symbol, you can animate them using a motion tween. To create the motion tween you need a start keyframe and an end keyframe containing the same symbol. You can then use a motion tween to fill the frames between the keyframes.

1. In the Right Eye layer, select frame **36** and choose **Insert > Timeline > Keyframe**. This will be the end keyframe.

   A keyframe signals Macromedia Flash that some animation action begins or ends at that frame.
2. In the Right Eye layer, select frame **36** and drag the right eye a short distance.
3. Select any frame between frames 1 and 36 in the Right Eye layer.
4. In the Property inspector, choose **Motion** from the **Tween** menu to create a motion tween.

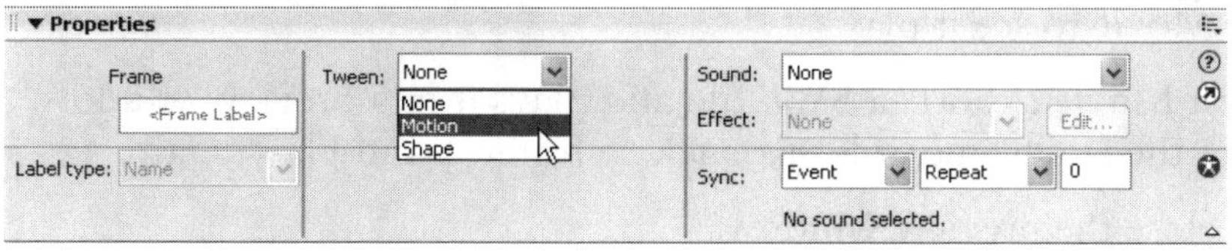

Note: You can also choose **Insert > Timeline > Create Motion Tween** or right-click (Windows) a frame between frames 1 and 36, and then choose **Create Motion Tween** from the context menu.

Notice the frames containing the motion tween are now light blue and contain a solid arrow running from the start frame to the end frame.

5. Position the playhead on frame 1 and choose **Control > Play** to play your movie and see the effect of the motion tween.

   The right eye gradually moves from its original position in frame 1 to the new position in frame 36. Notice that only the right eye moves.

   Note: If you want to change the motion, move only the symbol in keyframe 36.

6. Select frame **36** in the Left Eye layer and insert a keyframe.
7. Move the left eye the same distance as the right eye, and then create a motion tween between the first and last frames in the Left Eye layer.

Use a Shape Tween to Animate the Mouth

Because you created the mouth using one of the drawing tools (the Line tool) and have not converted the mouth to a symbol; it is still a shape. You can use a shape tween to animate the mouth.

8. Select frame **36** in the Mouth layer and insert a keyframe.

   Note: You can also right-click in frame **36** and choose **Insert Keyframe**.

9. With the **Selection** tool, click on the Stage away from the mouth line to deselect it. Then drag the mouth line into a bigger smile.
10. To create a shape tween between the first and last frames in the Mouth layer, click a frame between frames 1 and 36, and choose **Shape** from the **Tween** menu in the Property inspector.

    Notice the frames containing the shape tween are now light green and contain a solid arrow running from the start frame to the end frame.

11. Choose **File > Save.**

    This opens the Save As dialog box.

12. Using the Save in (Windows) or Where (Macintosh) drop-down menu, navigate to the drive and directory where you want to save the document. Name the document **Animated Face**, and choose **Save**.
13. Choose **Control > Test Movie** to see it play.

    Choosing **Control > Test Movie** exports a SWF file and plays it in a preview window. When the movie reaches the last frame, it loops back to frame 1 and plays again.

14. Choose **File > Close** to close the preview window.
15. Create any additional animated facial features as you choose.

Add User Control

In Flash, you can use ActionScript to enable the viewer to control a movie. You use *frame actions* to tell the movie what to do when it reaches a specific frame. You use *object actions* to associate the control with an object such as a button symbol. Object actions, such as button actions, let you give your visitors more control over your movie.

For example:

- You can attach a *stop* action to the first frame of your movie so the movie will not play past frame 1 until the viewer makes that happen.
- You can add a Start button in the first frame of your movie and attach a *goto* action so the movie will resume playing when the viewer clicks the Start button.
- When the viewer clicks the Start button, you can replace it with a Stop button. If you attach a *stop* action to the Stop button, the movie will stop when the viewer clicks the button.

Attach a *stop* Action to the First Frame

1. Select the top layer in the Timeline and insert a new layer.

   The new layer is inserted at the top of the list.

   Note: A new layer is always inserted above the currently selected layer. To change the order of layers in the Timeline, select a layer and drag it to the desired position in the list.
2. Name the new layer **Actions.**
3. Select the first frame of the Actions layer. This is where you will place the *stop* action telling the movie to stop and not begin playing automatically.
4. Choose **Window > Development Panels > Actions.**

   The Actions Panel opens. Notice the panel title bar reads Actions – Frame. This is because you are applying an action to a frame, not an object.

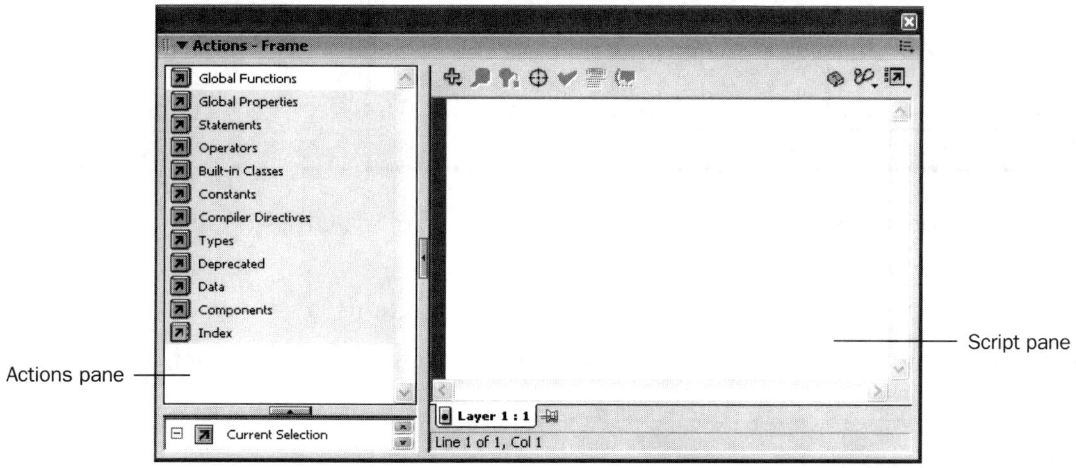

5. In the Actions pane, click the **Global Functions** category to display subcategories of actions.

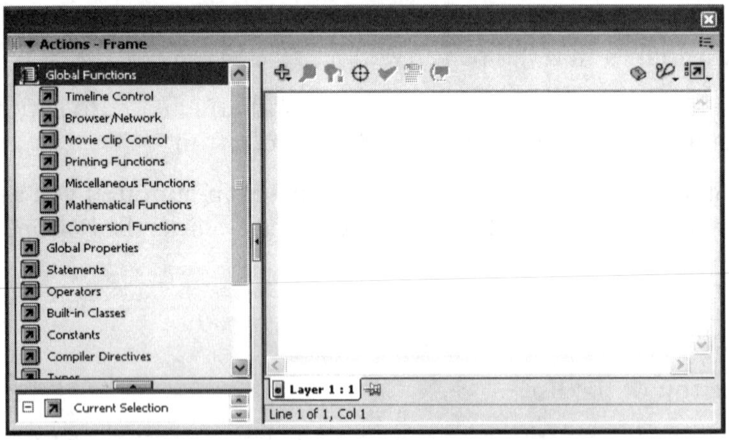

6. Click the **Timeline Control** category to expand it.

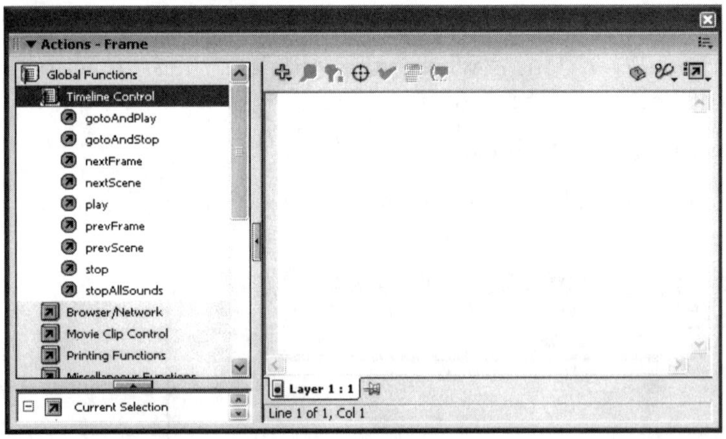

7. Select the **stop** action. To attach the *stop* action to frame 1, either double-click the **stop** icon or drag it to the Script pane.

8. Close the Actions panel and look in frame 1 of the Actions layer.

   The frame contains a small letter *a* indicating this frame contains an action.

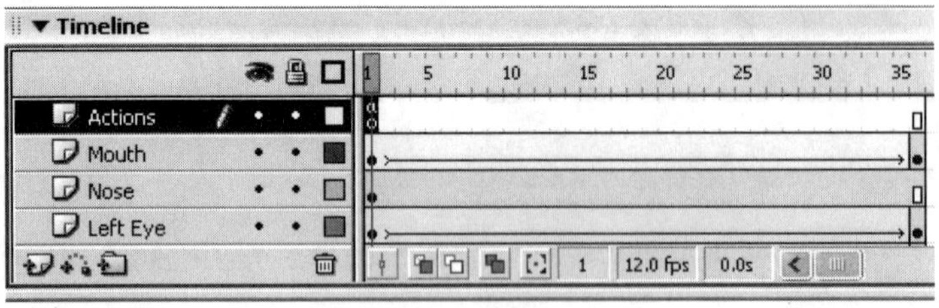

Create a Start Button

Now that you've placed a *stop* action in frame 1, you need to create an object action giving the user the ability to start the movie. The object action needs to be associated with an object, so first create a Start button.

9. Insert a new layer and name it **Buttons**.

10. Select frame **1** in the Buttons layer, and choose **Insert > New Symbol**.

    The Create New Symbol dialog box opens.

11. Name the symbol **Start**, select **Button** for the Behavior, and click **OK**.

Flash switches to symbol-editing mode, with a new blank Stage for your button symbol, listed with the name of your button in the information bar above the Timeline.

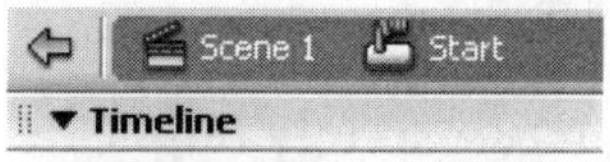

The Timeline displays four frames for the four states of a button.

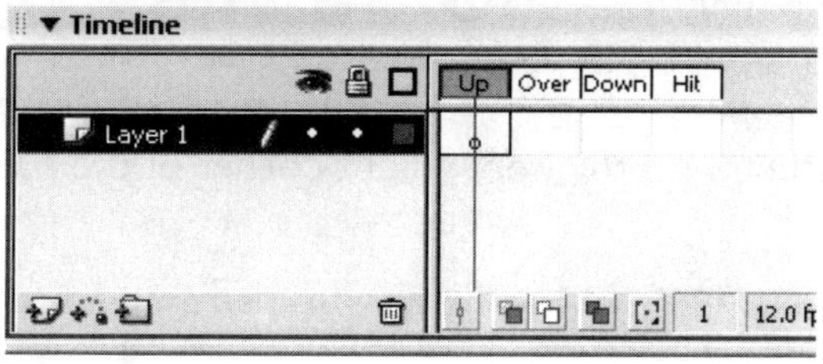

Each frame (also called a button *state*) has a specific function:

- The *Up* state represents the button's appearance when the pointer is *not* over the button.
- The *Over* state represents the button's appearance when the pointer is over the button.
- The *Down* state represents the button's appearance as it is clicked.
- The *Hit* state defines the target area that responds to a mouse click. This area is not visible when the movie plays.

12. Select the **Up** frame.

13. Use the **Rectangle** tool to draw a rectangular button on the Stage. Use the Property inspector to set stroke and fill colors for the Up state of the button.

14. Insert a keyframe in the Over, Down, and Hit frames.

    By inserting keyframes, you automatically copy the rectangle to the other states of the button.

    Note: Flash automatically inserts a keyframe in the Up frame.

15. Select the **Over** frame. Using the **Selection** tool, double-click the button on the Stage to select it, and change the stroke or fill color for the Over state in the Property inspector.

16. Select the **Down** frame. Using the **Selection** tool, double-click the button on the Stage and change the stroke or fill color for the Down state.

17. Select the **Hit** frame. Use the **Rectangle** tool to draw a rectangular target area that will respond to a mouse click.

Note: It doesn't matter what colors you use for the Hit area, because this rectangle is not visible to viewers of your movie. If you skip this step, Flash will automatically define the target area to be the same as the button shape.

18. Insert a layer and name it **Text**.
19. Select the **Up** frame in the Text layer and use the **Text** tool to key **Start**. Use the Property inspector to change the font, size, and color of the text. Center the text within the rectangle shape.
20. To exit symbol-editing mode and return to editing the movie, click **Scene 1** in the information bar at the top of the Stage or choose **Edit > Edit Document**.

    Your Start button does not appear on the Stage yet, but it is stored in the library.

Create a Stop Button

You could repeat the steps you used to create the Start button, or you can simply duplicate and then modify the Start button.

21. Choose **Window > Library** to open the Library panel, if necessary.
22. Select the **Start** button symbol in the library.
23. Select **Duplicate** from the Library panel Options menu (in the upper right corner of the panel).

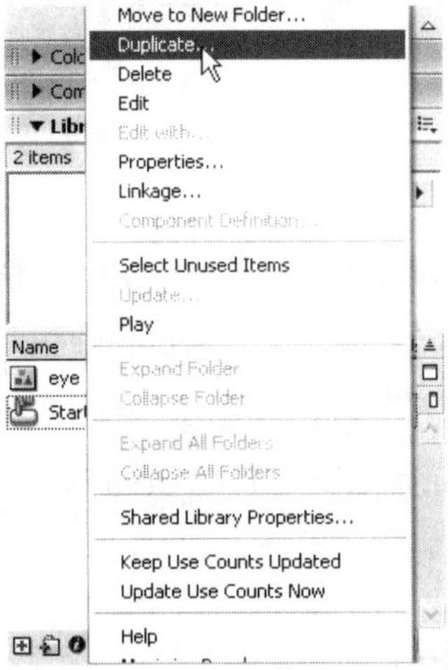

The Duplicate Symbol dialog box opens.

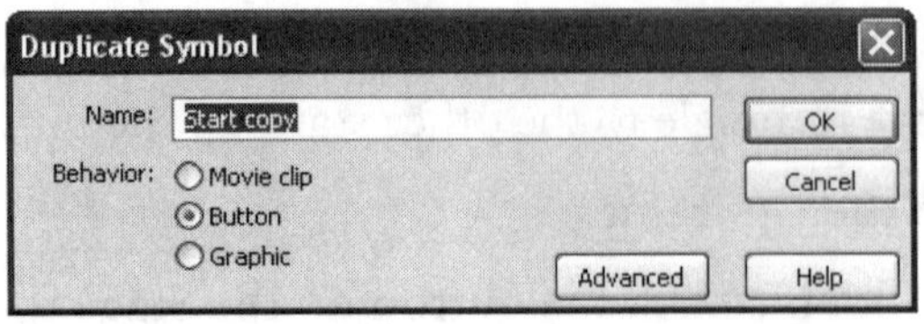

24. The Button Behavior is already selected. Name the new symbol **Stop** and click **OK**.

25. In the Library panel, double-click the icon for the **Stop** symbol to edit the symbol.

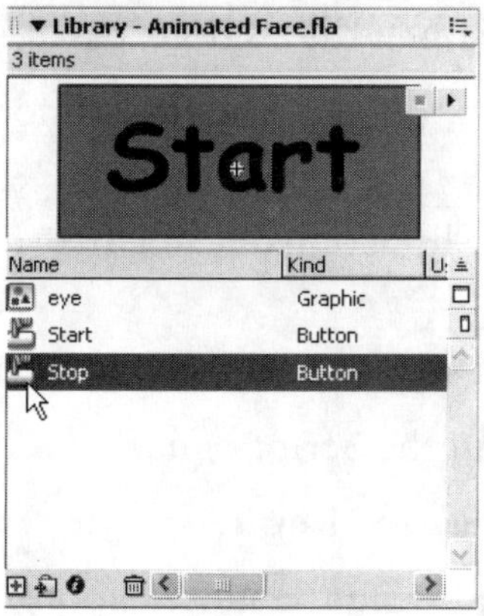

26. Select frame **1** of the text layer, and use the **Text** tool to edit the text to read **Stop**.
27. Click **Scene 1** or choose **Edit > Edit document** to exit symbol-editing mode.

Place the Buttons on the Stage

28. Select frame **1** in the Buttons layer.
29. Choose **Window > Library** to open the library, if necessary.
30. Drag the **Start** button from the library onto the Stage.
31. Select frame **2** in the Buttons layer and insert a keyframe.
32. Delete the **Start** button from frame 2.
33. Drag the **Stop** button onto the Stage.
34. Click the **Onion Skin Outlines** button at the bottom of the Stage.

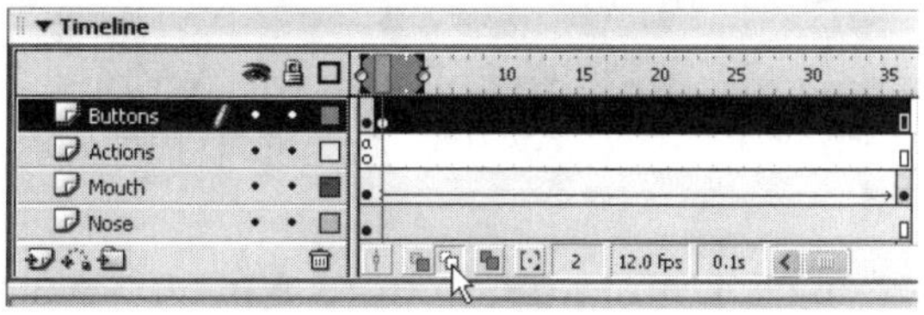

With onion skinning turned on you can view a range of frames. This will help you align the Start and Stop buttons.

35. Move the **Start** and **Stop** buttons so both of them are in the same position on the Stage.

Note: To fine-tune the position of the buttons, select a button and use the up, down, left, and right arrow keys.

36. Turn off onion skinning.

Add Button Actions

37. Select frame **1** in the Buttons layer, select the **Start** button, and open the Actions panel.

    Note: Be sure to select the **Start** button, or your action will be applied to the frame, not the button.

38. In the Actions pane, expand the **Global Functions** and **Movie Clip Control** categories and double-click **on**, located in the Movie Clip Control category.
39. Double-click **release** from the list of events.
40. Click to place the insertion point after the open curly bracket in the Script pane.
41. Double-click **gotoAndPlay**, located in the Timeline Control category. Key **2**.

    These actions tell the Start button to go to frame 2 and begin playing the movie upon release of the mouse button when the Start button is clicked.

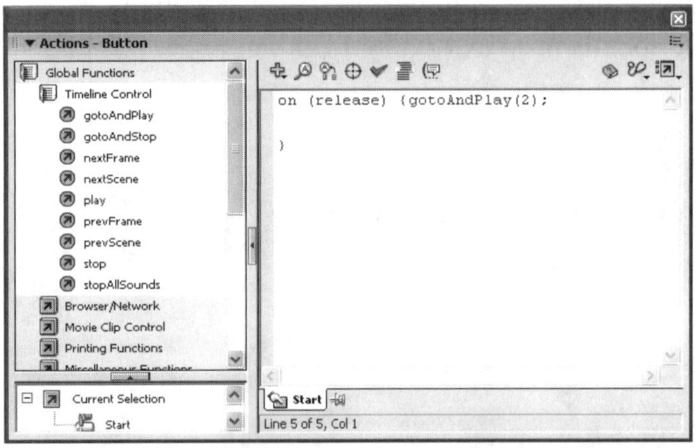

42. Select frame **2** in the Buttons layer and select the **Stop** button.

    Note: You may need to collapse the Actions panel to do this. To collapse the Actions panel, click the down-pointing arrow in the title bar. Be sure to select the Stop button to add actions to the button, not the frame.

43. Expand the Actions panel, if necessary, and double-click **on** in the Actions pane (Movie Clip Control).
44. Double-click **Release** in the Script pane.
45. Click to place the insertion point after the open curly bracket in the Script pane.
46. Double-click **gotoAndStop**, in the Actions pane (Timeline Control). Key **1**.

    This action will stop the animation and redisplay the Start button in frame **1**.

    Next, make the movie loop through frames 2–36 until the viewer clicks Stop. You can do this using a Frame action.

47. Insert a keyframe in frame 36 of the Actions layer.
48. Double-click **gotoAndPlay** in the Action pane. Key **2**.
49. Close the Actions panel, save your movie, and choose **Control > Test Movie** to test it.
50. Choose **File > Close** to close the preview window.

Add Sound

1. Insert a new layer below the Actions layer and name it **Sound.**
2. Choose **File > Import > Import to Library**.

   The Import to Library dialog box opens.
3. Locate and select a sound file saved on your computer. Click **Open** (Windows) or **Import to Library** (Macintosh).

   The sound is added to the library.

   Note: You can download free music loops and sound effect clips at *www.flashkit.com*, for example.
4. Select frame **2** in the Sound layer and insert a keyframe.
5. Open the library and drag the sound file from the library onto the Stage.

   Flash inserts the sound in the Sound layer, starting in frame 2.
6. Select frame **2** in the Sound layer. In the Property inspector, select **Loop** from the second Sync menu.

   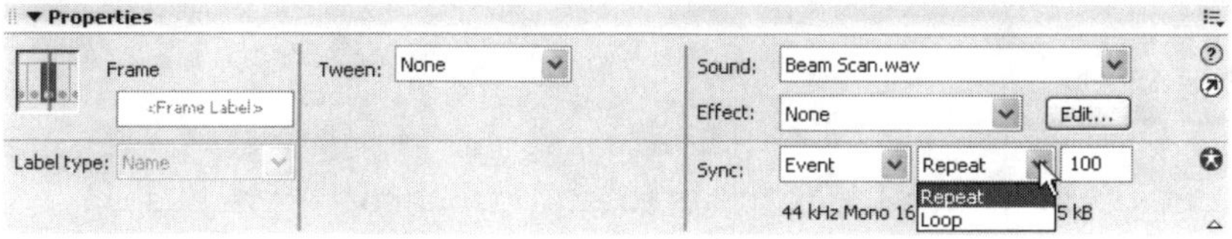

7. To stop the sound when the viewer clicks the Stop button:
   - Select frame **1** in the Actions layer.
   - Choose **Window > Development Panels > Actions.**
   - Double-click **stopAllSounds** in the Timeline Control category of the Actions pane.
   - Close the Actions panel.
   - Save the movie and test it. Close the preview window.

Publish Your Movie

When you're ready to deliver your movie to an audience, you can publish the Flash document (FLA file) for playback. The Publish command creates the Flash SWF file (playable with the Flash Player) and an HTML document that inserts your Flash movie in a browser window. For viewers who do not have the Flash Player installed, you can choose to publish the FLA file in alternative file formats—GIF, JPEG, PNG, or QuickTime—with the HTML needed to display them in a browser window.

1. Choose **File > Publish Settings** to open the Publish Settings dialog box.

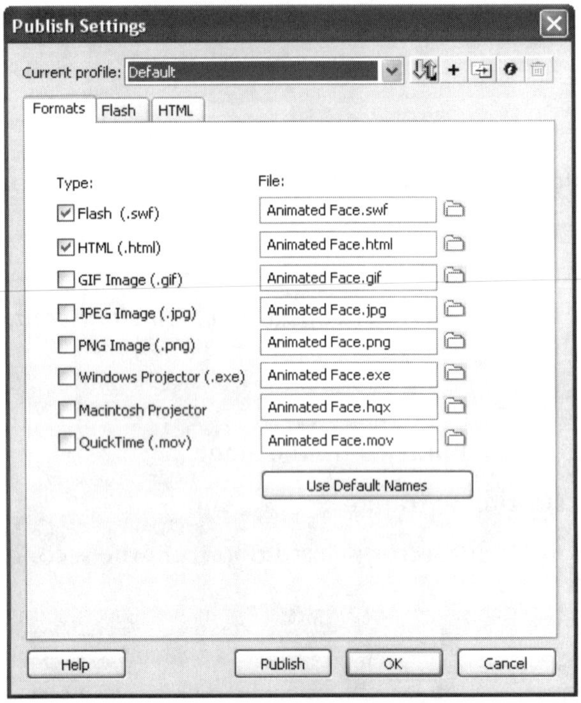

2. Use the **Formats** tab to determine which file formats to output when you publish.
3. Use the **Flash** tab to determine which Flash player you are publishing to. If you think your audience might not have the latest player, you might want to select an older player.

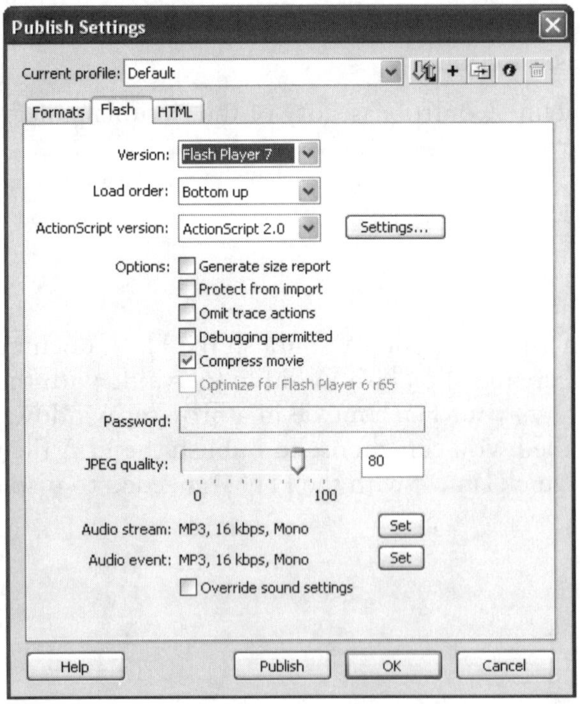

- Select **Generate size report** to see a detailed report of size for each asset in your movie.
- Select **Protect from import** to prevent anyone from importing your SWF file back into Flash and converting it back to an FLA file.
- Select **Compress movie** to reduce the file size of the exported movie.

4. Use the **HTML** tab to control settings for the HTML file.

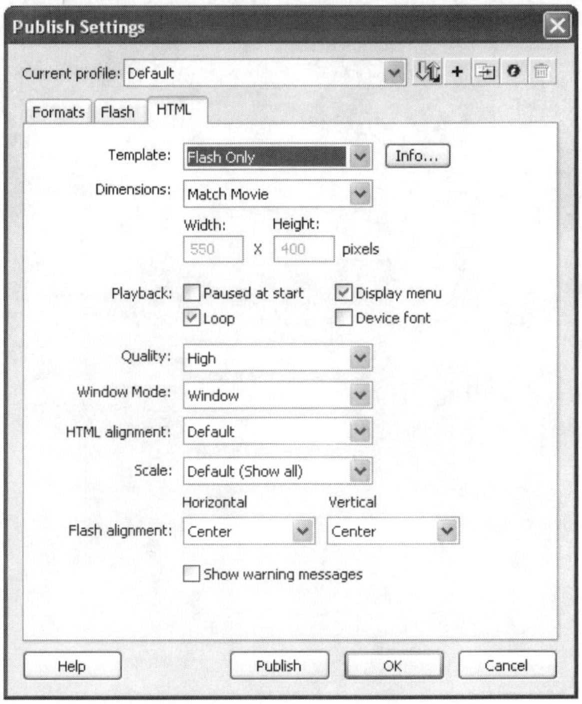

5. To publish your movie, click the **Publish** button. Click OK or Cancel to close the Publish Settings dialog box.

SYMBOLS, INSTANCES, AND THE LIBRARY

Symbols and Instances

A *symbol* is a graphic, button, or movie clip that you create once in Macromedia Flash MX 2004 and can use any number of times throughout your movie. Any symbol you create is automatically placed in a storage area called the *library* for the current document.

An *instance* is a copy of a symbol located on the Stage. An instance can be different from its symbol in color, size, and function. To create an instance of a symbol, drag the symbol from the library onto the Stage. Once you have created an instance you can use the Color options in the Property inspector to change its brightness, tint, Alpha, or RGB color settings.

Editing the symbol automatically updates all of its instances, but applying effects to an instance of a symbol updates only that instance.

One advantage of using symbols in your document is that it saves space and reduces the download time of your finished movie, since Flash does not have to save duplicate information for each instance. For example, if you create an animated wheel symbol, you can place several instances of the symbol in your document. The result is a file that is much smaller than if you had created each wheel separately.

When you create a new drawing in Flash, you're creating a shape, not a symbol. You can convert any shape to a symbol by selecting it and choosing **Modify > Convert to Symbol**.

Libraries

The library is a container where Flash stores and organizes symbols, sounds, bitmap graphics, video, and other elements. The library is attached to the document that you're working on. If you share your document with someone else, and they open it on their computer, they will see the same library objects. As your documents become more complex, you'll find it helpful to use folders to sort your symbols into related groups within the library.

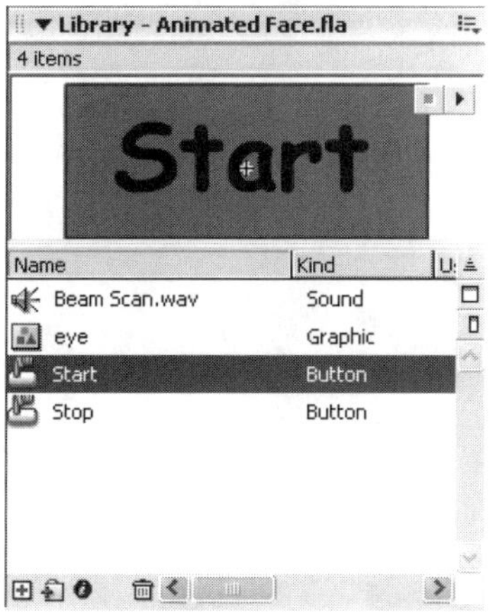

How to Create Motion and Shape Tweens

Overview of Tweening

Macromedia Flash MX 2004 provides two methods for creating an animation sequence: tweened animation and frame-by-frame animation. Frame-by-frame animation involves a series of keyframes with a different image in every frame. While this can be useful for complex animations, Flash is capable of automatically creating animation by tweening images. The word *tween* comes from an animation technique in which an artist draws the starting point of a motion—such as a dog wagging its tail to the left—and the stopping point of the motion—a wag to the right. Then the artist has to draw all the stages ***in between*** to make the tail appear to move. To tween an element on the Stage in Flash, you set the starting and ending frames for the element, create a tween between those frames, and Flash automatically fills in the frames between. There are two types of tweens in Flash: motion tweening and shape tweening.

Motion Tweening

You can use motion tweening to animate any of the following elements:

- A symbol (graphic, button, or movie clip)
- Grouped object (a collection of drawn shapes that have been grouped)
- A text block

When using a motion tween to animate a symbol, you can change the following properties:

- Color (tint)
- Alpha (fade or transparency)
- Position
- Size

For example, you can use a motion tween to create the effect of text floating across the Stage, but if you want the text to slowly fade as it moves across the Stage, you must first convert the text block to a symbol. You can then use the Color Alpha setting in the Property inspector to create the fade.

1. Start Flash and open a new blank document.
2. Draw a shape on the Stage or import an image by choosing **File > Import**.

   Notice that the shape appears in keyframe 1 of Layer 1.
3. If the object is a drawn object, select the **Selection** tool and double-click the object to select it.

   If the object is an imported image, select the **Selection** tool and just click the object to select it.
4. Choose **Modify > Convert to Symbol**.

   The Convert to Symbol dialog box opens.

   Note: You cannot apply motion tweens to shapes. To apply a motion tween, you must first convert the shape to a symbol.

5. Enter a new name for the symbol in the Name text box, select **Graphic** as the behavior, and click **OK**.
6. Select frame **10**.
7. Choose **Insert > Timeline > Keyframe**. (This will make the motion tween last for 10 frames.)

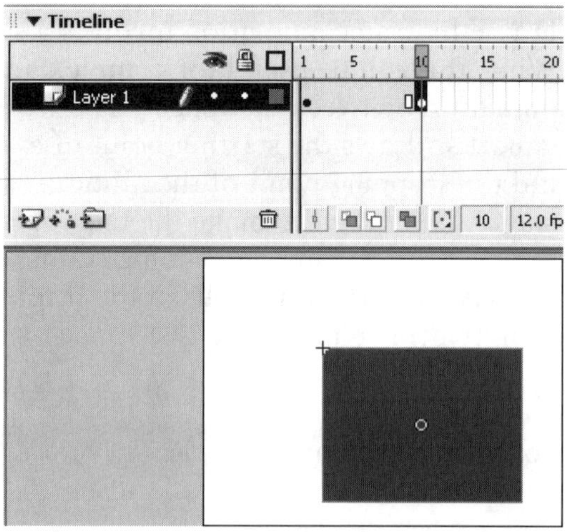

Notice that when you insert a keyframe, Flash fills the area between the last frame (in the current layer) and the new keyframe with the same content. Frames 1 through 10 all contain the new symbol.

8. Make sure frame 10 is selected. This is the end frame for the motion tween. Select the instance of the symbol in frame 10, then make one or more of the following changes:

Color change: In the Property inspector, choose **Tint** from the **Color** pop-up menu. Choose **100%** for the Tint Amount and change the color in the color box.

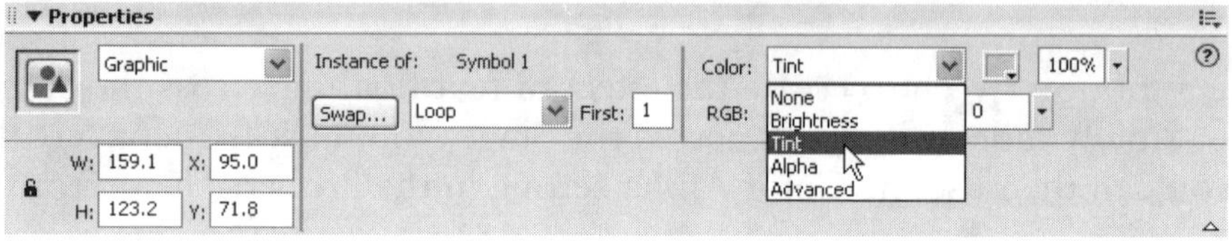

Fading: In the Property inspector, choose **Alpha** from the **Color** pop-up menu. Reduce the percentage of the Alpha amount for more transparency. For example, an Alpha value of 0% makes the object disappear.

Position: Use the **Selection** tool to move the object to a different position on the Stage.

Size: Select the object, then choose **Modify > Transform > Free Transform**. Drag the corners of the object to increase size, decrease size, or rotate the object.

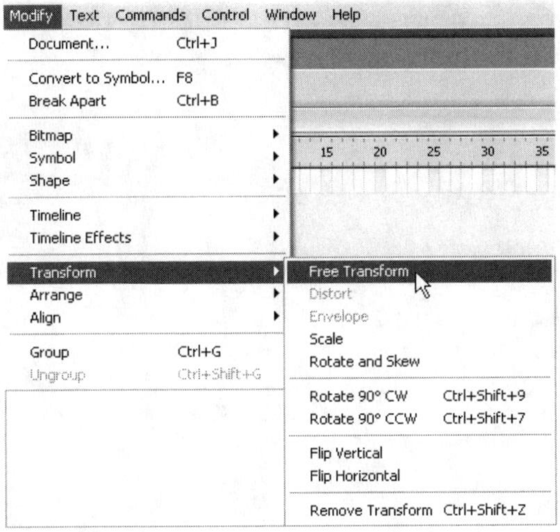

9. Select frame **1** in the Timeline.
10. In the Property inspector, click the arrow beside the **Tween** box and choose **Motion**.

    The tween is represented by a solid arrow on a blue background running from the start keyframe to the end keyframe.
11. In the Property inspector, adjust one or more properties of the Motion tween:

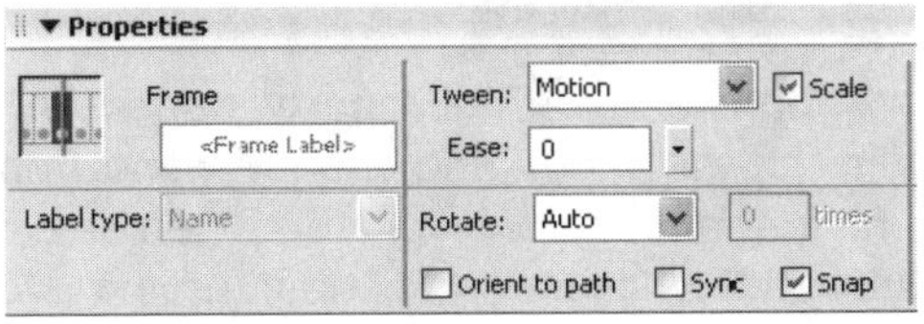

Ease: Controls how fast the object starts or ends the motion tween. For example, a high number for Ease makes an object begin tweening quickly but end tweening slowly.

Rotate: Rotates the object clockwise or counterclockwise a designated number of times.

Scale: Keeps the proportions of the object equal when the tween resizes the object.

Orient to path: If you have added a guide layer, the object is linked to the path drawn on the guide layer.

Sync: Starts and stops the tweening of all objects on the Stage at the same time.

Snap: Keeps the tweened object aligned to an invisible grid to control spacing.

12. Choose **Control > Test Movie** to test the movie.
13. Choose **File > Close** to close the preview window.
14. To see all phases of the tween at the same time, click the **Onion Skin Outlines** button at the bottom of the Timeline.

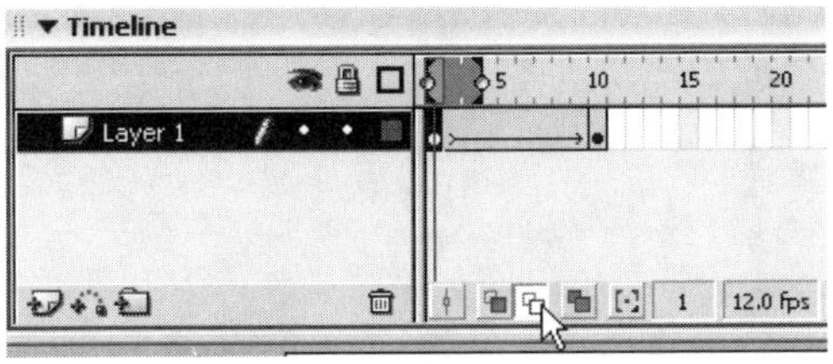

15. Drag the onion skinning frame handles (they appear as brackets with circles on them at the top of the Timeline) to span the frames in which the object appears.

    The steps of the tween are all visible on the Stage.

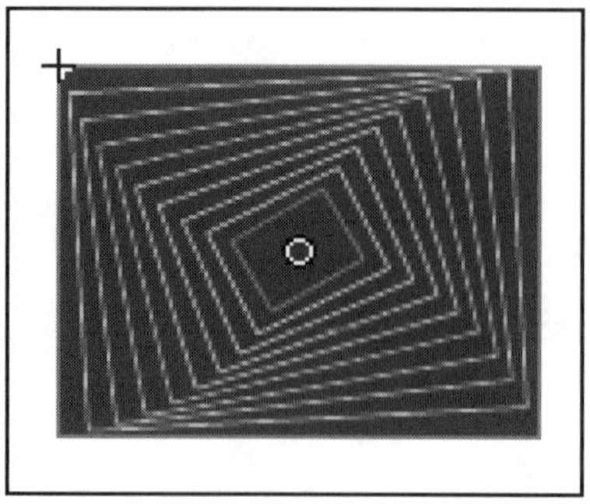

16. Turn off onion skinning.
17. Save the movie.

Common Motion Tween Problems and Solutions

The tween you created was indicated in the Timeline by a solid arrow on a blue background. If the tween is not working, the arrow is dashed. There are several ways to fix a broken motion tween.

Problem	Solution
No keyframe at beginning or end of motion tween.	Remove the motion tween in the Property inspector (select any frame of the tween and choose **None** from the **Tween** menu in the Property inspector). Then select the beginning or ending frame and choose **Insert > Timeline > Keyframe**. Add the motion tween again.
Objects in keyframes aren't the same.	Remove the motion tween in the Property inspector. Click the second keyframe (farther down the Timeline). Choose **Modify > Timeline > Clear Keyframe**. Make sure the first keyframe has the correct objects in it. Insert the second keyframe again and add the motion tween.
The two keyframes contain objects that aren't instances of symbols, grouped objects, or a text block.	Remove the motion tween and clear the second keyframe. If necessary, convert objects in the first keyframe to symbols or remove them from the Stage. Add the second keyframe again and re-create the motion tween.
More than one symbol is in the frame. Motion tweening will not occur on layers with more than one group or symbol.	Remove the motion tween and place each symbol on a separate layer, then create separate motion tweens for each symbol, on separate layers.

Shape Tweening

In Flash, a shape is a vector-based object or series of objects, such as anything you draw with the drawing tools. In order for a shape to be animated by shape tweening, it cannot be a grouped object, a bitmap, or a symbol. You can apply shape tweening to text, but you must first convert the text to a shape by breaking it apart.

For example, you could create a shape tween that turns the word "elephant" into an image of an elephant.

You can use a shape tween to:

- Tween the shape of an object (morph from one shape to another)
- Tween the color of an object (including a color with transparency)
- Tween the position of an object on the Stage (much like a motion tween, but between shapes rather than symbols)
- Tween text that has been broken apart
- Tween a bitmap that has been broken apart (converted to a shape)

You cannot use a shape tween to:

- Tween grouped objects
- Tween symbols
- Tween text that has not been broken apart
- Tween bitmaps that have not been broken apart

Note: Shape tweens can be much more memory-intensive than motion tweens.

In a shape tween, you can change the following properties.

- Color (tint)
- Alpha (fade)
- Shape

To change the color or alpha of a shape, use the Color Mixer panel.

1. Start Flash and open a new blank document.

   Frame 1 in Layer 1 already contains a blank keyframe.

2. Begin by adding a shape to the Stage:

   Drawn objects: Choose a shape tool (Rectangle or Oval) and draw an object on the Stage.

   Text: Choose the **Text** tool and key a word or phrase on the Stage. Then select the text and choose **Modify > Break Apart**. This breaks the words into separate letters. With the letters still selected, choose **Modify > Break Apart** again to convert the letters into shapes.

   Outside images: Choose **File > Import > Import to Stage** to import an image to the Stage. If the image is a bitmap, you must break it apart. If the image is a grouped vector drawing, you must ungroup it completely. To break apart a bitmap, choose **Modify > Break Apart**. To ungroup an image, choose **Modify > Ungroup**.

   Note: You might need to choose **Modify > Break Apart** or **Modify > Ungroup** multiple times until the object becomes a shape, as indicated in the Property inspector.

3. Select frame **10**.

4. Choose **Insert > Timeline > Keyframe.** (This will make the tween last for 10 frames.)
5. Make sure frame 10 is still selected and make one or more of the following changes to your shape:

   Amorphous shape change: Click the Stage with the **Selection** tool to deselect the object. Bring the Arrow tool close to the object to grab an edge. Click and drag the edge to change the shape of the object.

   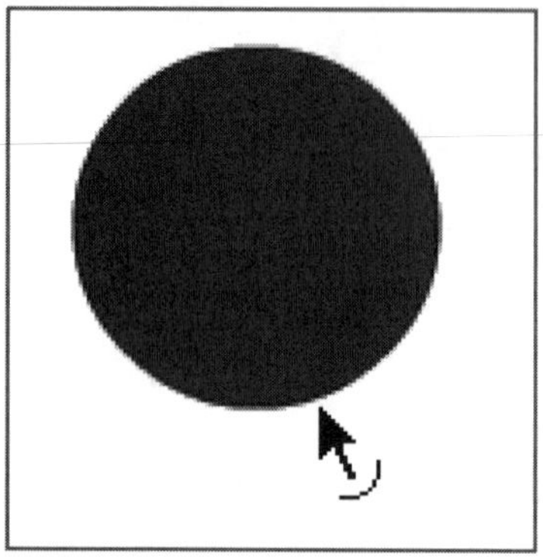

   Different shape: To morph between your original shape and a new shape, delete the object in keyframe 10 and draw a new object. Choose **Modify > Break Apart** if the drawn object is not a shape.

   Text: To morph between your original shape and text, delete the object in keyframe 10 and type text on the Stage. Choose **Modify > Break Apart** until the text block is a shape, as indicated in the Property inspector.

   Outside image: To morph between your original shape and a new image that you import, delete the object in keyframe 10 and choose **File > Import** to bring in an outside image. Choose **Modify > Break Apart** to make the object a shape, if it is not already.
6. Select frame **1** in the Timeline (in the current layer). This is the frame containing your start frame for the animation.
7. In the Property inspector, choose **Shape** from the **Tween** pop-up menu.

   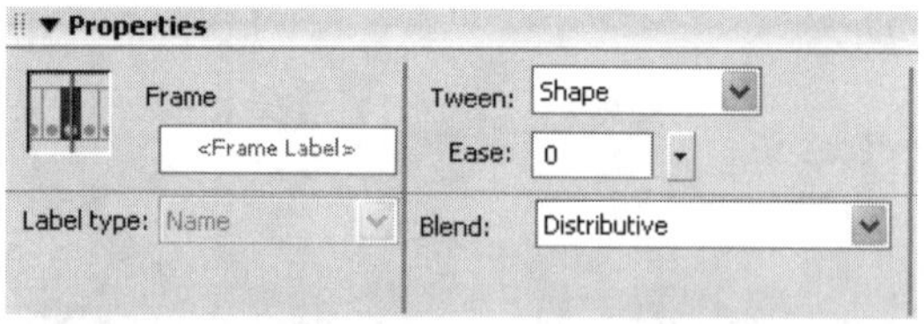

8. Adjust one or more properties of the Shape tween:

   Ease: Controls how fast the object starts or ends the shape tween. For example a high number for Ease makes an object begin tweening quickly, but end tweening slowly.

   Blend (Distributive): Creates an animation in which the intermediate shapes are smoother and more irregular.

   Blend (Angular): Creates an animation that preserves corners and straight lines in the intermediate shapes.
9. Choose **Control > Test Movie** to test the movie.
10. Choose **File > Close** to close the preview window.

11. To see all phases of the tween at the same time, click the **Onion Skin Outlines** button at the bottom of the Timeline.
12. Drag the frame handles (they appear as brackets with circles on them at the top of the Timeline) to span the first 10 frames of Layer 1.

    The steps of the tween are all visible on the Stage.
13. Save the movie.

Shape Tweens versus Motion Tweens

The following table is helpful in deciding which type of tween to choose when animating objects.

	Shape	Group	Symbol	Text Block	Broken-apart Text
Shape Tween	Yes	No	No	No	Yes
Motion Tween	No	Yes	Yes	Yes	No

How to Import Sound and Video

In Macromedia Flash MX 2004 you can import sound and video to integrate them into the Timeline. You can create media-rich content with very precise control.

Importing Sound

Sound can be used for many purposes in Flash. Some examples include soundtracks, narration, and sound effects that complement objects, such as rollover buttons.

You can import the following sound file formats into Flash:

- WAV (Windows only)
- AIFF (Macintosh only)
- MP3 (Windows or Macintosh)

If you have QuickTime 4 or later installed on your system, you can import these additional sound file formats:

- AIFF (Windows or Macintosh)
- Sound Designer II (Macintosh only)
- Sound Only QuickTime Movies (Windows or Macintosh)
- Sun AU (Windows or Macintosh)
- System 7 Sounds (Macintosh only)
- WAV (Windows or Macintosh)

When you import a sound file, it's placed in the library. Then you can drag an instance (copy) of the sound onto the Stage. Sound files must be tied to keyframes.

You can synchronize a sound to your movie in several ways (Sync Options):

- *Event:* An event sound plays when the playhead reaches the first keyframe containing the sound. It plays in its entirety, independently of the Timeline, even if the movie stops. If a different instance of the same sound is started, the sounds will overlap.
- *Start* is the same as Event, except that if the sound is already playing, no new instance of the sound will begin playing.
- *Stop* silences the specified sound.
- *Stream* forces the movie to keep pace with the sound. If Flash can't draw animation frames quickly enough, it skips frames. Unlike event sounds, stream sounds stop if the movie stops. Stream sounds can also produce a much smaller file size, although their quality tends to be poorer than event sounds.

Import a Sound

1. Start Flash and open your movie, or open a new blank document.

2. Insert a new layer.
3. Double-click the new layer name, and rename it **Sound**.
4. Choose **File > Import > Import to Library**.

   The Import dialog box opens.

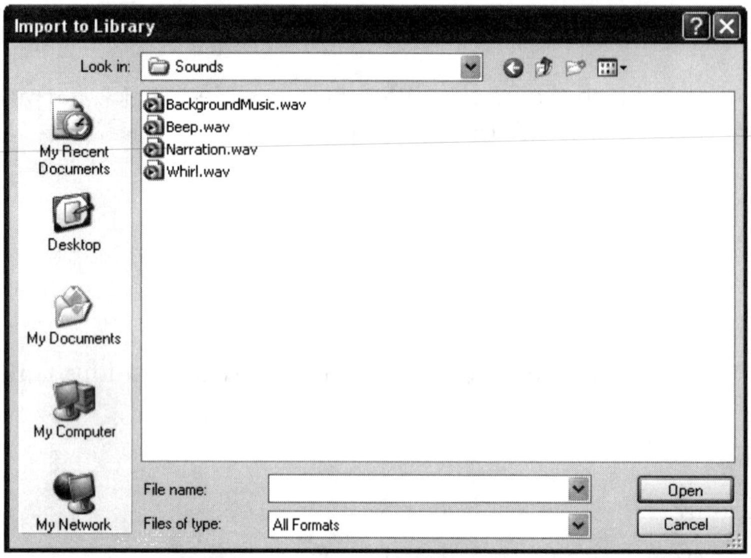

5. Locate a sound file, select it, and click **Open** (Windows) or **Import to Library** (Macintosh).

   Note: You can download free music loops and sound effect clips at *www.flashkit.com*, for example.

6. Select frame **1** in the Sound layer.
7. Choose **Window > Library**.

   The sound appears in the Library panel. To preview the sound, click the **Play** button in the preview (upper) pane of the Library panel.

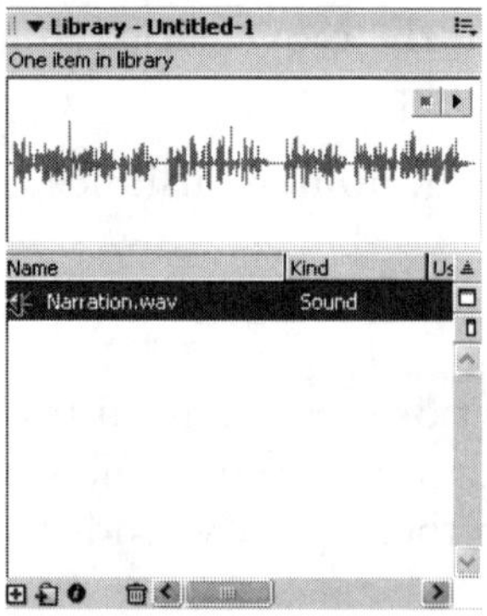

   Note: You must select the sound to see the waveform of the sound in the preview pane.

8. Drag the sound file from the library onto the Stage.

   Note: The Sound layer must contain enough frames to play the entire movie. For example, if your movie is set for 12 frames per second and your sound is 2 seconds long, the Sound layer must contain at least 24 frames. If you are adding sound to an existing movie, your movie might already be long enough to accommodate the sound.

9. If necessary, add frames to the Sound layer. To do this, click a frame on the Timeline for the Sound layer, such as frame 24 for a 2-second movie at 12 fps, and choose **Insert > Timeline > Frame.**

   The sound does not appear on the Stage, but does appear in the Timeline as a waveform.

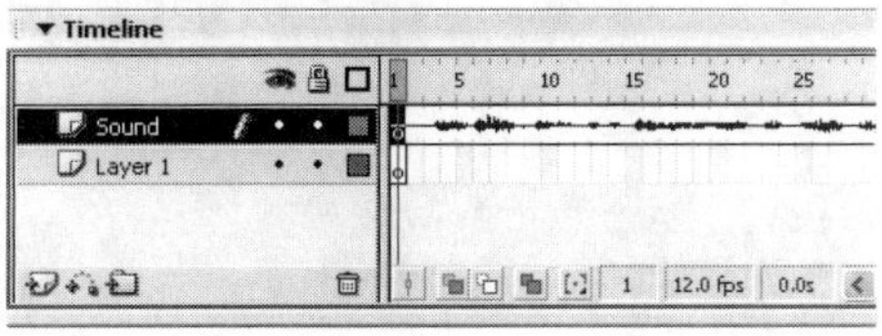

10. Select the first keyframe and adjust the settings for the sound in the Property inspector:

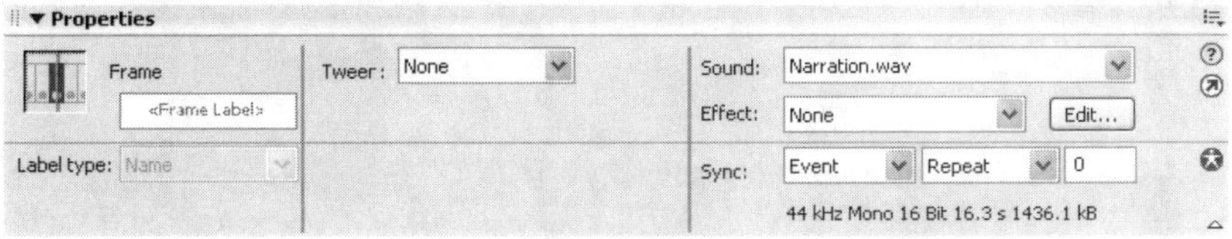

- *Effect:* Choose from previously created effects such as Fade In, Fade Out, keeping sound in only one channel (left or right) or fading sound from one channel to the other. Choosing Custom opens a sound-editing window for creating your own fading effects. In the sound-editing window, called the Edit Envelope, adjust the sound handles to control sound volume in each channel.

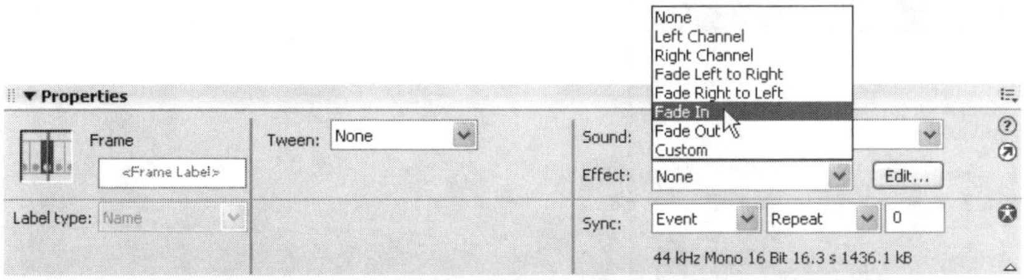

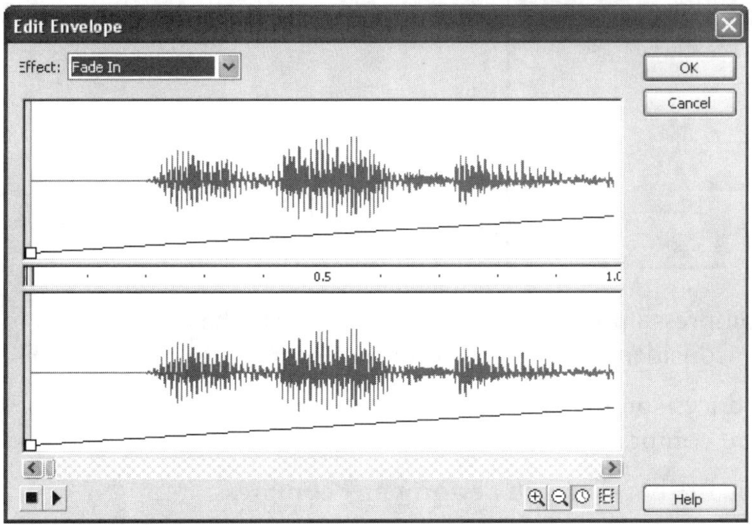

- *Sync:* Choose Event, Start, Stop, or Stream. You can also choose to have the sound repeat or loop.

Sound Compression

Sound files can drastically increase the file size of your movies. One way to control this is to set the compression for the sounds in Flash.

1. Open the **Library** panel, if necessary, and select the sound file.
2. Click the **Properties** button in the Library panel.

The Sound Properties dialog box opens.

3. Choose a compression option from the Compression menu and click **OK**.

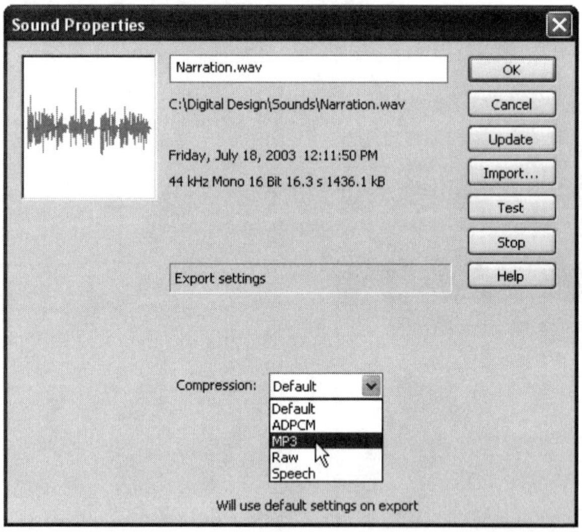

- *ADPCM:* This is the compression method from Flash 3. It sets the compression for 8-bit and 16-bit sound data. Consider using this if you need to open your movie in Flash 3.
- *MP3:* This method produces sounds that can be heard only by users with Flash 4 or higher, but it offers good compression and sound fidelity.
- *Raw:* This resamples the file but does not perform any compression.
- *Speech:* A good compression to use for speech sound files.

4. Save the movie.
5. Choose **Control > Test Movie**.

Importing Video

You import video straight into the Timeline and it plays when you play your movie.

You can import the following video formats if QuickTime 4 is installed (Windows and Macintosh):

- Audio Video Interleaved (.avi)
- Digital Video (.dv)
- Motion Picture Experts Group (.mpg or .mpeg)
- QuickTime Movie (.mov)

You can import the following file formats if DirectX 7 or higher is installed (Windows only):

- Audio Video Interleaved (.avi)
- Motion Picture Experts Group (.mpg or .mpeg)
- Windows Media File (.wmv, .asf)

Import a Video Clip

1. Choose **File > Import > Import to Library**, then locate a video file, select it, and click **Open** (Windows) or **Import to Library** (Macintosh).

   The Video Import Wizard opens.

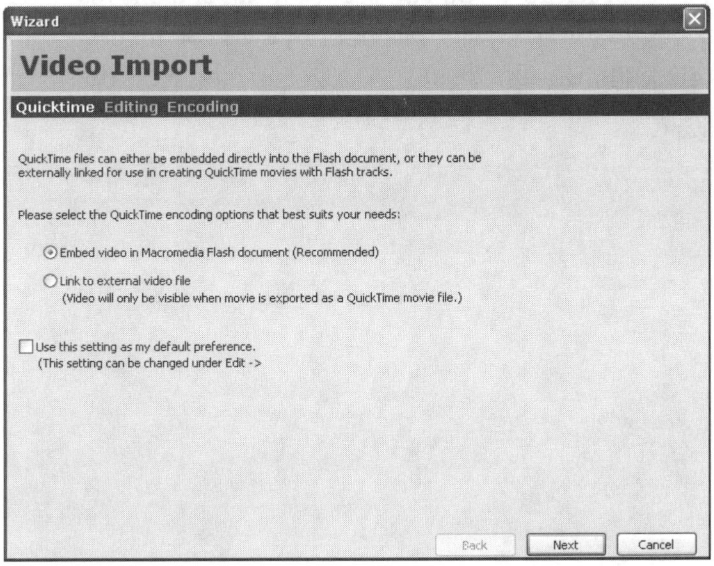

   The steps might differ depending on which video format you are importing.

2. Select the option to embed the video in Flash and click **Next**.

The second step of the Wizard appears. In this step you select a compression profile for the video depending on the estimated connection speed of your target audience.

Note: If you choose to import a .mov file, you may be asked if you would like to import the entire video or edit the video first. Choose to import the entire video.

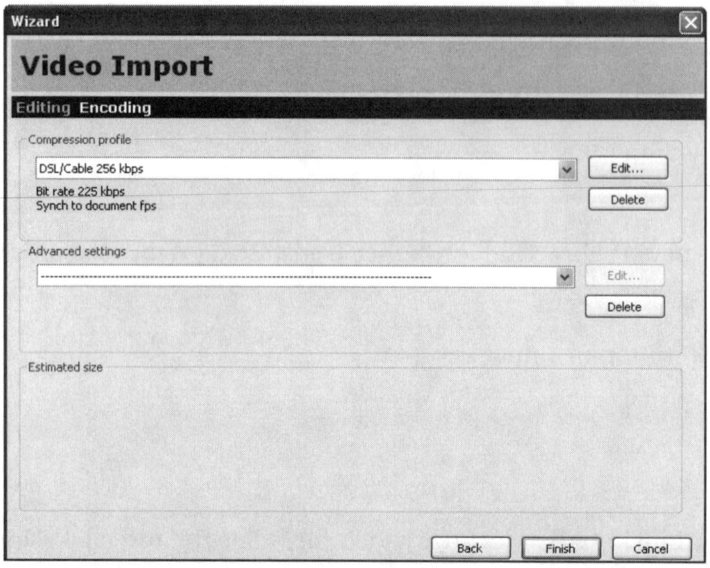

Note: Although embedding the video creates a larger SWF file, it allows you more design control over the appearance of the video because you can see it on the Stage. This saves time and usually improves the layout for the video in Flash.

3. Select a compression profile and click **Finish**.

   The video is imported to the Library.

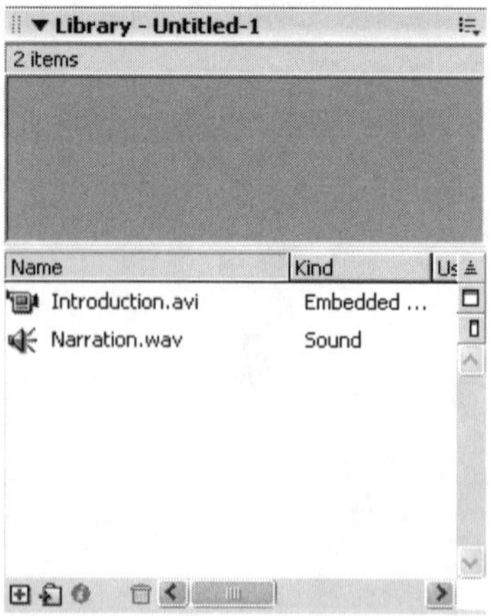

Note: If you import directly to the Stage, you will receive a message showing the number of frames that must be inserted in the timeline to accommodate the video. Click Yes to insert the correct number of frames for the video to play.

4. Save the movie.
5. Press **Enter** (Windows) or **Return** (Macintosh) to play the video.

How to Create a Button Symbol

Button Symbols

Buttons allow users to control parts of a movie. Use button symbols to create interactive buttons that respond to mouse clicks, rollovers, or other user interaction. Button symbols are four-frame interactive movie clips. The first three frames display the button's three possible states—Up, Over, and Down; the fourth frame, Hit, defines the active area of the button. The Timeline for a button doesn't play like other movies; it reacts to pointer movement and actions by jumping to and displaying the appropriate frame.

You can create the image that will represent your buttons in several ways. For example, you can use an existing graphic as the button, or you can create a shape using the drawing tools.

Create a Rollover Button

Create a new button symbol that contains two layers. One layer will contain a shape representing the background of the button. The second layer will include a text label for the button. You will change the background and text label in the Over and Down states of the button to create the rollover effect.

1. Start Flash MX 2004 and open a new blank document.
2. Choose **Insert > New Symbol.**

   The Create New Symbol dialog box opens.

   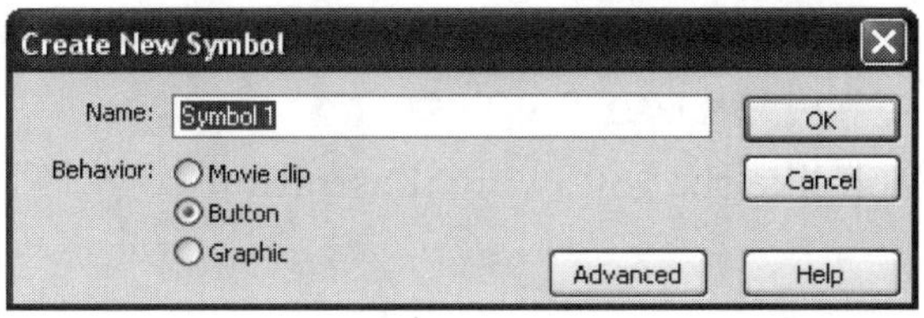

3. Select **Button** as the behavior type, name the button, and click **OK**.

   You are now in symbol-editing mode and viewing a separate Timeline for the button symbol. The Up frame contains a keyframe.

   Each frame in the Timeline of a button symbol has a specific function:

   - *Up* state represents the button whenever the pointer is not over the button.
   - *Over* state represents the button's appearance when the pointer is over it.
   - *Down* state represents the button's appearance as it is clicked.
   - *Hit* state defines the area that will respond to a mouse click. This area will be invisible in the movie.

4. Select the **Up** frame.
5. Use the Drawing tools to create a shape for your button. Use the Property inspector to set the fill and stroke colors for the Up state of the button.

6. Select the **Over** state and choose **Insert > Timeline > Keyframe** to add a keyframe.

   Adding this keyframe copies the button from the Up frame to the Over frame.

7. Select the **Over** keyframe and use the **Selection** tool to select the button.
8. Change the fill or stroke color of the button shape.

   When the user rolls the pointer over the button, the button will appear as you see it in the Over frame.

9. Insert keyframes in the Down and Hit frames.

   This copies the button from the Over frame to the Down and Hit frames.

10. Insert a new layer and name it **Text**.
11. Select the **Up** frame of the Text layer. This frame already contains a keyframe.
12. Use the **Text** tool to key text on the button shape.
13. Use the Property inspector to adjust the font, size, and color of the text so it fits nicely on your button shape.
14. Use the **Selection** tool or the up, down, left, and right arrow keys to position the text on the button shape.
15. Insert a keyframe in the Over frame of the Text layer.
16. Select the text and use the Property inspector to change some feature of the text in the Over frame, such as color.
17. Insert a keyframe in the Down frame. If you want the text to change appearance when the button is clicked, edit the appearance of the text in the Down frame.

    The Timeline for the button symbol should look like the following illustration.

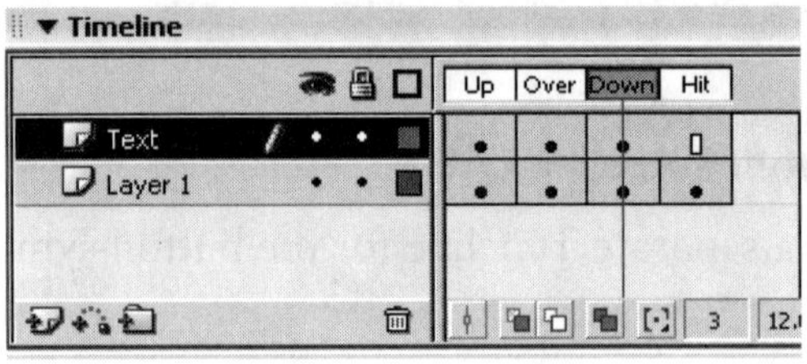

    Now you can insert an instance (copy) of the button symbol into the main Timeline of your movie.

18. Click **Scene 1** to exit symbol-editing mode and return to the main Timeline.
19. Choose **Window > Library** to open the Library panel.

The new button symbol appears in the Library panel.

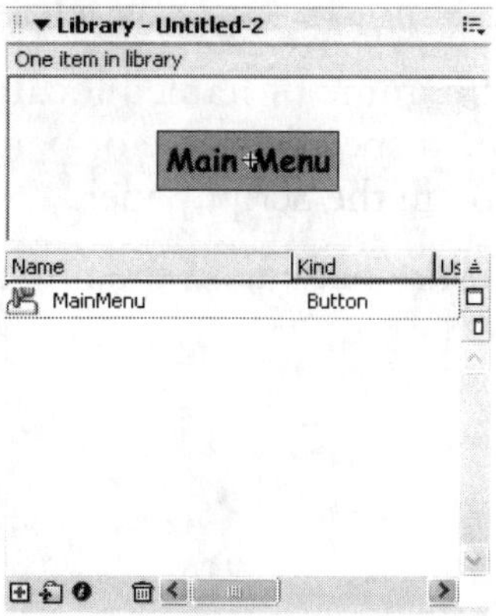

Note: You must select the symbol in the library to see the symbol in the preview pane.

20. Drag the button symbol from the library onto the Stage.
21. Choose **Control > Test Movie** to test the movie.

    When you roll over the button with the pointer, you see the changes you defined in the Over frames for the button. If you edited the Down state of the button, this will be visible when you click the button.

    Right now the button looks great, but it doesn't perform any action. You can remedy this by adding ActionScript to the button.

22. Close the preview window.

Add User Control with Actions

Buttons give users control over the movie. You can apply actions to your buttons that will stop the movie, stop sounds, restart the movie (after stopping it), or jump to different frames within the movie and begin playing. You add actions to any instance of the button symbol that you've placed in your movie.

1. Click the instance of the button to which you want to add an action.
2. Choose **Window > Development Panels > Actions** to open the Actions panel.
3. Click to expand the Actions and Movie Control categories.
4. Double-click an action to add it to the selected button symbol.

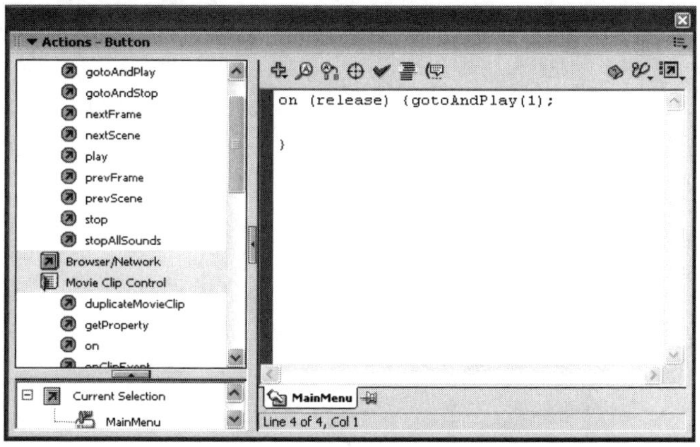

- *on:* Allows you to select an event on which the next action occurs. For example, you can select on *Release*, which will perform an action when the mouse button is released.
- *gotoAndPlay:* Enables users to go to and play from a specific frame or named location in the movie. You can also select an action to gotoAndStop on a specific frame or named location in the movie. You must also enter the desired location in the Script pane.
- *stopAllSounds:* Enables users to stop playing all sounds that are playing in the movie.

5. Close the Actions panel.
6. Save the movie.

ANALYZING MACROMEDIA FLASH ON THE WEB

This sample analysis of a Macromedia Flash Web site illustrates some techniques designers use to target a specific audience.

URL: *georgewashington.si.edu/*

Name of the site: *George Washington: A National Treasure*

What is the main type of audience the site is targeting? How does the site target this audience?

The main audience is teachers who might choose to use the information on this site for a unit on George Washington, history, culture, or art.

Identify the following Macromedia Flash techniques and explain what part of the site uses them:

- Motion tweens

  On the initial screen, the white and red bars that expand and contract are motion tweens, as is the white star that appears.

- Shape tweens

  The white star that turns into the profile of George Washington is possibly a shape tween.

- Movie clips

  The rotating star that appears when your pointer is over the words "Explore the Portrait" is a movie clip.

- Buttons

  After you enter the portrait and click "Explore the Portrait," the boxes at the top of the portrait, labeled Symbolic, Biographic, and Artistic, are all buttons.

  The numbers that appear on the portrait are also buttons.

- Sound (How many sounds do you hear? How many times does the sound seem to loop?)

  There are no sounds in the portrait.

- *stop* actions

  There is probably a stop action placed after the red and white stripes complete their motion tweens, to hold the user at a screen before deciding to enter the portrait.

- *go to and play* actions

  There is most likely a go to and play *action set on each of the main buttons over the portrait and the numerical buttons on the portrait.*

- Combinations of symbols (such as buttons that contain animated movie clips)

  The "Explore the Portrait" button on the initial screen is a combination of a button and a movie clip, since the movie clip appears only when the pointer is over the button.

Challenge:

- For the complicated effects you see, suggest combinations or types of technical techniques that might be involved to create them.

  When the pointer rolls over one of the numbers on the portrait, these buttons fade out the other parts of the image and highlight the section of the image to which the number is attached. These buttons most likely contain an action that calls a movie clip to begin playing when the Over state of the button is activated. The movie clip fades out all aspects of the picture except for the aspect related to the number you choose.

- Describe a surprising technique.

  The magnifying glass is a surprising technique that adds to the overall feel of the site. Drag the pane up from the bottom of the portrait to magnify the portion of the portrait under the pane.

- Describe a challenging technique.

  The magnifying glass is a challenging technique. It most likely involves the use of complicated ActionScript.

- Describe unidentified techniques.

  It is difficult to tell how the magnifying glass might be achieved.

- Describe a creative design.

  A creative effect is the fading out and zooming in on aspects of the portrait when you click a number button.

How to Apply Colors and Gradients

The Color Mixer enables you to apply colors that aren't in the standard palette. You can use the Color Mixer to create new colors and add them to the palette, which you can save for later use. You can also incorporate new colors into gradient fills and store your gradients for repeated use.

Gradients can be helpful when creating effects, such as glows, photo-realistic spheres, solar flares, and glowing buttons. Macromedia Flash MX 2004 lets you create two types of gradient fills—linear and radial.

Create Colors

1. Start Flash and open a new blank document.
2. Use the **Oval** tool to create a simple shape on the Stage.

   You can adjust the fill and stroke colors using the Property inspector. To apply a color that is not in the current palette, use the Color Mixer panel.
3. By default, the Color Mixer panel is open. If it is not, choose **Window > Design Panels > Color Mixer**.

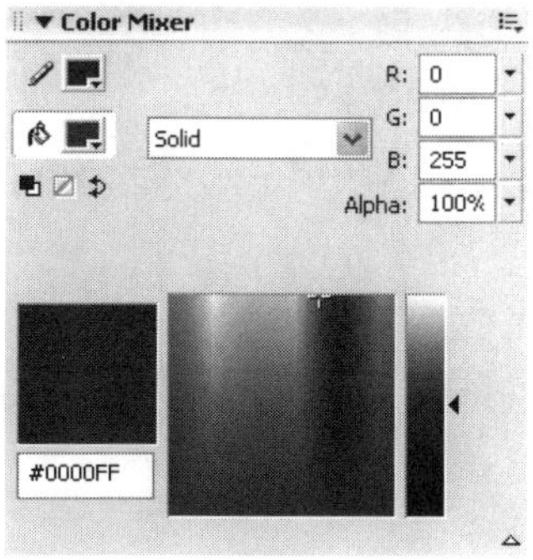

4. Make sure that both the stroke and fill of your shape are selected.

   Note: To select the stroke and fill of your shape, double-click the shape with the **Selection** tool.
5. Click the paint bucket icon (not the Color box) to select the Fill Color section in the Color Mixer.

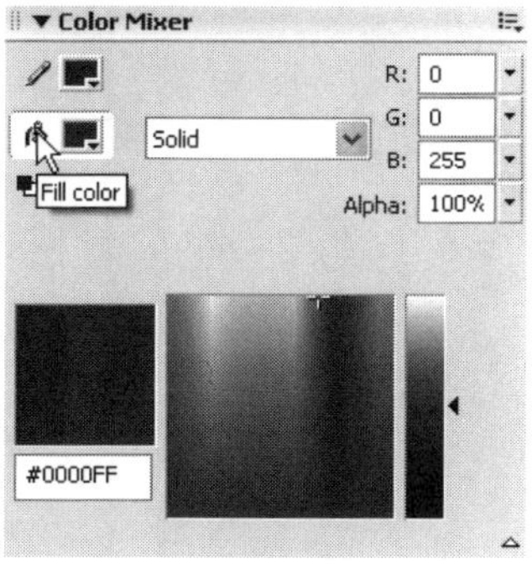

You can select a new fill color from the palette by clicking the **Fill Color** box, or you can enter precise RGB values. You can also enter these values as hexadecimal numbers. This is helpful if a client provides RGB or hexadecimal values for colors. Use the **Alpha** slider to adjust the level of transparency.

6. To browse for a color, click and drag in the color bar. As you drag, the colors you point to are shown in the preview area and on the Fill Color box.

Add Colors to the Palette

Once you mix your own colors, you can use them to create a custom palette. You do this with the Color Mixer and Color Swatches panels.

1. Make sure the Color Mixer and Color Swatches panels are both visible.

   If they are not, choose **Window > Design Panels > Color Mixer** and **Window > Design Panels > Color Swatches**.

2. Use the Color Mixer to create a new color using the color bar or the RGB boxes.
3. From the Color Mixer Options menu, choose **Add Swatch**.

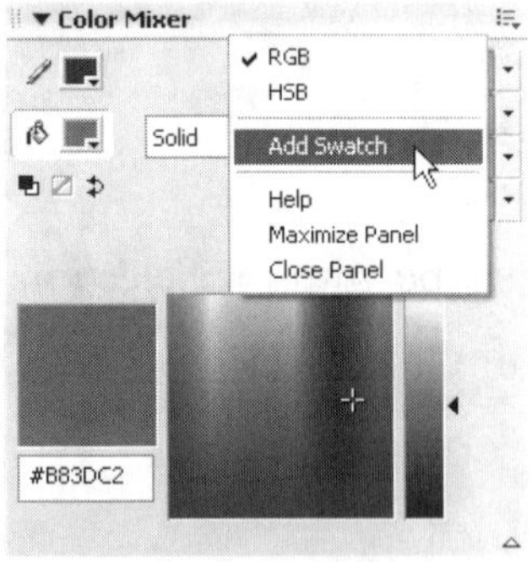

The new color is added to the palette in the Color Swatches panel.

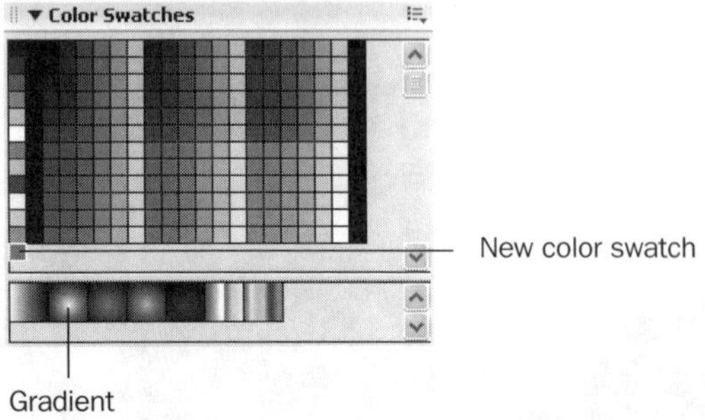

Create Gradients

1. Make sure the Color Mixer and Color Swatches panels are both visible.

   If they are not, choose **Window > Design Panels > Color Mixer** and **Window > Design Panels > Color Swatches.**

2. Use the **Selection** tool to double-click the oval shape on the Stage.

3. In the Color Mixer, choose **Radial** from the **Fill style** menu.

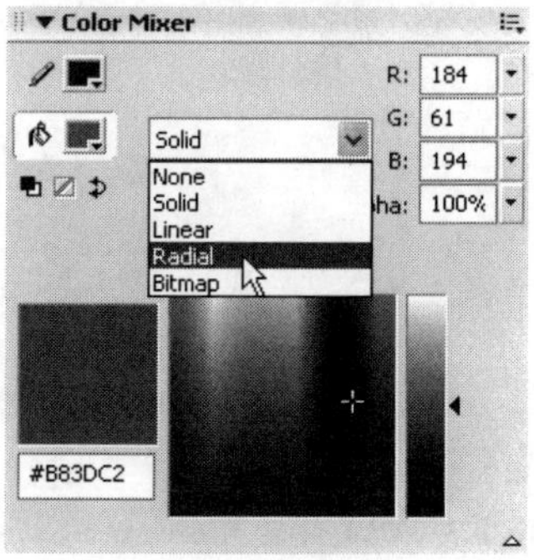

   This fills the selected shape with a black and white radial gradient.

   Note: Radial gradients work best on elliptical shapes.

4. Click the left pointer in the Color Mixer.

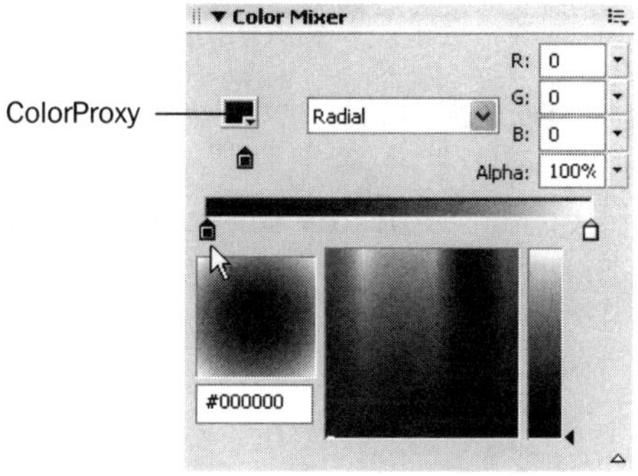

   The gradient starts out black in the center and transitions to white. With the left (black) pointer selected, use the ColorProxy box to change the inner color of the gradient.

5. Click the ColorProxy box and select a new color.

   The new color is applied to the gradient. You can also select colors by keying numbers in the RGB and hexadecimal boxes.

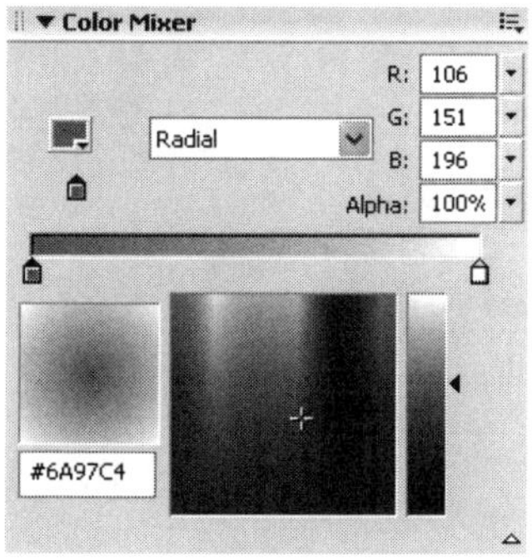

You can also change the color of the right (white) pointer to change the outer color of the gradient. You can even click along the gradient definition bar to enter additional colors.

6. Click along the gradient definition bar to place an intermediate color and change the color to black.

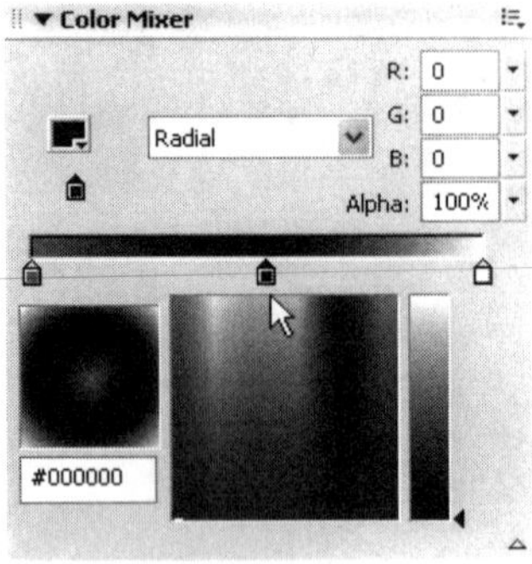

7. From the Color Mixer **Options** menu, choose **Add Swatch**.

   The new gradient is added to the gradients in the Color Swatches panel.

8. Deselect the shape on the Stage to see the new gradient applied to your shape.

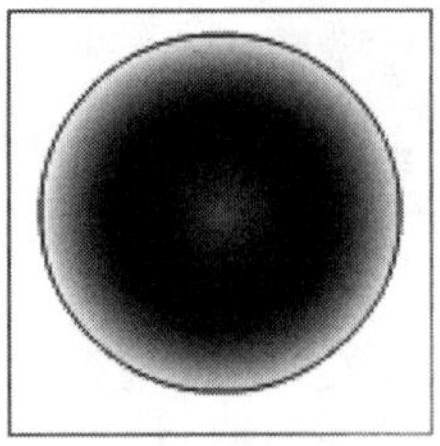

You can now add this gradient to other shapes by selecting it in the Color Swatches panel and using the Paint Bucket tool to apply the gradient.

How to Create Transitions with Motion Tweens

You may have noticed from watching television or movies that transitions are a subtle, but very important part of telling a story. For example, dissolving between images can indicate a passage of time. On the Web, transition effects can be used to create moods and they can help to keep your visitors interested. You can use them to focus the visitor's attention or to indicate a preferred path through your site. One way to create transitions in Macromedia Flash MX 2004 is to apply effects to a motion tween.

Rotation

In the Property inspector, you can add rotation to any motion tween. Rotation can be used to draw attention to content that is entering or exiting the Stage.

1. Start Flash and open the document you want to edit.
2. Locate the layer and keyframe that contain the symbol you plan to transition to the Stage or from the Stage. This will be the starting keyframe for the motion tween.
3. Make sure the symbol is alone on its own layer.
4. Decide how much time is required for the symbol to move to or from the Stage. This tells you where to place the ending keyframe for the motion tween.
5. Insert the ending keyframe accordingly in the Timeline.

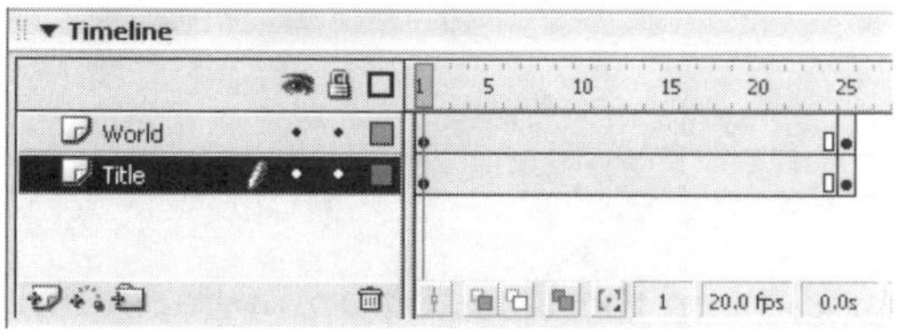

Note: If you are calculating in seconds, be sure to note the frame rate (fps) at the bottom of the Timeline. By default, Macromedia Flash sets new movies to 12 frames per second.

6. Select the starting keyframe for the transition and select the symbol.
7. Use the **Selection** tool to move the object to its starting position—on the Stage (ready to exit) or off the Stage (ready to enter).

Note: You might want to add multiple effects, such as changing size or fading, to make the object grow or fade in as it enters, or fade out and shrink as it exits.

- *Changing size:* Reduce or increase the image percentage in the Transform panel with the **Constrain** box selected.
- *Fading:* Select the symbol and choose **Alpha** from the Color pop-up menu in the Property inspector. Adjust the alpha setting to increase or decrease transparency.

8. Select the ending keyframe for the transition.
9. Use the **Selection** tool to move the symbol to its ending position (on or off the Stage).

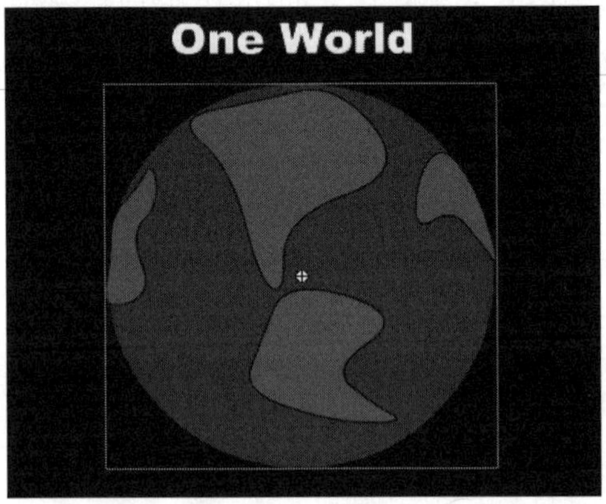

10. Click anywhere between the starting and ending keyframes. Choose **Motion** from the Tween pop-up menu in the Property inspector.

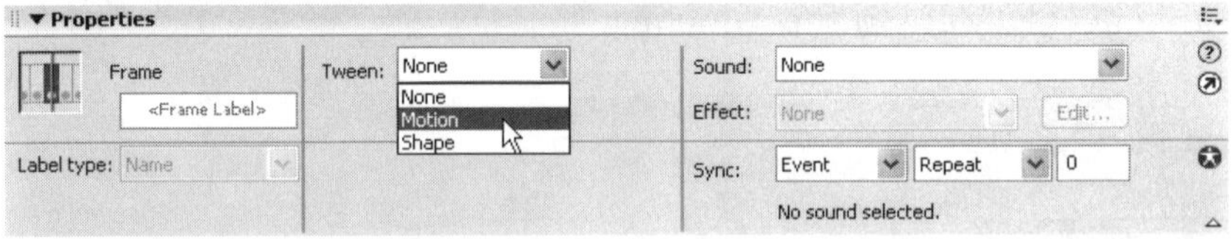

11. Choose **CW** (clockwise) or **CCW** (counterclockwise) from the Rotate pop-up menu in the Property inspector.

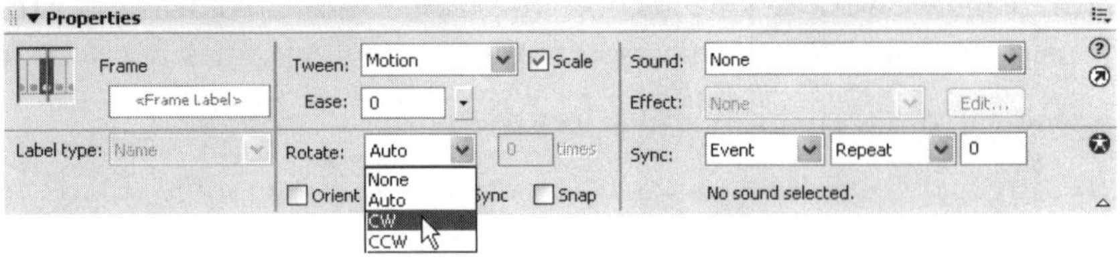

12. In the Rotate times box on the Property inspector, enter the number of times you want the symbol to rotate.
13. Select the **Sync** check box.

    This synchronizes the motion to the number of frames in the Timeline.

    Note: You can also synchronize sound with this tween by choosing a sound from the **Sound** pop-up menu. To have choices on the Sound pop-up menu, you must first import sounds, either from an external source or from the common libraries in Flash.

    If you synchronize sound, choose **Stream** from the **Sync** pop-up menu in the Property inspector. Now the sound will only play with the motion tween.

14. Save the movie.
15. Choose **Control > Test Movie** to test the movie.

16. Choose **File > Close** to close the preview window.

Fading

By creating a motion tween with different alpha settings, you can fade images in and out.

1. Start Flash and open the document you want to edit.
2. Locate the layer and keyframe that contain the symbol you plan to fade. This will be the starting keyframe for the fade.
3. Make sure the symbol is alone on its own layer.
4. Decide how much time is required for the symbol to complete the transition. This tells you where to place the ending keyframe for the motion tween.
5. Insert the ending keyframe accordingly in the Timeline.

   Note: If you are calculating in seconds, be sure to note the frame rate (fps) at the bottom of the Timeline. By default, Flash sets new movies to 12 frames per second.
6. Select the starting keyframe for the transition and select the symbol.
7. In the Property inspector, choose **Alpha** from the **Color** pop-up menu.

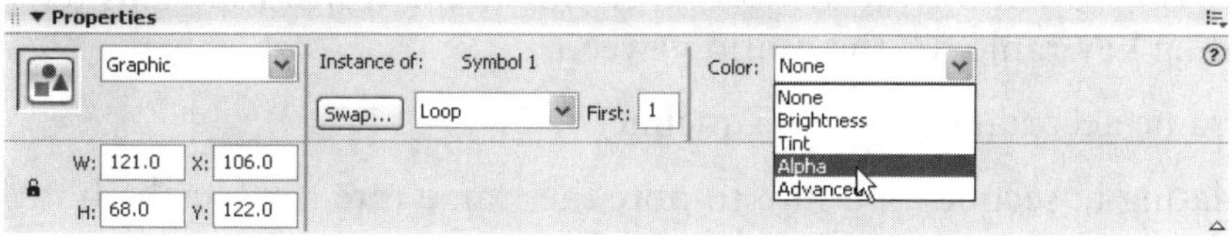

8. Drag the sliding Alpha amount (to the right of the Color menu) down to 0%.

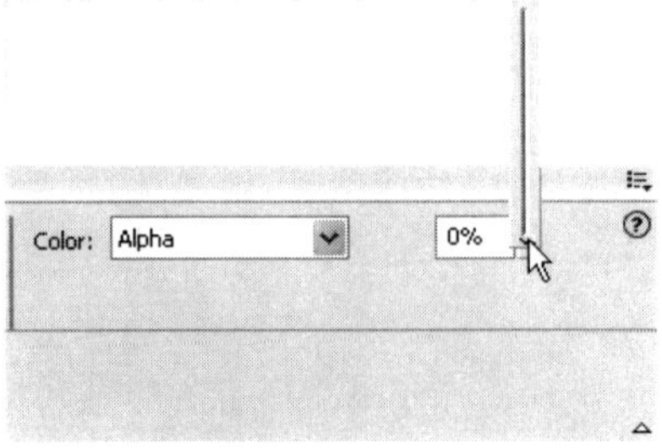

Note: The object will disappear from the Stage, but the blue outline will be visible when the symbol is selected.

9. Right-click (Windows) or Control-click (Macintosh) anywhere between the two keyframes and choose **Create Motion Tween** from the context menu.
10. Save the movie.
11. Choose **Control >Test Movie** to test the movie.

    You see the image fade in or out.

    Note: To create a fade-out, leave the alpha setting at **100%** on the starting keyframe and change the alpha setting on the ending keyframe to **0%**.
12. Choose **File > Close** to close the preview window.

Color Fades

You can use color fades to draw the viewer's attention to an object on the screen. To create a color fade, apply a motion tween between two instances of the same symbol, and then change the color of the instances in the starting and ending frames.

1. Start Flash and open the document you want to edit.
2. Locate the layer and keyframe that contain the symbol. This will be the starting keyframe for the color fade.
3. Make sure the symbol is alone on its own layer.
4. Decide how much time is required for the symbol to complete the transition. This tells you where to place the ending keyframe for the motion tween.
5. Insert the ending keyframe accordingly in the Timeline.

   Note: If you are calculating in seconds, be sure to note the frame rate (fps) at the bottom of the Timeline. By default, Flash sets new movies to 12 frames per second.
6. Select the starting keyframe for the transition and select the symbol.
7. In the Property inspector, choose **Tint** from the **Color** pop-up menu.

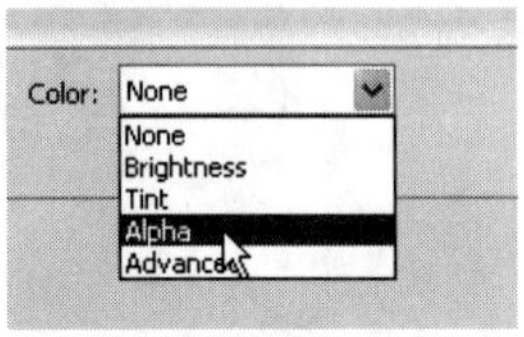

8. Use the **Color** box to select a new color and enter **100%** for the tint amount.

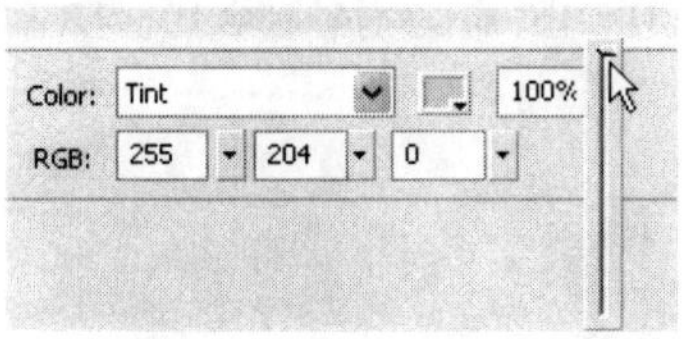

9. Right-click (Windows) or Control-click (Macintosh) between the two keyframes and choose **Create Motion Tween** from the context menu.

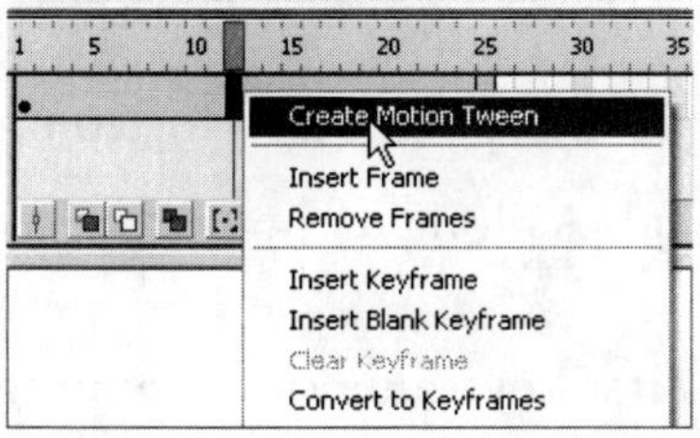

Note: You can also synchronize sound with this tween by choosing a sound from the **Sound** pop-up menu. To have choices in this pop-up menu, you must first import sounds, either from an external source or from the common libraries in Flash.

If you synchronize sound, choose **Stream** from the **Sync** pop-up menu. Now the sound will only play with the motion tween.

10. Save the movie.
11. Choose **Control > Test Movie** to test the movie.
12. Choose **File > Close** to close the preview window.

Flipping Images

Flipping images and then creating a motion tween can create an effective transition between images of roughly the same size. The trick is to flip the first image halfway and then start fading in the second image while the first image is still flipping to make a smooth transition.

1. Start Flash and open the document you want to edit.
2. Locate two symbols on different layers that you plan to transition between: the entering object and exiting object. Position the symbols in roughly the same position on the Stage.
3. Decide how much time is required to complete the transition. This tells you where to place the ending keyframe for the motion tween.
4. Insert keyframes in both layers accordingly in the Timeline.

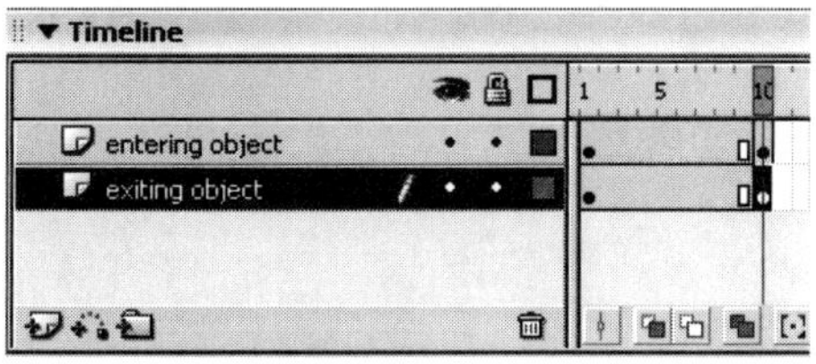

5. Insert a keyframe in the entering object's layer one frame after the first keyframe of the exiting object. For example, the exiting object will exit from frame 1 to 10, so insert a keyframe in frame 2 of the entering object's layer.

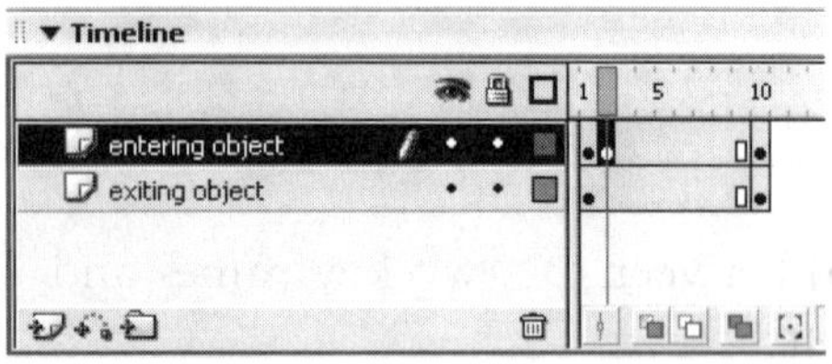

6. Select the last keyframe of the exiting object.
7. Select the exiting object on the Stage and choose **Modify > Transform > Flip Horizontal**.

   Note: Instead of Flip Horizontal, you can choose **Flip Vertical**. As long as both exiting and entering objects flip the same way, the transition will work.
8. Right-click (Windows) or Control-click (Macintosh) in the first keyframe of the exiting object and choose **Create Motion Tween** from the context menu.
9. Insert a keyframe in the midpoint of the tween for the exiting object to cut the flip tween in half.
10. Click and drag to select all frames after the midpoint keyframe, then right-click (Windows) or Control-click (Macintosh) the selected frames and choose **Remove Frames** from the context menu.

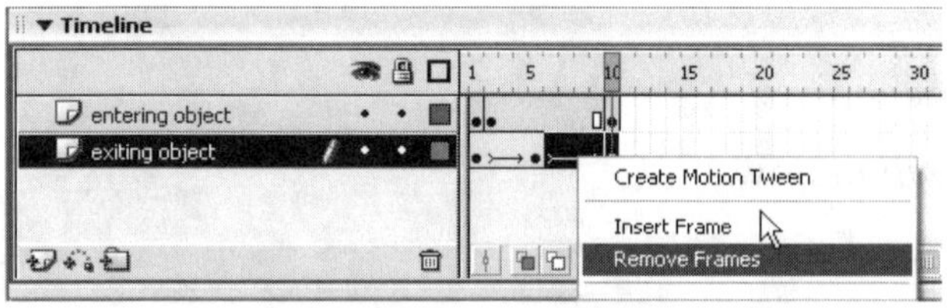

   The second half of the flip is removed.
11. Select the last keyframe of the entering object and choose **Modify > Transform > Flip Horizontal**.

    Note: Choose the same type of flip for the entering object as for the exiting object.
12. Right-click (Windows) or Control-click (Macintosh) between the second keyframe and the last keyframe of the entering object and choose **Create Motion Tween** from the context menu.

    The entering layer still contains a symbol in the first keyframe. This frame should be empty.
13. Right-click (Windows) or Control-click (Macintosh) in the first keyframe of the entering layer and choose **Clear Frames** from the context menu.

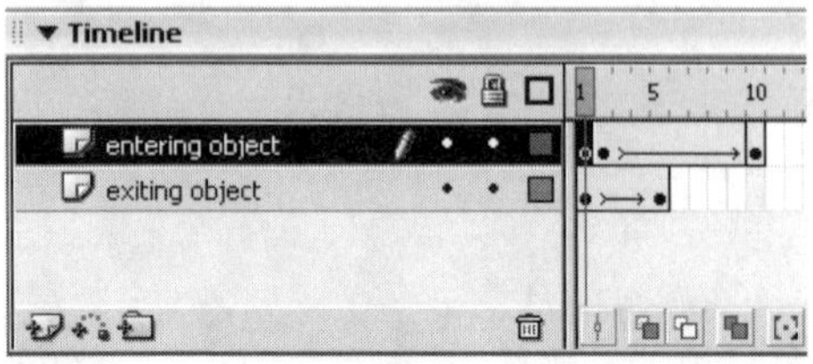

14. Select the first keyframe of the entering object's motion tween and click the symbol on the Stage to view its properties in the Property inspector.
15. In the Property inspector, choose **Alpha** from the **Color** pop-up menu and set the alpha to 0%.
16. Click the first frame of the entering object's motion tween and, in the Property inspector, change the easing to **–100%**.

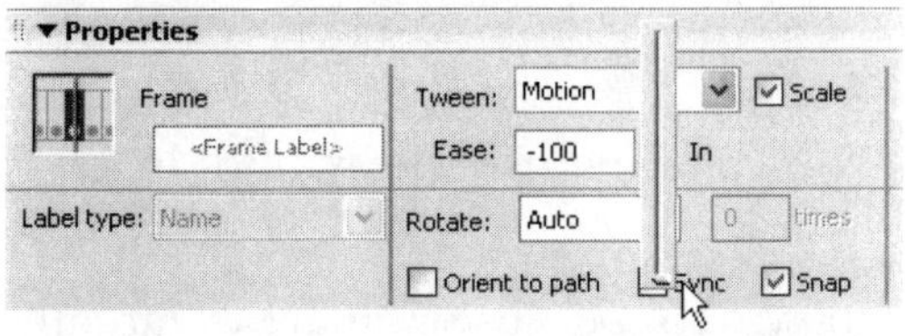

The fade begins slowly.

Note: You can also synchronize sound with this tween by clicking in the entering object layer and choosing a sound from the **Sound** pop-up menu. To have choices in this pop-up menu, you must first import sounds, either from an external source or from the common libraries in Flash.

If you synchronize sound, choose **Stream** from the **Sync** pop-up menu.

17. Save the movie.
18. Choose **Control > Test Movie** to test the movie.
19. Choose **File > Close** to close the preview window.

Text Transitions

A good technique to introduce text is to distribute the letters of the text to separate layers. Then you can animate the individual letters to create interesting effects and personality.

1. Start Flash and open the document you want to edit.
2. Create a new layer on which to insert the text.
3. Use the Text tool to type the text approximately where you want it to start, on or off the Stage.

4. Select the text and choose **Modify > Convert to Symbol**. Enter a name for the symbol, select **Movie clip** as the behavior, and click **OK**.

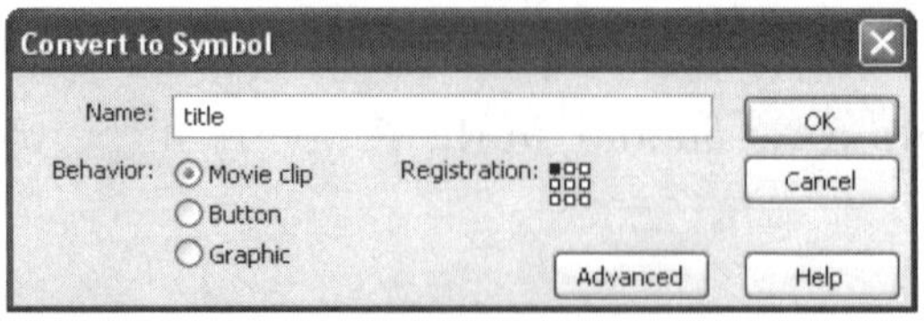

This converts the text into a movie clip symbol. You can now use the symbol in a motion tween.

Note: It is easier to work on the text in a movie clip symbol because you are eventually going to generate a layer for each text letter. This would clutter the main Timeline. Also, if you want the text animation to run longer than the main Timeline, it must be in a movie clip symbol. (Graphic symbols are limited by the length of the main Timeline.)

5. Choose **Window > Library** to open the Library panel, and double-click the movie symbol to edit the symbol (not just the instance of the symbol on the Stage).

The symbol appears in its own Timeline.

6. Insert a new keyframe in frame 10.

This will be the ending point for the first part of your text animation.

7. Right-click (Windows) or Control-click (Macintosh) in frame **1** and choose **Create Motion Tween** from the shortcut menu.

8. Drag the text in frame 1 up about three inches.

9. Insert a keyframe in frame 11.

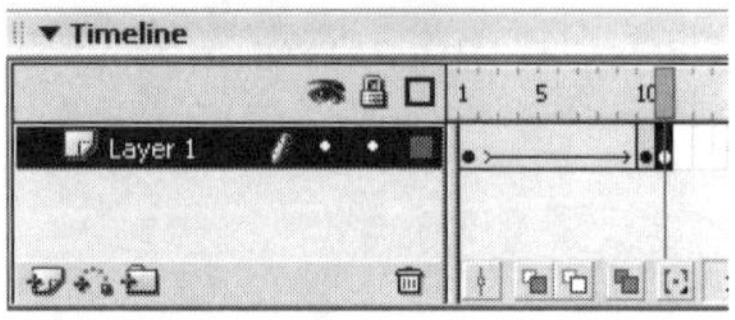

10. Select the text and choose **Modify > Break Apart**.

The text is divided into separate letters.

11. With the letters still selected, choose **Modify > Timeline > Distribute to Layers.**

    Each letter is now on its own layer in frame 1.

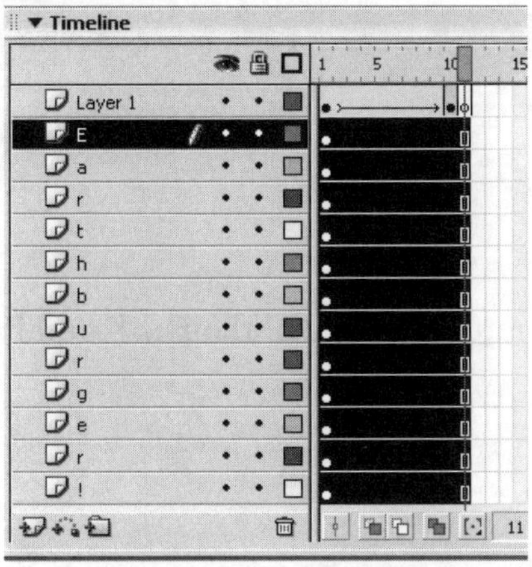

12. With all of the letter layers selected, click and drag their keyframes from frame 1 to one frame past the end of your initial motion tween.

    You now have each letter in position to begin any individual motion tweens or effects. Each letter layer contains a starting keyframe.

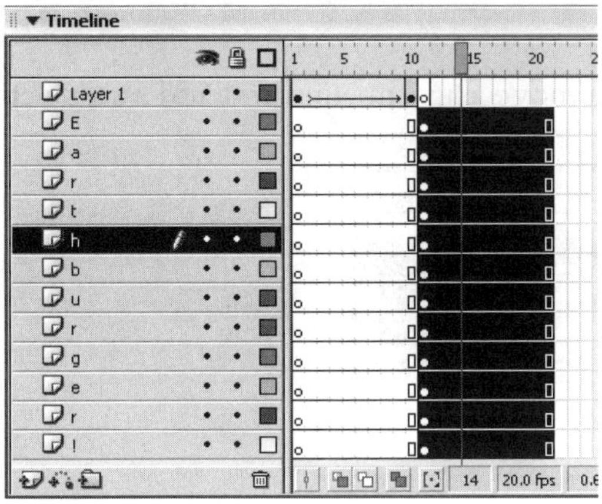

13. Add an ending keyframe for each letter.
14. Apply one or any combination of the following animation ideas to the letters:
    - *Rotate:* To make the letters rotate, create motion tweens with the **Rotate** option selected.
    - *Move:* Create motion tweens and move the letters in the ending keyframes off the Stage. For example, you could have every letter exit the Stage in a different direction.
    - *Fade:* Convert the letters in the starting keyframes to symbols. Then create the ending keyframes for each letter at different positions on the Timeline. Apply motion tweens. Use the **Color** pop-up menu in the Property inspector to change the alpha for the symbols in the ending keyframe to **0%**. Adjust the starting and ending keyframes for each letter so they fade out at different points along the Timeline. You can also apply a color fade instead of a fade to 0% alpha.

The following example illustrates a combination of move and fade:

The following example illustrates tweening an "E" shape into an image of the Earth and back:

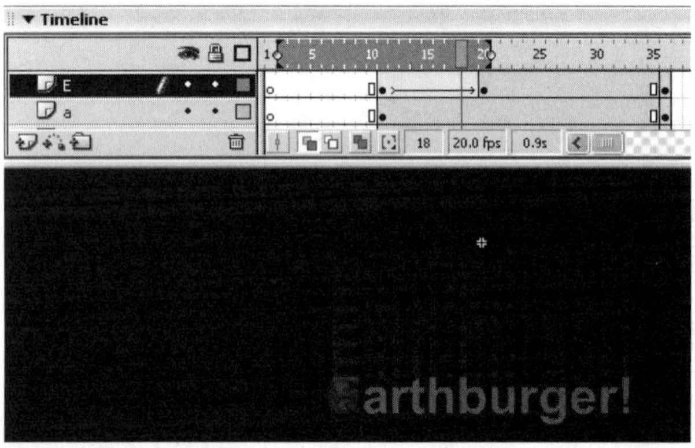

15. Insert a keyframe at the end of the text animation movie clip Timeline and add a *stop* action.

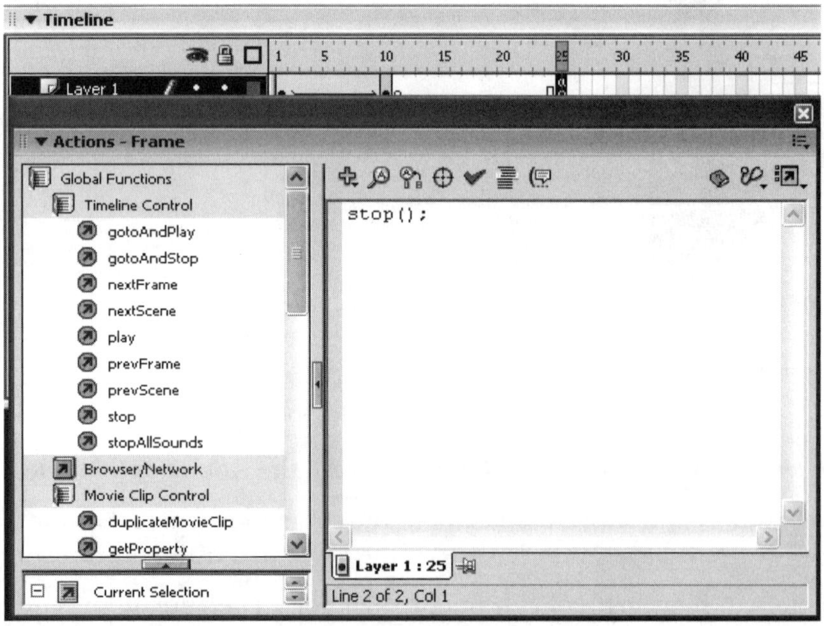

Note: If you don't add the *stop* action, the movie clip will keep running continuously, even after the main Timeline animation is finished.

16. Click **Scene 1** in the information bar to return to the main Timeline.

17. Drag the keyframe holding the text animation movie clip to the appropriate starting point in the main Timeline.

18. Position the text animation movie clip instance in the correct starting point on the Stage.
19. Choose **Control > Test Movie** to test the movie.
20. Choose **File > Close** to close the preview window.
21. Save the document.

Other letter animation ideas:

- Break the letters apart and distribute them to layers before they enter the Stage. Have the letters fall onto the Stage in different ways.
- Bring letters on the Stage as one unit and then have all the letters do a trick, one-at-a-time.
- Create a movie clip out of a single letter and have that letter constantly running a shape or motion tween. For instance, you could have the letter "i" in "Lighthouse" continuously change into a little lighthouse, send out a beam of light, and then change back into an "i."
- Break the letters apart to convert them to shapes and create shape tweens that morph the letters into other images.

How to Use Filmmaking Techniques

Web designers have an entire history of filmmaking techniques to draw from and inspire them when creating Web sites and digital movies. Macromedia Flash MX 2004 enables you to simulate traditional film techniques. As you design Flash movies, think of creative ways to incorporate these effects and look for opportunities to create new effects that may in turn inspire traditional filmmaking.

Four popular filmmaking techniques include:

- *Pan, Tilt, and Zoom Effects:* Moving the camera horizontally across a scene is known as a *pan*. Moving the camera up or down across a scene is known as a *tilt*. Moving the camera away from or toward a subject in a scene is known as a *zoom*.
- *Camera Angles:* The rule of thirds and adjusting the viewing *angle* can help emphasize a certain aspect of the subject.
- *Cross Fades:* This technique appears to fade in one image while another fades out, a transitional effect for moving from one image to another.
- *Bounce Effect:* A moving object rebounds before stopping. This technique grabs attention and can focus the viewer on an area of the screen. This effect is sometimes combined with a sudden sound effect, such as a "boing" or "tire screech."

Create a Pan, Tilt, or Zoom Effect

To set a scene in a movie, the camera moves over a large scene and then zooms in to a specific point. A pan (or tilt) followed by a zoom is a good technique to introduce a digital narrative. Zooming in focuses the viewer's attention on a particular part of the image.

1. If your image is not already a symbol, convert it to a movie clip symbol. Place the symbol on the left side of the workspace.
2. Insert a keyframe in the Timeline where you want the pan to end.

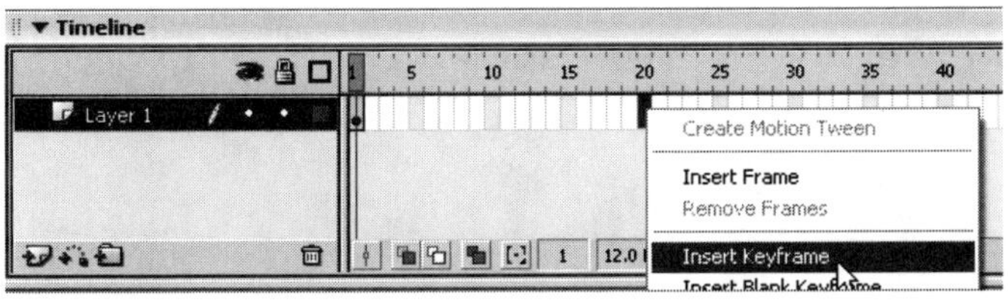

3. Select the ending keyframe. Drag the instance of the movie symbol to the opposite side of the workspace.
4. Click in the **Outline** column to the right of the layer name for the layer that contains the movie symbol.

Note: It is easier to see the border of an image if you set the layer holding the image to outline mode (especially if the image contains a lot of grays that can fade into the area outside the Stage). Be sure that, during a pan, the image does not slide off the Stage.

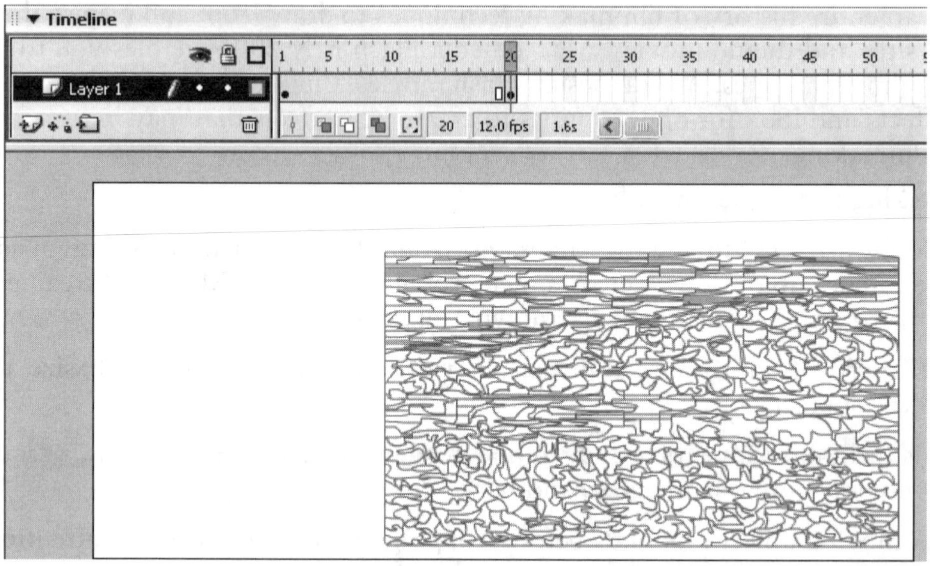

5. Select the starting frame and choose **Insert > Timeline > Create Motion Tween.**

   This motion tween moves the movie symbol horizontally across the Stage (a pan). The ending keyframe for this motion tween will be the starting point for another motion tween that zooms the image 300%.

6. Add a keyframe for the ending point of the second motion tween (the zoom).

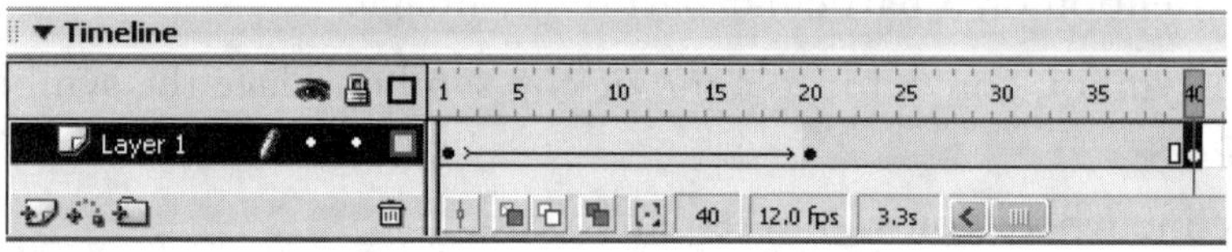

7. Select the ending keyframe and choose **Window > Design Panels > Transform** to open the Transform panel.

8. Increase the magnification in the Transform panel to a specific percent of its original size (such as 300%). Make sure **Constrain** is selected.

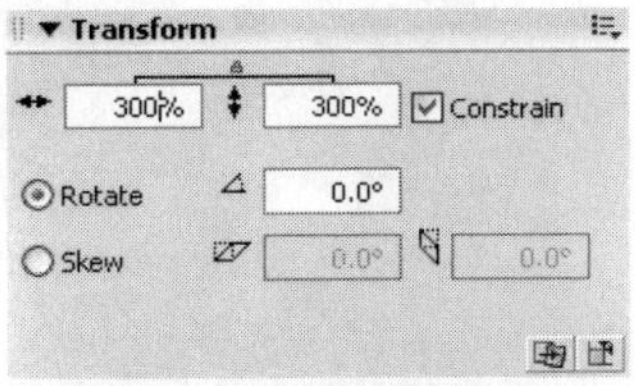

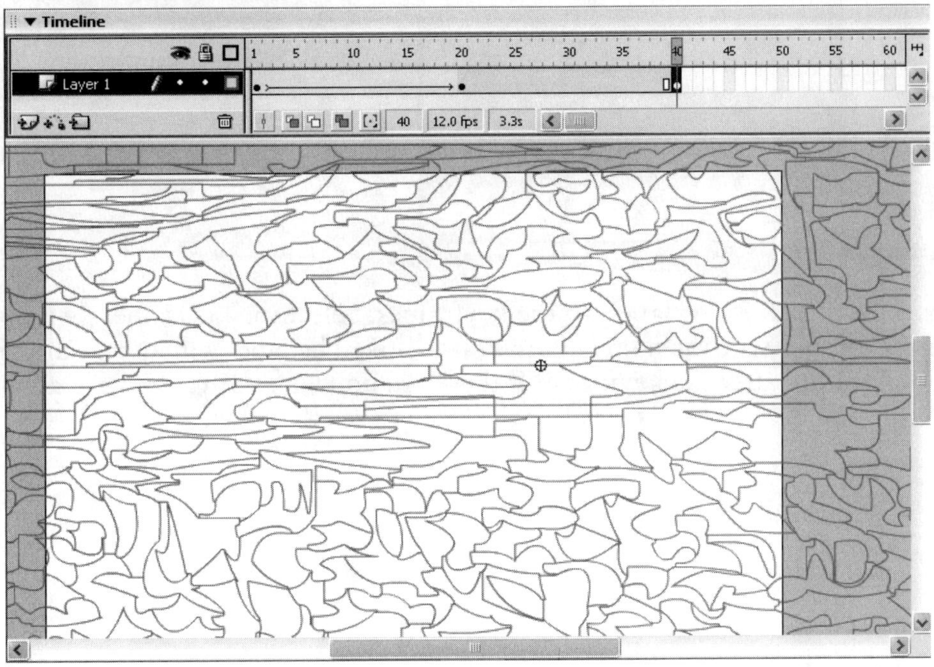

9. Create a motion tween between the second and third keyframes.

10. In the Property inspector, increase the easing to a value between 60 and 100 for the motion tween. This will cause the zoom to start quickly and slow down as it arrives at the resting point.

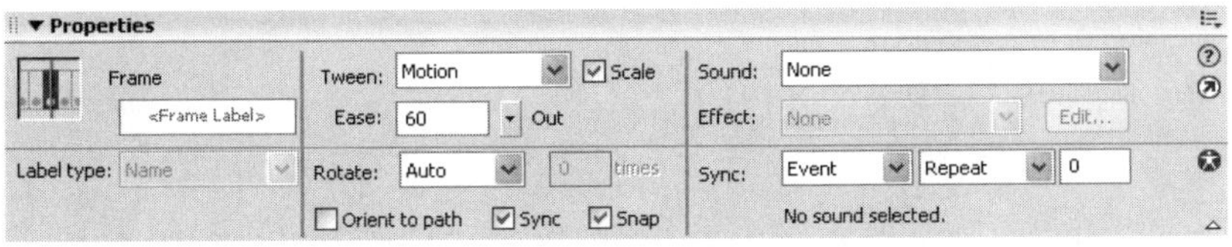

11. Insert a keyframe after the last frame of the movie and add a *stop* action.

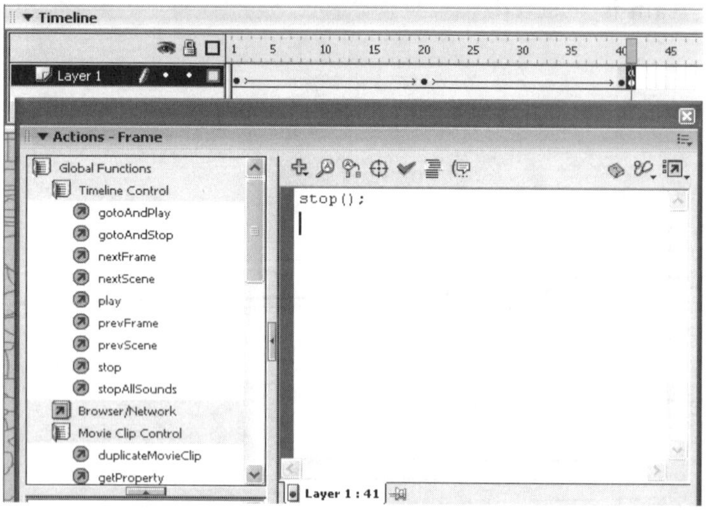

Note: You may want to add frame labels to the keyframes. Select the keyframe, then open the Property inspector and type the name in the Frame box. The label will appear along the Timeline in the frames after the keyframe. If there are no frames after the keyframe, insert a blank keyframe in the same layer after the label to see the label.

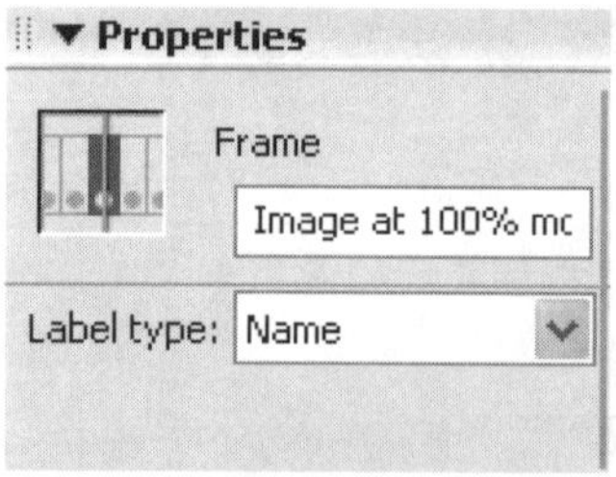

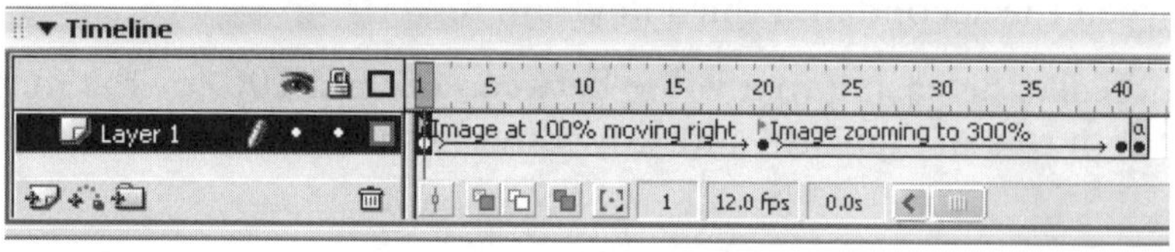

12. Turn off outlining, save the file, and choose **Control > Test Movie.**

Further ideas:

- *For a documentary:* Slow the process down to reflect the pace of the narrative. In *www.becominghuman.org*, for example, a slow pan and zoom goes well with a documentary-style narrative.
- *For humor or action:* Make the zoom-in portion of the pan quick and somewhat unsteady, as if looking for the subject of the scene. You might zoom in and out several times during a pan, to show you are looking for something in the scene.
- *For drama:* Pan or tilt the scene without a zoom. This method presents a sweeping landscape, such as a mountain range leading to the ocean. Since it takes in the majority of the landscape, it adds depth and seriousness to the tone of the narrative.

Camera Angles

When you have several images on the screen in a digital narrative, there are certain tricks you can use to emphasize aspects of the subject. Use the rule of thirds and adjust the viewing angle to emphasize a certain aspect of the subject.

- The *rule of thirds* states that, if you divide the screen into a 3-by-3 grid, the intersections of the lines are areas where the eye will focus. Line up the items of focus at these intersections on the screen.
- You can add importance to a subject by presenting the subject as seen from below. Likewise, you can diminish the importance of a subject by presenting it as seen from above.

Even though the girl isn't in the center of the image, the eye is drawn to her because she is near the intersection of the rule-of-thirds lines.

Looking up at this man having a moment makes him look powerful. If the camera angled down on him, he would look smaller and less powerful.

Cross Fades

A transitional effect for moving from one image to another is to fade one image out as you fade the other in.

1. Convert two images that will be cross-faded into symbols and place them on separate layers.
2. Insert keyframes in both layers at the same point in the Timeline to mark the beginning of the fade-out of the first image and fade-in of the second image.
3. Decide the length of the transition and insert keyframes in both layers at the same point in the Timeline to mark the end of the fade-out of the first image and fade-in of the second image.
4. Select the first keyframe for the image that will fade out, select the image, and use the Property inspector to set its alpha level to **100%**.

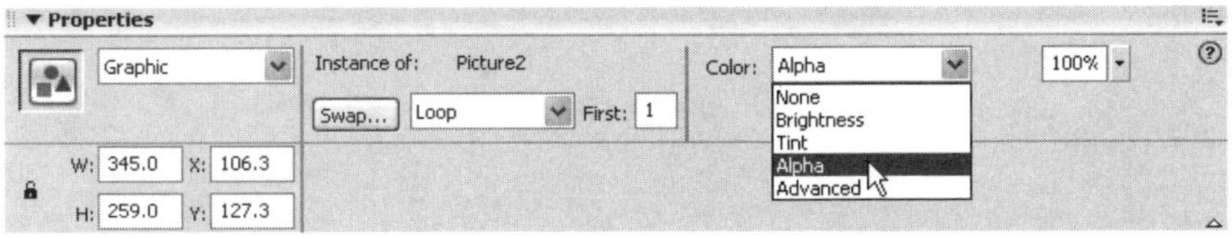

Note: If your images are in the same position on the Stage, you will need to hide the top layer in order to select the symbol in the bottom layer. It is easier to select your images if they are offset on the Stage.

5. Select the first keyframe for the image that will fade in and set its alpha level to **0%**.
6. Select the last keyframe for the image that will fade in and set its alpha level to **100%**.
7. Select the last keyframe for the image that will fade out and set its alpha level to **0%**.
8. Select the first keyframe for each image and insert a motion tween.

   Note: You can do this by right-clicking (Windows) or Control-clicking (Macintosh) and choosing **Create Motion Tween** from the shortcut menu, by choosing **Insert > Create Motion Tween**, or by using the **Tween** pop-up menu in the Property inspector.
9. Add Frame labels to the first keyframes of each motion tween.

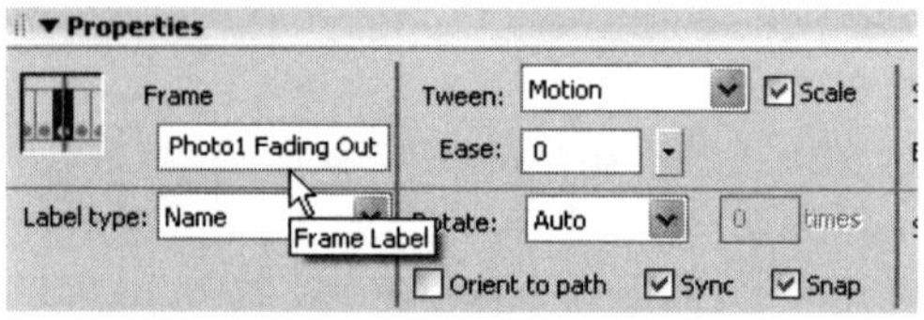

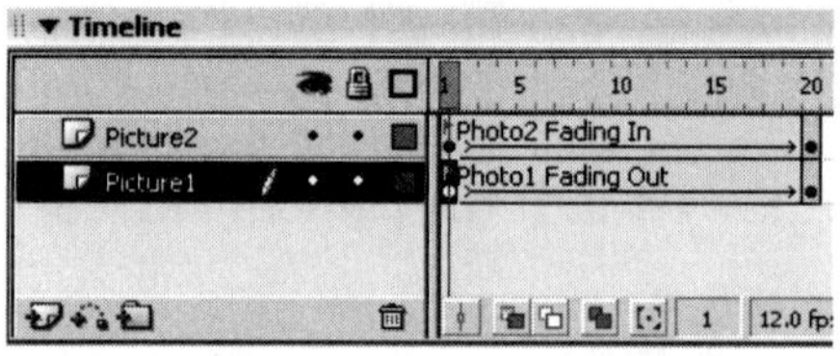

Note: You can also make the fade-out start after the fade-in or vice versa. Or, you can extend the fade-out to end in the same frame as the end of the fade-in.

If the images zoom in or out before the fade-out, you probably want to continue the zooming process during the fade.

10. Save the movie.
11. Choose **Control > Test Movie** to test the movie.
12. Choose **File > Close** to close the preview window.

Bounce Effect

Some animated text and images that move onto the Stage will seem more lifelike if you add a little bounce to them when they reach their stopping point. This is an old animation technique acknowledging that any moving object carries momentum and thus rebounds a bit before it comes to a stop. This technique also grabs attention and can focus the viewer on an area of the screen.

1. Motion tween a symbol so that it moves across the Stage.

   Note: When dragging the symbol to its ending point, hold down the **Shift** key to constrain the symbol so it moves only in the direction you drag, without shifting up or down.

2. Label the starting keyframe for the motion tween **Moves Right** or **Moves Left** and the second keyframe **Bounce**.

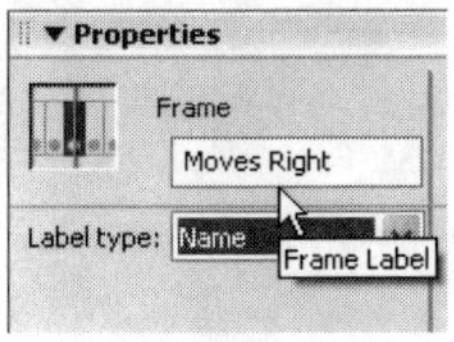

3. Insert a keyframe 3–5 frames after the end of the motion tween. Label this frame **Back**.
4. Insert another keyframe 8–10 frames after the end of the original motion tween. This will be the final resting point of the image.

   Note: You can make the final bounce back into place take longer by inserting the keyframe in this step farther along the Timeline. Because the animation occurs over more frames, the object moves more slowly.
5. Select the keyframe labeled **Back**.
6. In this keyframe, click the symbol instance on the Stage and use the arrow keys to move the instance 5–10 key presses back in the direction it came from.
7. Create motion tweens between all the keyframes.
8. Insert a keyframe after the last frame and add a *stop* action.

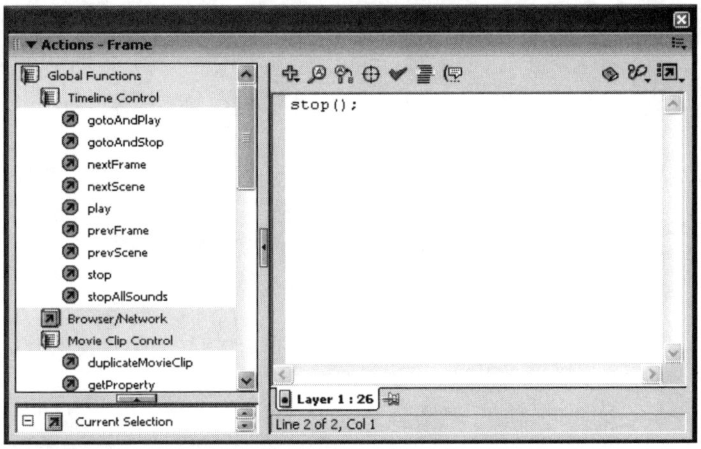

9. Save the movie.
10. Choose **Control > Test Movie** to test the movie.
11. Choose **File > Close** to close the preview window.

SAMPLE NARRATIVE SUMMARY AND STORYBOARD

NARRATIVE SUMMARY AND STORYBOARD

Student Name: Jane Smith Date: 4/2/2002

To help your producer create your narrative, provide the following information:

- Description of the overall movie in the form of a rough flowchart
- List of the filenames and general settings for the movie
- Detailed storyboard sketches and descriptions for each section of the movie

Narrative Flowchart

General Movie Settings

Filename: sf_fog.fla

Main folder (contains all files for the movie): js_narrative

Image source folder: images

Video source folder: videos

Audio source folder: music

Document size: 780 pixels wide by 438 pixels high

Background color: white

Frame rate: 12 frames per second

Storyboard # 1

Student Name: Jane Smith   Movie Title: San Francisco Fog

To complete the storyboard, draw and describe the initial and final state of each section. Then describe the transition from the initial to the final state.

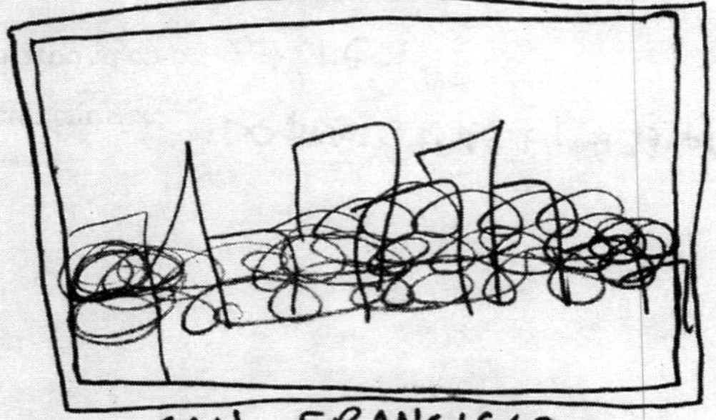

Description of Initial State

Drawn images:
–

Imported images:
Sunny photo of San Francisco

Audio (music or sound effect loop):
–

Audio (spoken text):
–

Displayed text:
SUNNY
SAN FRANCISCO (Black text)

Other:

Description of Transition

Describe objects that change and how they change.
Estimate the time for each change in seconds.

- sunny photo fades into foggy photo
- "Sunny" text moves up to exit the stage
- "FOGGY" text falls in from top and stops with a bounce on top of photo
- Spoken: Why does San Francisco get foggy?

Description of Final State

Drawn images:
–

Imported images:
Foggy photo of San Francisco

Audio (music or sound effect loop):
–

Audio (spoken text):
–

Displayed text:
SAN FRANCISCO (Black text)
FOGGY

Other:

Storyboard # 2

Student Name: Jane Smith Movie Title: San Francisco Fog

To complete the storyboard, draw and describe the initial and final state of each section. Then describe the transition from the initial to the final state.

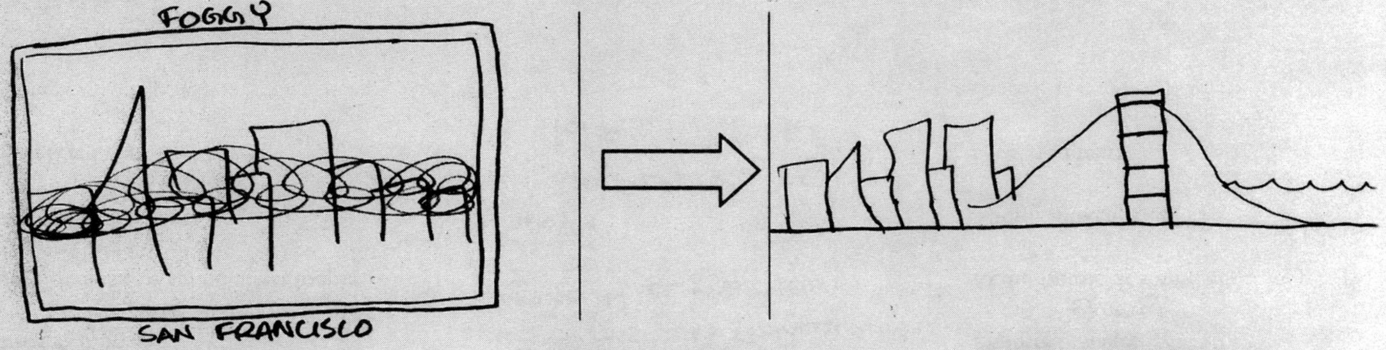

Description of Initial State

Drawn images:

—

Imported images:

Foggy photo of San Francisco

Audio (music or sound effect loop):

—

Audio (spoken text):

—

Displayed text:

FOGGY
SAN FRANCISCO (Black text)

Other:

Description of Transition

Describe objects that change and how they change.
Estimate the time for each change in seconds.

- "FOGGY" text flys up to exit the stage
- "SAN FRANCISCO" text falls down to exit the stage
- Foggy photo moves left to exit the stage
- San Francisco skyline picture enters from right side of the stage

Description of Final State

Drawn images:

—

Imported images:

sf_skyline.gif

Audio (music or sound effect loop):

—

Audio (spoken text):

—

Displayed text:

—

Other: —

Storyboard # 3

Student Name: Jane Smith Movie Title: San Francisco Fog

To complete the storyboard, draw and describe the initial and final state of each section. Then describe the transition from the initial to the final state.

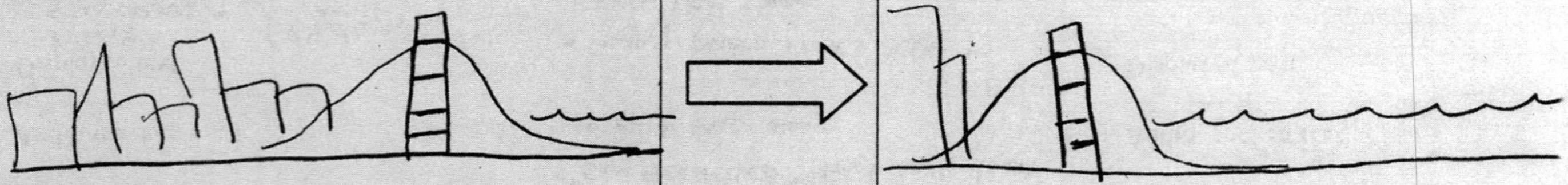

Description of Initial State

Drawn images:
–

Imported images:
sf_skyline.gif

Audio (music or sound effect loop):
–

Audio (spoken text):
–

Displayed text:
–

Other:
–

Description of Transition

Describe objects that change and how they change.
Estimate the time for each change in seconds.

- pan across San Francisco skyline to see the ocean
- Spoken:
  San Francisco fog forms...

Description of Final State

Drawn images:
–

Imported images:
sf_skyline.gif

Audio (music or sound effect loop):
–

Audio (spoken text):
–

Displayed text:
–

Other:
–

Storyboard # 4

Student Name: Jane Smith Movie Title: San Francisco Fog

To complete the storyboard, draw and describe the initial and final state of each section. Then describe the transition from the initial to the final state.

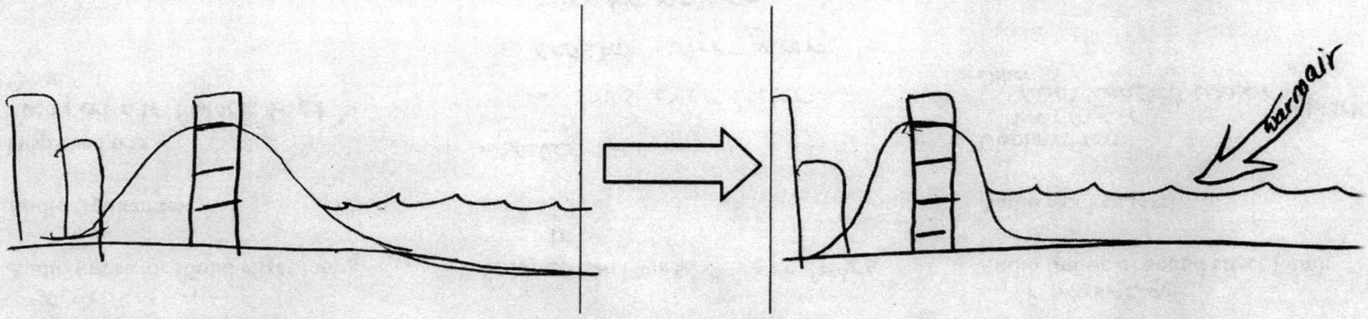

Description of Initial State

Drawn images:
–

Imported images:
sf-skyline.gif

Audio (music or sound effect loop):
–

Audio (spoken text):
–

Displayed text:
–

Other:
–

Description of Transition

Describe objects that change and how they change.
Estimate the time for each change in seconds.

- red/orange arrow fades in
- "warm air" text fades in
- Spoken:
  When warm, moist air above the Pacific ocean...

Description of Final State

Drawn images:
red/orange arrow

Imported images:
sf-skyline.gif

Audio (music or sound effect loop):
–

Audio (spoken text):

Displayed text:
warm air (black text)

Other:
–

Storyboard # 5

Student Name: Jane Smith Movie Title: San Francisco Fog

To complete the storyboard, draw and describe the initial and final state of each section. Then describe the transition from the initial to the final state.

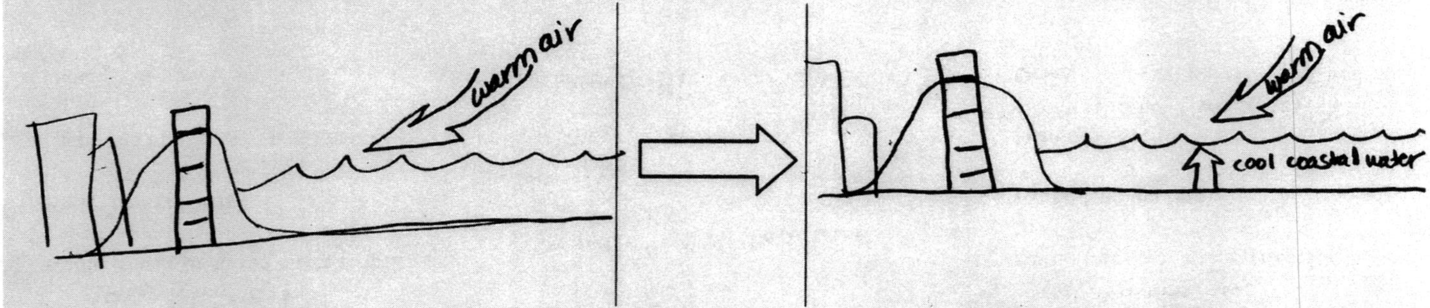

Description of Initial State	Description of Transition	Description of Final State
Drawn images: red/orange arrow Imported images: SF_skyline.gif Audio (music or sound effect loop): – Audio (spoken text): – Displayed text: warm air (black text) Other:	Describe objects that change and how they change. Estimate the time for each change in seconds. • blue/white arrow fades in • "cool coastal water" text fades in • spoken: ...blows over cooler coastal waters near San Francisco...	Drawn images: red/orange arrow blue/white arrow Imported images: SF-skyline.gif Audio (music or sound effect loop): – Audio (spoken text): – Displayed text: warm air Cool coastal water (black text) Other:

Storyboard # 6

Student Name: Jane Smith Movie Title: San Francisco Fog

To complete the storyboard, draw and describe the initial and final state of each section. Then describe the transition from the initial to the final state.

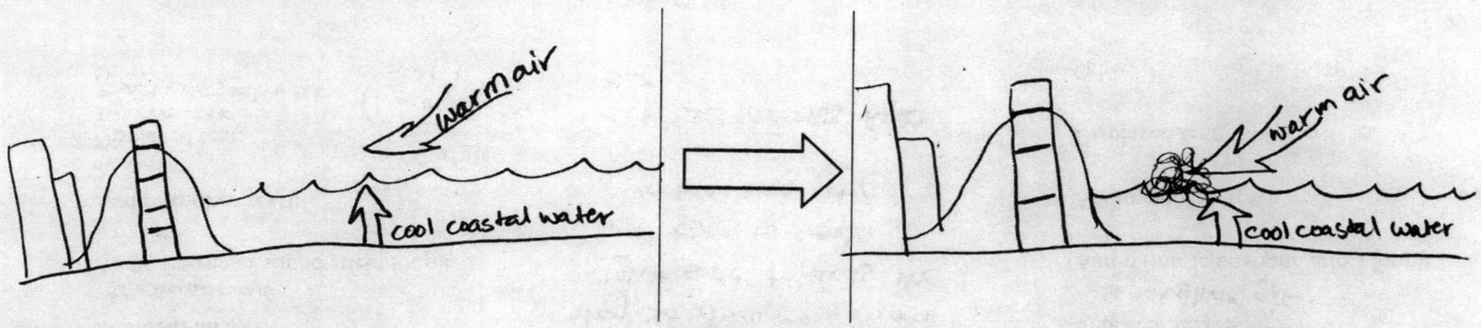

Description of Initial State

Drawn images:
red/orange arrow
blue/white arrow

Imported images:
sf_skyline.gif

Audio (music or sound effect loop):
-

Audio (spoken text):
-

Displayed text:
warm air
cool coastal water (black text)

Other:
-

Description of Transition

Describe objects that change and how they change. Estimate the time for each change in seconds.

- fog barely starts to fade in but does not completely come in
- Spoken: Air temperature drops to dew point...

Description of Final State

Drawn images:
red/orange arrow
blue/white arrow
very light, nearly transparent fog

Imported images:
sf_skyline.gif

Audio (music or sound effect loop):
-

Audio (spoken text):
-

Displayed text:
warm air
cool coastal water (black text)

Other:

Storyboard # 7

Student Name: Jane Smith Movie Title: San Francisco fog

To complete the storyboard, draw and describe the initial and final state of each section. Then describe the transition from the initial to the final state.

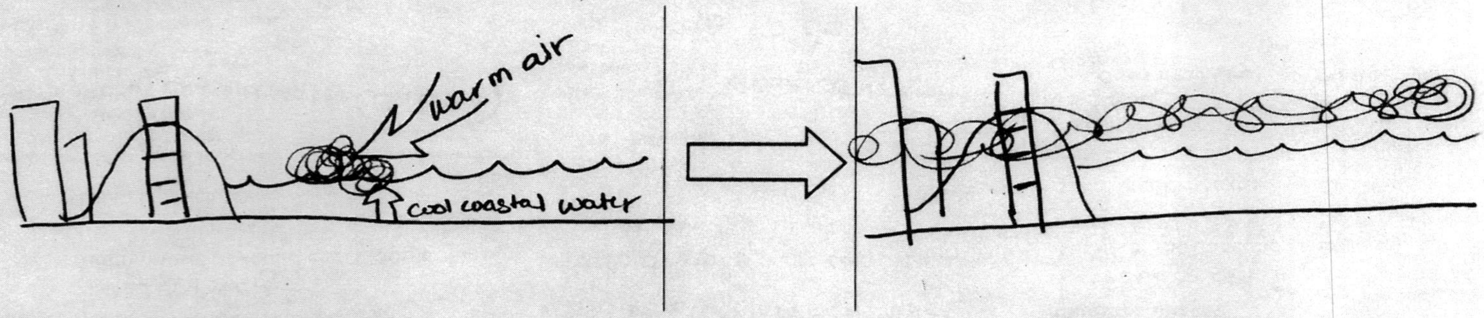

Description of Initial State

Drawn images:
red/orange arrow very light, nearly
blue/white arrow transparent fog

Imported images:
SF_skyline.gif

Audio (music or sound effect loop):
-

Audio (spoken text):
-

Displayed text:
warm air
cool coastal water (black text)

Other:

Description of Transition

Describe objects that change and how they change.
Estimate the time for each change in seconds.

- fog cloud moves in from right side towards the left side to begin covering the city
- text and arrows fade out
- Spoken:

Then, fog!

Description of Final State

Drawn images:
fog cloud

Imported images:
SF_skyline.gif

Audio (music or sound effect loop):
-

Audio (spoken text):
-

Displayed text:

Other:

Storyboard # 8

Student Name: Jane Smith Movie Title: San Francisco Fog

To complete the storyboard, draw and describe the initial and final state of each section. Then describe the transition from the initial to the final state.

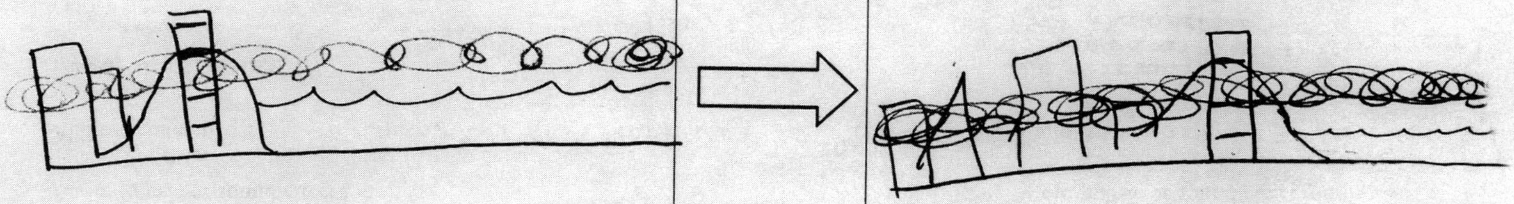

Description of Initial State

Drawn images:
fog cloud
Imported images:
sf-skyline.gif
Audio (music or sound effect loop):
–
Audio (spoken text):
–
Displayed text:
–
Other:
–

Description of Transition

Describe objects that change and how they change.
Estimate the time for each change in seconds.

- image pans to view most of skyline
- fog moves to cover the entire city

Description of Final State

Drawn images:
fog cloud
Imported images:
sf_skyline.gif
Audio (music or sound effect loop):
–
Audio (spoken text):
–
Displayed text:
–
Other:
–

Storyboard # 9

Student Name: Jane Smith Movie Title: San Francisco fog

To complete the storyboard, draw and describe the initial and final state of each section. Then describe the transition from the initial to the final state.

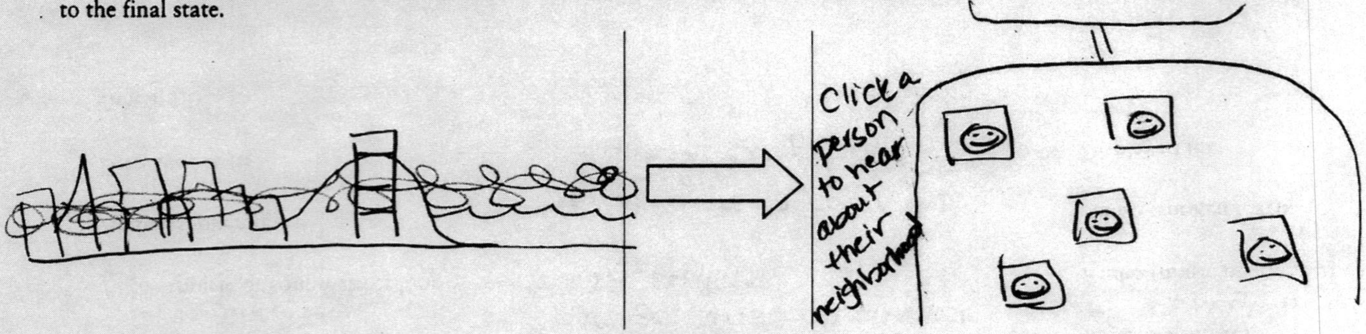

Description of Initial State

Drawn images:
fog cloud

Imported images:
sf_skyline.gif

Audio (music or sound effect loop):
-

Audio (spoken text):
-

Displayed text:
-

Other:
-

Description of Transition

Describe objects that change and how they change. Estimate the time for each change in seconds.

- San Francisco skyline and fog fade out together
- San Francisco map fades in
- Each person's face (buttons) fade in
- Spoken:
  What's the fog like where you live?

Description of Final State

Drawn images:
-

Imported images:
sf_map.gif, rus_face.jpg, al-face.jpg, rich_face.jpg, soma-face.jpg, noe-face.jpg

Audio (music or sound effect loop):
-

Audio (spoken text):
-

Displayed text:
Click a person to hear about their neighborhood (black text)

Other:
each face is a button that plays different videos

Storyboard # 10

Student Name: Jane Smith Movie Title: San Francisco Fog

To complete the storyboard, draw and describe the initial and final state of each section. Then describe the transition from the initial to the final state.

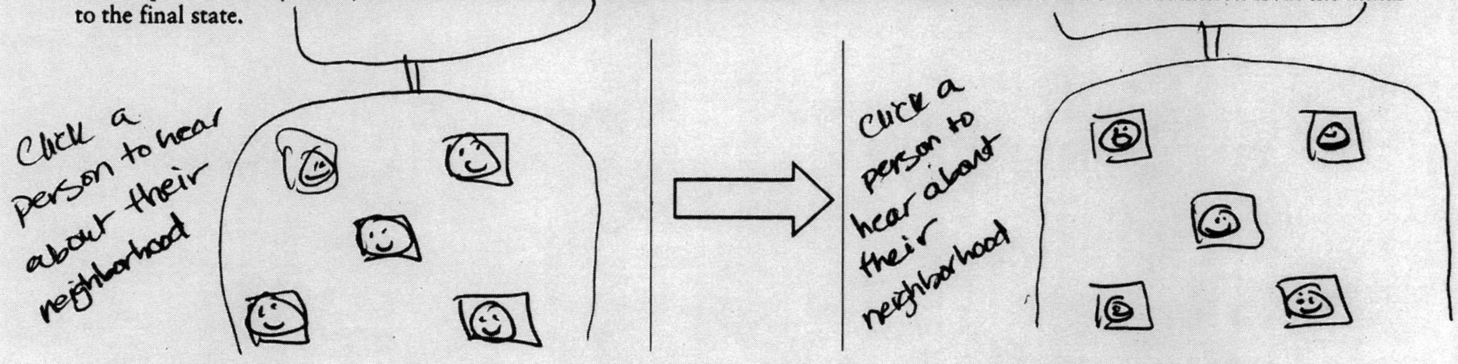

Description of Initial State

Drawn images:

–

Imported images:
sf_map.gif, rus-face.jpg, al-face.jpg, rich-face.jpg, soma-face.jpg, noe-face.jpg

Audio (music or sound effect loop):

–

Audio (spoken text):

–

Displayed text:
Click a person to hear about their neighborhood (black text)

Other:
Each face image is a button that plays different videos

Description of Transition

Describe objects that change and how they change. Estimate the time for each change in seconds.

- Clicking a photo of a person triggers a video to play in the place of the photo
- The photo returns when the video is done playing

Description of Final State

Drawn images:

–

Imported images:
sf_map.gif, rus-face.jpg, al-face.jpg, rich-face.jpg, soma-face.jpg, noe-face.jpg

Audio (music or sound effect loop):

–

Audio (spoken text):
Foggy (said in video)

Displayed text:
Click a person to hear about their neighborhood (black text)

Other:
rich-vid.mov, al-vid.mov, rus-vid.mov, noe-vid.mov, soma-vid.mov

How to Organize Movie Content

Organize the Library

You can create folders to organize your files in the library.

1. To create a folder in the library, choose **New Folder** from the **Options** pop-up menu (upper right corner of the Library panel).

   The new folder is added to the library.

   Folders are represented by orange file folder icons.

2. Name the folder and drag files into the folder. You can even store folders within other folders.

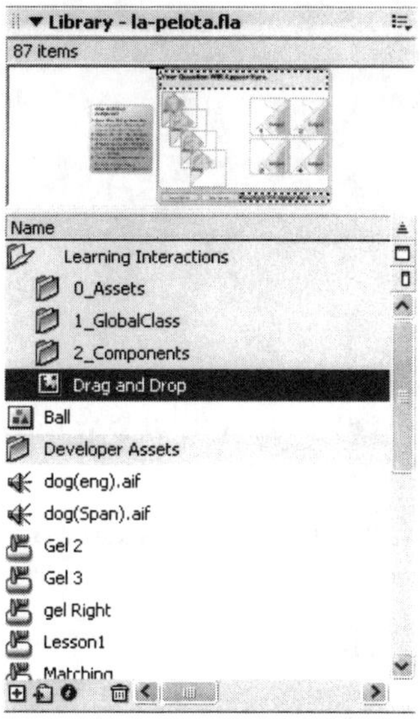

3. Double-click a folder to see or hide its contents.

Organize Layers

Organize your layers by using descriptive layer names, putting layers in a logical order, and creating folders.

1. To change the name of a layer, double-click the name and enter a new name.
2. You can change the order of layers by dragging them up or down in the stack.

   Note: ActionScript should be placed in a layer named Actions, typically at the top of the layer stack. Background layers typically go at the bottom of the stack.

3. To create a layer folder, click the **Insert Layer Folder** button and give the folder a new name.

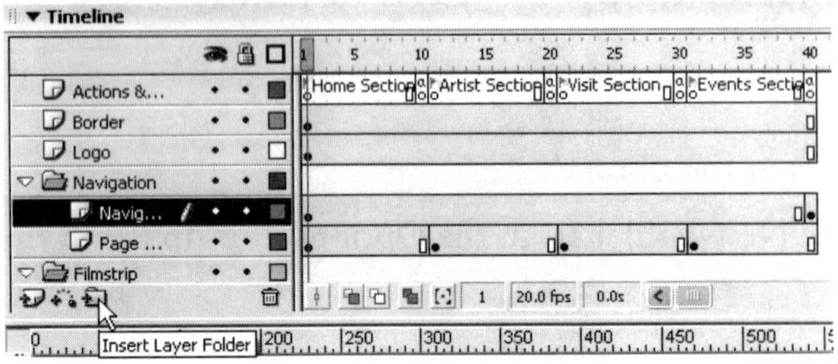

4. Drag layers into folders to keep them organized.

Set Audio Compression Options

1. Import audio into the Sound layer in the digital narrative.
2. In the Property inspector, set Sync to **Stream**.

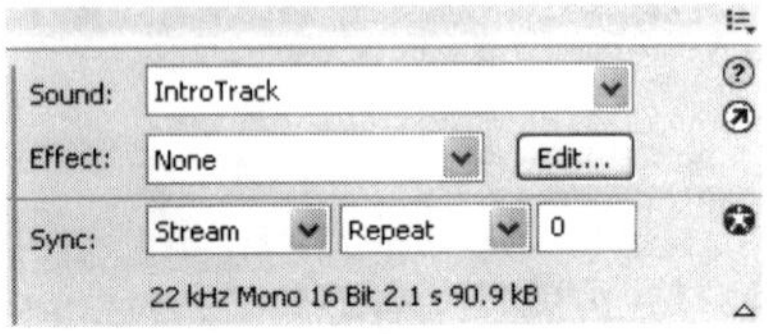

Note: Although streaming means losing some audio quality, it creates a smaller SWF file and synchronizes the audio to the object movements on the Stage.

3. Use the frame rate and the length of the audio to determine how many frames down the Timeline to extend the sound.
4. Select the frame and extend the Timeline in the sound layer by choosing **Insert > Timeline > Frame**.

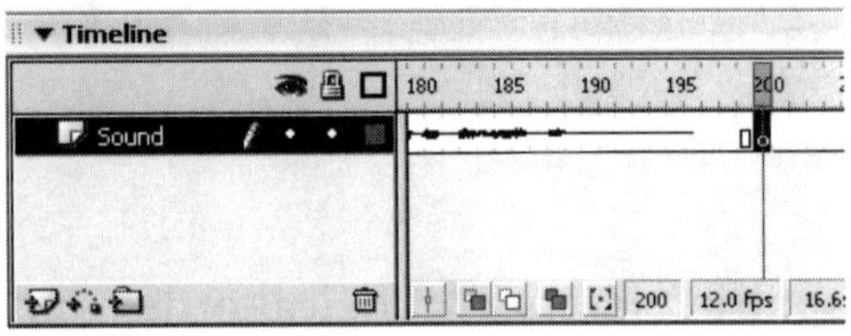

All the audio will be visible in the Timeline.

Note: Do not use Insert > Keyframe because a new keyframe would stop the audio before it is finished.

Label Keyframes

You can label frames to indicate when changes occur on the Timeline.

1. Select a frame you want to label.
2. In the Property inspector, enter the label in the Frame Label text box.

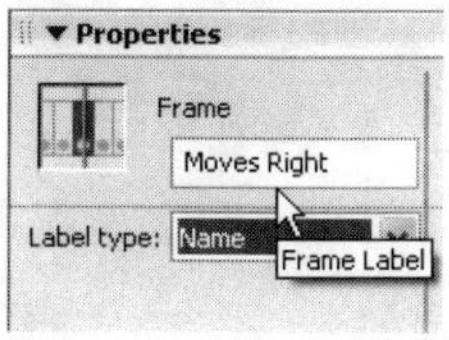

Note: Frame labels are included when you publish a document as a Flash movie, so avoid long names to minimize file size and also keep the label from spanning too many frames.